MEN
TALK

Given half a chance!

Sam Bunch

First Published by Parks Publications
in London 2022
Sam Bunch © 2022

A CIP catalogue record for this book is
available from the British Library.
ISBN 978-1-9998804-2-2

Printed and bound in Poland

Illustrations **Ruth Allen**
Design **Alison Gardner**

Follow me
@collectingconversations.com

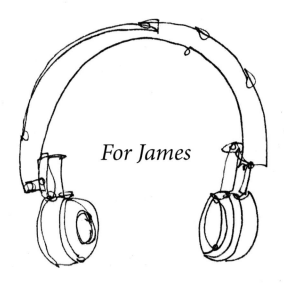

For James

'The Marriage of Heaven and Hell'
William Blake

*The man who never alters his opinion
is like standing water, and breeds
reptiles of the mind.*

Contents

Foreword

In the summer of 1987, I was in Corfu with a bunch of fellow backpackers. One of them told us about a cool place on the island where she knew the waitress. The venue was a roadside petrol station by day that transformed into a bar after working hours. We decided to go. It was rocking. A lively crowd dancing, drinking and smoking around the petrol pumps to the DJ spinning the best of the '80s. The waitress came over, holding a tray, notepad and pen and in the strongest of no-nonsense Lancashire accents said, 'Right you lot, what can I get you?' This was the first time I met Sam Bunch. As I saw how a forecourt could transform into a cool outdoor dance club, I understood how, out of the ordinary something quite extraordinary can happen. It is precisely this that Sam achieves in 'Men Talk' as she travels around the globe (albeit via Zoom) asking men the most ordinary of questions. 'How are you?' She then waits and listens - really listens - for the answers that start to come.

Sam interviewed both my Dad, Chris, and me for this book. From her simple opening question, 'How are you?', Dad and I respectively found ourselves reflecting upon what it was to be a father who struggled to understand his son, and to be a son who struggled to be understood. Dad and I talked at length afterwards about what an incredibly intimate experience this had been for us both and how, when we read each other's interviews, we understood and accepted each other more fully. This, in essence appears to be one of the unforeseen outcomes of this work - and in our case, this was rendered even more poignant by the fact that Dad died just over a year later.

Sam's final question is, 'What have you taken from doing this today?' Many of the men say they feel lighter, more aware and somehow a little freer, unburdened, as a result of having gone through this process. As a psychotherapist, a man, and a dad, I know the 'script' that is handed down to us men, right from the start. And that is, 'Boys don't talk about feelings'. The gender roles that we are assigned lead us to collude with this repressive 'script' and before we know it, we've inadvertently created a self-fulfilling prophecy that repeats itself through generations. My many years of practice as a psychotherapist have taught me that when we repress our feelings, thoughts, beliefs and ideas, they tend to fester in the depths of our experience and to gather shame, guilt and fear. These feelings, among others can translate into actions and behaviours that can be damaging for both the person and for society. Substance misuse, OCD (Obsessive Compulsive Disorder), suicide attempts, violence, and bullying, to name just a few.

By giving men the chance to talk and really be heard, 'Men Talk' creates an opportunity for this cycle to be broken, reminding us men that we can talk about how we feel and at the same time reminding society that when someone stops to listen - to really listen - we've actually got a lot to say.

Phil Georgiou
Psychotherapist UKCP/EAP/ECP

Introduction

Let's be honest: men aren't renowned for talking. 'They never open up, or express their feelings,' is often women's complaint. I beg to differ. They might not offer their thoughts on a plate, but when asked - they do tell.

I've lived most of my life listening to women criticising men for one reason or another, but when you've asked a hundred men how they are, or how they feel about something, you find their thoughts, dreams and desires aren't far away from women's.

There's been a lot of conditioning, lack of male role models, a bit too much linear thinking perhaps? Not much self-reflection, self-questioning or a 'best friend' to air their concerns with. Men go inwards. It can get muddled in there. Lack of clarity and harsh societal pressures might be the reason why. It's no wonder mental health issues are at an all time high. But it's not all about mental health, although it's certainly a theme. Men have so much more going on…

Listening to a hundred people is a lot of spoken words, three million in fact, and believe you me, men can and do talk. Throughout this book we've covered a lot. We've talked about life, death and everything in between, and lots of tears have been shed.

Thousands of hours have been put into this project. These conversations weren't a quick chat, they were soulful! One fella said, 'It's been an amazing experience. If you take all the excess out of the things that you're saying you can really hear yourself - there's a truth here. I've learnt so much and I feel very empty in a good way. It's like a clear-out, sorting out the rubbish.'

As you read through the commentaries you will see how men adapt and change as they grow older. Priorities shift. 'Men Talk' is a sort of 'how to' book for men, but showing rather than telling men how to! All 100 men answered the same 18 questions. I've picked commentary that gives a flavour of everything I've heard. While transcribing and listening, I'd sometimes get overwhelmed, and find myself with a lump in my throat, a tear in my eye or an outburst of laughter. It's been a really lovely experience.

Whilst telling people about my book, men have said to me, 'Who's going to buy your book? Men won't read it!' Rude, but I think they're right. Men aren't on the whole that interested in how other men think. Women are! This is a book about men, for women to read, then tell men about.

But if only men could hear what I've heard. Men really ought to read this book, if only to show them that they are not alone. To realise that most of what swirls around in their heads is actually very common, and that there is something 'connecting' about that. Men tend to suffer alone in their thoughts and carry a hefty burden because of it. Men tend not to share, women share. It somehow comes more naturally to us. But, give them a chance.

A bit of background as to why I wrote this book...

Book writing was never on my bucket list but I have an insatiable curiosity and even more of a one to share. Where best to direct that energy? Into a book of course! And, isn't that the beauty of life? You never know what's coming next. Oscar Wilde said, 'If you want to be a grocer, a politician, or a judge etc., you will invariably become it; that is your punishment. If you never know what you want to be, if each day you are unsure of who you are and what you know, you will never become anything, and that is your reward.' I like the essence of what he's saying - you don't have to stick at one thing and be labelled as such - I'm always up for new challenges and for me, the current one is book writing.

My first book, 'Collecting Conversations', which in essence is the prequel to the book you have in your hands was inspired by the 25 years worth of diaries my Mum left me after she died. She talked about daily life in all its mundanity. I used some of the topics she mentioned and came up with a list of questions that we don't usually get asked and I set out on a mission to find out how 100 women think and feel about their daily life.

It was a long process. Seven years 1,000 books, printed, bound and tightly packed in a container, sailed from China, arriving on my doorstep several weeks later. The enormity of what I had done struck me - I was an author, publisher and soon to be bookseller! What on earth had I done? (If you want to know more about my self-publishing adventure, go to collectingconversations.com on the 'About Me' page).

Then the hard work really started! Radio interviews, writing articles for newspapers and magazines. Giving talks up and down the country in bookshops and libraries, at quiz nights and at book clubs. I even gave a TedX talk in front of over two hundred people, which was the most anxiety-provoking time of my life! In just eight months I'd sold out and went for a second print run. I was on a roll.

At the same time, the menopause smacked me in the face. Just for fun, I quickly and explosively vented my hormones into a tiny book, 'Menopause - A Hot Topic'. Now I now had two books to sell. I'd also started interviewing 100 men for this book too. I must be bonkers.

By the end of 2019, I was up to my eyes in sweat, books and interviews. I'd interviewed 30 of the intended 100 men but it had taken me three years. I needed to knuckle down and get some focus.

That focus came in March 2020 and boy did it all change. Covid and lockdown! Discipline, routine and focus became my new norm. No more distractions. And now I had access to men from all over the world thanks to ZOOM! Where did all these men come from I hear you ask? All over the place. Some were men I already knew. Some were friends or relatives of friends. Some were straight off Twitter and Instagram. My postman took part as did the man that came to cut the trees back. A man in the local coffee shop. I even got random emails asking if I would talk to such and such a person. It wasn't hard getting people to come forward and I'll talk to anyone. It's a Sagittarius thing! I have no problem interacting. It's part of who I am. I'm so comfortable chatting that people naturally warm to me - for that, I am blessed.

There was this one bloke on Twitter, his feed said, 'I'm bored.' I happened to be scrolling, saw it and messaged him, 'Fancy having a chat then?' That conversation developed over four weeks. Two hours every Thursday morning - he said it was like counselling, sort of, and for me, it was like chatting to an old mate. By the time we'd finished I'd sent him a gift of an Eric Morecambe postage stamp (he likes Eric otherwise that would have been weird!) from an inherited stamp collection, and he sent me a bottle of wine from the vineyard his family runs. So you see - conversations are very connecting. Another fella found me, again on Twitter. He messaged me, 'I like what you're doing, can I be part of it?'. I was a bit shocked as he has thousands of followers and my 'reach' on Twitter is tiny. We arranged a time, plugged into Zoom and once again started chatting like old friends. There's something indescribable about having a good old chat - no agendas, no judgments, it just feels right and... you learn so much.

The interviews took between two and eight hours each, and transcriptions were roughly between 20,000 and 80,000 words. (By the way, an average book is around 80,000 words). In just 18 months I had interviewed the remaining 70 men and transcribed those THREE MILLION words - did I mention that already?

I hate labels and boxing people into categories but I do have a wide demographic. The youngest man I spoke to was two weeks off his 20th birthday, and the oldest, 92. They came from all over the place. Australia, South America, across Europe, the Caribbean, India, America and every corner of the UK.

The chapter titles are the questions I asked. I've also woven 17 longer conversations aptly titled 'A longer conversation' throughout the book to give you a flavour of what a fuller conversation was really like. There are five word-clouds too. These questions provoked shorter answers. I've had to edit hard here and reduce their answers to single word adjectives they used, without any detail - sadly there's just no room. I've highlighted the top words that were most said.

This book contains a plethora of experiences. A cacophony of words that I've had to reduce to a mere 95,000 but I hope what these men have shared gives you an insight into how they feel and think. It's unclarified, it's messy, but so are we.

So if you're new to my books - hello and welcome. If we're old friends - welcome back and thank you, your support means a lot. I know you've paid for this book (thank you) but please see 'Men Talk' as a gift from me and these 100 men, a labour of love. A companion, a dialogue, an offering of hope and connection, something us humans always need. I ask only that you please share it with the men in your life. They need to know it's not just them who think as they do!

How are you?

'I'm content but I haven't always been'

Ever wondered why we greet people with, 'Hi, how are you?' And then more often than not the response is, 'Fine, thanks!' So, how are you? Yes, YOU there, reading this book. How are you? I'm interested to know. I know most of us don't consider how we are. We wake up, jump out of bed (okay, that's not quite true) and get on with the day. But I loved the reactions this question revealed. While many men are content and full of zest for life, I had no idea there was so much depression and anxiety out there. I knew it was a 'thing' but when over a quarter of the men I spoke with actually told me about their mental health problems, I was shocked. I kept hearing it, over and over again. I hope by reading this you won't feel down but feel inspired to listen, help and take charge of anything that comes your way, hopefully sooner rather than later, but also know that it's 'normal' to have these feelings and complexities. Just knowing that might help?

The 20s

Last night I picked up my friend from the Eurostar and coincidentally bumped into my ex-girlfriend who I hadn't seen for ages. It was so weird. I gave her a hug and we chatted for a while. After I was like, 'Oh fuck, I thought I was further along.' I spent a lot of time thinking about her and I was hit by that drug all over again. I had a night full of weird dreams. It's clouded my morning today.

I've been overthinking my future. I feel like I'm having to prove myself to myself. Who am I - what do I do? It's absurd. Somehow I feel I'm running out of time, I'm 26! I scramble to get everything done, rushing because there's a clock ticking.

My idea of success has been distorted by the fact that both my ex-partners have gone on to have global notoriety and huge success. Both have been able to buy their first homes at a young age. I'm thinking that's what success looks like and anything that isn't that, isn't success! I have to keep reminding myself that success comes in many different forms. I can't forget these women either because their faces are plastered on posters and our TV screens. I can't block them out. I am forever reminded about what I don't have.

■

I've definitely been better. I have an existing health condition. It flared up recently. I've been on medication for anxiety, depression and a bit of psychosis, too. I've had various services involved along the way. I feel well versed on the subject but this time I feel more engulfed by it all. It's taken everything out of my control. I'm not very good at asking for help. It's a bit of a shock not to be in control any more.

■

I'm better than I was. I was in a really dark place. I'm not back to where I want to be. I still have days when I'm down. What lifted me was spending time at home with people I trusted. Those I knew would always have my back and loved me. There are always people to talk to, people who care. It showed me not everyone in this world is out to get me. Now if something happens, I have a sequence of things that I do, if that fails, I call Mum!

■

The best I've been in a long time. I'm beginning to understand who I am a bit more now. My second year at uni was very difficult for me. A while ago I watched a documentary about people who committed suicide from the Golden Gate Bridge in San Francisco. The only two survivors both said as soon as their hands left the rails they realised, everything is reversible!

■

In my mind there is an underlying discontentment. I think it's to do with being in London and my job. Initially I could see the real purpose of doing what I was doing but when we didn't win any further contracts I ended up doing projects just for growth and profit. The weekend arrives. I go out, have a few drinks and repeat. I don't know how to get my head around it. I need to do something else.

■

A year ago I had a fairly loose idea of what I was going to do for the foreseeable future. I had a steady job in farming and a house that came with it. I got bored. I got into tree surgery for the sake of variety. I broke up with my long-term girlfriend. It's all chaos when things change isn't it? I guess life has been about ticking boxes and figuring out what I don't want. I've had big ups and downs over the last six years. I'm getting used to not being as happy as I was when I was a kid. My childhood was spent fucking about in the woods with my mates. Riding bikes, making dens, being boys. Then we all got out of uni and had to find something to do for the rest of our lives. Life gets a bit more challenging, doesn't it? My anxiety kicked off when I was about 22. I don't know where it came from. I think quite a lot of it was seasonal. It was winter and the weather was shitty. I was working on a farm. I started feeling morose. It was bad for about three months. I've learnt how to deal with it. It's knowing the triggers.

The 30s

I used to walk with my head down and never smile. When you're 15, you really want to be 18, you think you'll be happy. I got to 18, now I could buy alcohol but I wasn't happy. Then it was, 'Hey, 21 – I'll be happy when I get there.' But then you realise you have to grow up, there's a lot of pressure; to find a companion, get a good education, but still I wasn't really happy. Ten years ago I became interested in meditation. I try not to have too many expectations now. Now I'm very happy.

∎

Exponentially better than I was this time last year. Last year was a hard year. I separated from my wife. Being a musician is an extremely unconventional life. There's not a steady flow of income. A lot of my friends my age have wives, mortgages and children, I don't have any of that. I don't want it. There's nothing wrong with convention, I'm just not a conventional person.

∎

I've been out of work for a year now. It's getting a bit boring. I teach martial arts twice a week. If I didn't do that I would literally be doing nothing else. I used to be a solicitor. My Dad was a solicitor. I'm one of three brothers. It was expected that one of us would go into the family business but law wasn't for me. I got into digital marketing but it all got a bit stressful. I've had a few interviews recently but I don't interview well. I can't see a path ahead at the moment.

■

My emotions are nearly non-existent. For the most part I don't share how I'm feeling. I'd love to be able to but growing up we didn't show emotion. We didn't cry and if you did, the old man would say 'Don't be a pussy.' That's just the way it was. The older I get, the more I realise it's good for you to share your emotions.

■

I was at a crossroads. I'd had enough. I'd been running a couple of pubs for years and it wasn't satisfying anymore. I want to make a difference. I used to live on a boat, there was a lovely feeling of community. It's very important for me to find community. I am ready for the next stage in life. There's a pressure to earn some money now there's a baby coming!

The 40s

I feel very happy. Not having a kid till you're 41 is pretty good. I did a lot of things between 17 and 41. I've had a massive amount of freedom. I don't feel I've missed out. I'm here with my daughter. That's what I do every day.

■

I'm trying to figure out how I am. I've been put in the slow lane recently. A few months ago I had a major accident (I tore my heart). Just before that life-changing moment I'd been doing what I love best - organising events that bring communities together. The driving force for me is about finding connection. Having proper conversations, connecting with people and feeling part of the community - it makes me feel alive. The way a lot of people live, especially in cities, can bring isolation and loneliness. I like to create a community, to fill in the void for the lack of extended family around me. It's my way of feeling connected.

·

I came to the UK when I was 25 to study. I'm grateful to live here although learning how to survive in Britain can make you quite hard. London is lovely but there's an issue in Britain. The whole Brexit thing feels like we've cut off one leg. I wonder who actually really cares and what was the point of it all?

I'm from Barbados. As a black person coming from a black majority county, I feel different to a lot of black people here in the UK. I only discovered I was actually black in a very racial sense when I came here. I never used to wake up thinking, 'Oh, I'm black.' I have a black majority mindset. Although Barbados is a small island, my upbringing is similar to a white person's growing up here in Britain, where white people are the majority. Because I grew up in a majority, I grew up confident and strong. Sometimes I find black minorities in scenarios when they get into arguments which they think are racist but I don't think they are. They are marginalised. There is this idea of what it is to be English but at the same time fighting with a more modern idea of what it means to be British.

I have dreams and aspirations, things I want to achieve. Sometimes it's a burden to have dreams; to be the best dad, to achieve your goals. I'm 40, it's a funny age, you could easily get into having a mid-life crisis. There's a catharsis too, accepting life as it is and living one day at a time.

·

I'm happily married and happy in my job. I have a better appreciation of the parts of my job I don't like and why I don't like them. I suppose that's normal. At the end of the day, it's work and they pay you to do it. A few years ago I had a bout of depression. We moved house, I'd just got married and things weren't great. We had marriage counselling. It was a rocky road for a while.

·

Bored and average. I have low-level depression. I take antidepressants. I am afraid to come off them, which is frightening. I've been taking them for a few years. I have a stigma about it. What is it that I am depressing? What am I not addressing? We are so quick to label depression. One in four of us have depression. Pills are a quick fix answer. We have sanitised our emotions through pills. We all need to scream and wail from time to time.

■

Over the last few years I've found myself in a downward spiral physically. I have high blood pressure. It's made me much more careful about what I eat. I feel the physical decline. I've had two new knees too. You know when some people say they feel exactly the same as they did when they were 18? I don't! I'm 50 this year, I've got 12 years to pay off my mortgage. I can't see me retiring any time soon. The burden is huge, it occupies my thoughts day and night. My time is dedicated to work, family and friends. I haven't got time for everyone else's problems. I am pretty content with my lot but saying that, if I lost my job our lives would be fucked. Fear is the single biggest motivation. There's an expectation from myself that I will provide. We have chosen the lifestyle we have and the big part of that is, it has to be paid for.

The 50s

The older I've got I feel I have less purpose. When the boys were dependent (they've now left home) it felt rewarding. There's a lack of reward in my life at the moment. Work doesn't do it for me anymore. I worry about getting older. I need to keep busy. I've started to think about how long I've got left but I don't wake up thinking, 'Christ, I made it to another day!' I take work more seriously nowadays. I try to be on top of everything. I finish one job then someone rings and I go straight onto the next - that's rewarding. Someone wanting you is too much to turn down. There's a need to be needed.

■

Two years ago I went for therapy. Work was getting me down as was my mother. My mother was where I wanted to start the therapy because she had been bothering me my whole life. I came out of the first session, sat in the car and cried for 15 minutes. I was 52, the co-head of global real estate at one the world's top 10 law firms. I was paid a fortune. I travelled to America six times a year, staying in top hotels, playing top golf courses. On one level I was living the dream but inside I wasn't. Alcohol became a release. I wasn't an alcoholic but it was the trigger.

■

My great-grandad was the first to settle down, he came from travelling stock. There's something in my blood. I love the idea of jumping in the campervan and setting off. I am a free spirit at heart. I've always done different things with my life. I am very hands-on. I bought my first house when I was 19 and I'm on my third property now. I enjoy my work. I do company clearances and liquidations, and sell the stuff through auctions. I love rooting around. I started my working life as a baker. I enjoyed getting up early. Then I became a long distance truck driver, carrying scrap metal and steel around the country. I'd sleep in my cab most weeks. Later I started driving for the milk board. Then moved on to being a sign writer. I never entertained the idea of working in an office.

■

I promised myself that by the time I was 50 I would have left my secure, mundane job with the pension and the trappings. Teaching was like prison. I would have had a heart attack if I'd have stayed any longer. On my walk into school in the mornings I'd ask myself, 'Why am I doing this?' That awful nine-to-five routine. I felt crushed. I had to hide the way I felt. It was a performance every day. Eventually I couldn't hide it any more. I felt people could see that I didn't want to be there. As a society we are so used to routine and security blankets so when you throw it off it's scary, but it's nice to have freedom of thought.

■

Being made redundant changed me, you have to re-evaluate what's important. I went from earning half decent money to nothing overnight and I went into a mad panic. But quite quickly I got a few clients and things are okay now. I've never been money-oriented, it doesn't bother me. There are more important things in life. Just as long as I can pay my bills and go on holiday, I am happy with my lot. I've noticed people look down on you because you don't have what they have. I don't give a shit how much money anyone has, I will treat you the same as you treat me, rich or poor makes no difference.

■

There's not much structure to my day. I walk the dog and that's about the only thing I do that's routine. I sold my business last year so I suppose I'm semi-retired. Every day is different. I like fluidity. I'm not too keen on structure. I have engineered my life towards that. I didn't want to be a nine-to-five person.

■

You know the idea that people get happier the older they get, but as a young person you think, 'Bollocks,' because in your youthful innocence you assume you can't be happy looking like 'that'! Well, it's true. I am very happy. I gave up my job two years ago. The first three months felt like I was on low dose of MDMA. I was ecstatic. I'd never had that feeling before without a chemical enhancement. It was literally like I was floating on air. I'd been ready to give up my job for a while. It was all-consuming. I spent most of my time in my head. That horrible phrase that everyone talks about being present, I never was. If I was sat next to you at a dinner party there would be a part of me that wasn't there. Whenever I met anybody new I'd do a quick interview, checking them out. Am I going to give this person real space, time and my attention? I already have my family and my work which takes so much of my time. I had no time for other people. I became very good at being glib. When the job went, I had space. I had energy and time. I started meeting people for what they were and not for what I could get out of them. I learnt to become a functioning human being again. I'm becoming a nice person again.

■

I'm physically hanging in there. It's a difficult period. We had our two girls quite late. I was 39 and 41 when we had them. They're good kids, they take over our life like everyone's do. I'm really glad we did all the things we did before we had kids because having kids doesn't come at the best time money-wise, they cost us a bloody fortune. I'm probably on the downside of my financial power so that's a bit of a strain. My wife's a teaching assistant, she doesn't get paid a lot, and that puts extra pressure on me.

■

I stopped working 10 years ago after the economic crisis in 2008. I hated my job. I used to have this Sunday night feeling while watching the 'The Antiques Road Show,' a moment of dread about going to work the next day. I got a good pay-out so I left. At the same time my Mum was dying in a home. She had Alzheimer's and I thought I'd spend some time looking after her. Sadly, she died within a month of me leaving work.

■

I can feel some depression coming on. I've suffered with depression for the last four years. I was feeling okay but this virus situation has made me feel moody again. I've been furloughed. I've never felt so vulnerable in my life. I can't control anything. The whole of my industry is making cuts. I've never been in a position where people won't consider talking to me about job opportunities. It's not good.

■

Five years ago I believed I was invincible then got clobbered with depression. I never dreamt I'd end up in that place. I had to change my thinking massively. It's as if all my adrenaline is stuck inside me and has nowhere to go. It feels like dead butterflies in my body. I thought I was in a better place than I am. In my working life I've been off work with depression twice. One time I was working on a huge construction project and it wasn't going to plan. Fingers were pointing in my direction, it was stressful. I was on site. The stress was getting to me. I had pins and needles in my fingers. I was bent over trying to put my boots on and the tears were pouring. I didn't want anyone seeing me like that so I had to walk away. I couldn't work out what was going on. I didn't feel well at all. I went into the bathroom and looked in the mirror. I saw a face staring back at me that I didn't recognise. I knew I wasn't right. I sent an email to my boss. He told me to take some time off. He spent a lot of time with me. He was very supportive. By the end of that first week I was lying on the settee. I couldn't even be arsed to brush my teeth or shave. I didn't want to do anything. The saddest thing about it was looking at my wife and seeing what it was doing to her. I could tell she was looking at me wondering if I was going to do something to myself. I'd always had a disdain for people who committed suicide because I couldn't understand how they got into that position but when my depression came on I understood because I felt close to it. That was a scary moment.

■

If you'd asked me on the 22nd of August I'd have said I never felt better. I don't want to bore you with all my ailments but on the 23rd of August I had a stroke - totally out of the blue. Fortunately it happened on a Sunday morning. I collapsed in the bathroom. If it had happened in the night my brain would have been severely affected. I am on sick leave. I can't drive but I work from home anyway. I feel very fortunate, even after my stroke. We were in a good place. We live in a nice house. Our kids are healthy and happy. My wife and I are good mates. We have a good life. What could be better?

■

I think of Walt Whitman in that I contain multitudes. I feel so many things now. In fact 54 is probably the best time of my life but paradoxically the worst too. I'm being over-dramatic but it's the most confusing time of my life. I hit my 50s and looked in the mirror and thought, I don't feel 50. I still feel like I'm in my 20s. That's the confusing bit. I think about silt on the river. I think I've silted up a lot of knowledge, insight and pain. I think it could be baggage. It feels to me like a bedrock now. Who is this person in front of me with bags under their eyes and a whole lot of stuff still being worked out?

I've been in a relationship for 25 years. I love my wife very much but we've grown apart while our situation has stayed the same. We've changed. We've morphed. When my daughter went to university, the sense of change was enormous. That horrible phrase, empty nesters. I'm genuinely confused about everything at the moment. My wife's going through major changes. She's on an emotional rollercoaster too.

■

I've been an active hands-on dad since I was 23. I've always had at least one child at home. Then it was just me and my wife for the first time since 1986. I felt bereft. I was very, very sad. In many ways it feels very melancholic, just us in the house. Although there's something really lovely about it too - playing cards, chatting and watching TV. Making meals for just the two of us.

■

I'm excessively happily married to my second wife. Having spent 35 years in the world of finance, I've become a farmer. I'm excited. It has given me a new lease of life. I'm doing something that really excites me. I'm an enthusiast.

■

A lot of people slow down at my age. I'm just gearing up. I got to a point in life where I've achieved a lot. I got the house paid off, I've got the car I wanted, I've got the work that I absolutely love. In 2016 I thought, 'It's time to start giving back.' I started raising money for charities by doing extreme, crazy adventures, while wearing funky hats! It gives me an opportunity to interact with people, face-to-face. I give talks in schools. I tell the kids, 'In life you're going to be judged - don't be scared to be different, or to look different because they are the things that will get you noticed and give you opportunities.'

For me it all started when I was 16. My Dad, who passed away about a month ago, wanted me to work at ICI where he worked. He wanted me to follow in his steps. I had different ideas. He made me sit the exams and I purposely failed them. He said, 'You're going to be a failure in this life. You're going to amount to nothing!' That comment changed my life, it was the kick up the arse I needed. I'd left school and the world was my oyster. I wondered how I, this young kid with a chip on his shoulder, was going to survive in the world? I rapidly became independent. I left home, lived in Spain for five years. Came back and bought my own house. I didn't have a pot to piss in, all my mates were out drinking and I was just working. That was kind of the path I took. My life literally just grew and grew and grew. I started off sweeping shop floors. I wanted to become the manager. I looked at the boss and thought, 'He's no different to me - if he can do it, I can.' And that's what I did.

∎

We are heading towards being empty nesters. My wife and I are going to have to get to know each other again. We knew each other 20 years ago, then we had children and our life has been centred around them. There are very few compensations for getting older but one of them is you have more self-revelation. You learn and change over the years. Things happen to us - we do change. I think life is too bloody short not to be conscious of what you're doing and how you respond.

∎

We've always been happy but we seem to be getting happier as we get older. In the early days we'd have our arguments and now we're just getting on with it. There might be a bit of shouting but it's usually over something silly, like, 'You didn't sugar my brew!'

The 60s

I'm enjoying life. I am very happy. Less stressed these days. I never want to be miserable, it's too much hard work. Sometimes I meet people who are hard work. Always moaning - 'My cats died, I lost my job!' Keep those things to yourself and deal with them. I absorb people's energy. I try to swerve people who moan.

∎

I am content but I haven't always been. It's taken a long time. Making a break in my mid-50s from the rut I was in with my marriage was immensely uncomfortable. Those years of transition were quite difficult but now it's all settled down. I'm motivated by an internal sense of duty. For example, five years before our separation I said, 'We can't go on like this, by the time our son is 18, if our situation hasn't changed...' We didn't separate overnight. We had therapy. We tried. The other pattern I broke out of, which I partly came to realise through therapy, was pleasing my mother and fulfilling her unfulfilled ambitions! My mother would have been 'something' if she'd been born in another time. She poured into me her unfulfilled stuff. I went around achieving endlessly, to fulfil her unspoken ambitions. A few years ago she said, 'I always thought you'd become a member of the Cabinet!' My contentedness is related to my mother's lack of contentedness.

■

I woke up this morning thinking, 'Fuck, I'm old!' I feel a bit of gratitude. After 27 years of Buddhist practice you realise your life isn't that bad and no one gets out of here alive anyway.

■

I am now unable to see being alone as anything other than loneliness and something very stressful and difficult. I didn't notice it but in recent years it's become much more threatening.

■

I always appear to be full of life and vim but deep down I'm probably full of angst and misery. I've always been like that. I'm not exactly pushing back the frontiers in my life.

My friend is dreading turning 60 but I think turning 60 gives you opportunities - a free bus pass. It's fantastic. You get a bowel screening kit through the post. I've just sent my sample off! I got a letter asking if I'd like to take part in a prostate cancer screening. Society tells you you're old, irrelevant of how you feel.

■

I am not doing miserable. I have to stay fit as I will be having my 100th birthday! There will be no wheelchairs or zimmer frames as they get in the way of the dancing.

■

I would say as I've got older the burden of expectation is slipping away. I've never really felt as though I've fitted in - I would like to fit in. I am not a father or a husband. I live alone in a council flat. I have no car. I'm an eccentric, I suppose. I have felt very isolated. If I could choose, I would have more love in my life.

■

Life is tolerable. I'm reasonably happy. I've spent the last 10 years living back at home in London, caring for my Dad. Things came to a head when my Dad got broken into by the infamous 'Night Stalker' in 2008. The attacker went on a series of attacks in South East London back in the '90s. He broke into elderly people's homes, sexually assaulting both men and women. They didn't catch him for 20 years. Thankfully he didn't assault my Dad but he did break in, dressed in full biker leathers. He stayed for a couple of hours, eventually leaving, taking four bottles of champagne. My Dad was 86 at the time and said it was the most exciting thing that had happened to him since the war. After that I moved back in with him. He died last year.

■

I've had a rough time with my brother's death recently. That was tough. He was a year older than me. After his wife left him he completely changed. He became bitter. And my Mum is 89 and has dementia. One minute you're talking, having a laugh and joke, then she turns around and says, 'Those birds are back.' I'm like, 'What birds?' And she'll say, 'Those on top of the wardrobe. Give them some bread.'

■

I'm lonely but content. I've always lived alone and always been fairly lonely. I can't figure out why. I have good friends. I think it's just my nature. I'd like to have a relationship but I think it would do my head in. I don't have that anchoring. I worry I don't have roots.

The 70s

I'm trying to pack up work but it's difficult because I've been a barge engineer and sailor for a long time. The people I help have chosen a lifestyle that harks back if you like. They all live on old boats and nobody has taught them about old boats. There isn't a course to learn about them, either. When I say I'm trying to retire, I'd like to stop helping them but I don't feel I can. They're trying to cope with something they don't understand. I'm quite happy to carry on explaining, fault-finding, troubleshooting but I don't want to get a spanner out and fix it for them any more.

∎

I've been doing my job and been self-employed most of my life which presents its own challenges when you're trying to bring up five children! I'm used to managing that burden. I have to make provision for my wife who is 18 years younger than me.

∎

I'm 75 and rapidly approaching the departure lounge! I'm absolutely fantastic. I've always had a positive disposition. I'm still busy.

∎

If I'm working on a project I'm okay but if there's nothing going on I can slump, and slip into depression. I've been like this on and off for 20 years. In the early days it could last two to three weeks and I'd be really down. These days I've got more of a grip on it. If it lasts more than a couple of days I can talk myself out of it. I blow small things out of proportion. When it was bad I didn't want to associate with anyone, which I don't think is the right thing to do. Going for a walk and being with people is much better for you.

∎

I am happy and physically fit. I have no real complaints. I retired from being a postman eight years ago. I was happy being a postman. My Dad was a postman too. I didn't want too much stress or too much responsibility in my life. The job changed so I packed up early, I was 63. My wife retired, too. People say, 'What you gonna do with yourself when you retire?' We are actually busier now than we were when we worked. I had no idea what life would be like but things evolved. I found the transition very easy. I am content with my life.

∎

I've worked through some of my insecurities. I don't have to worry about my career path any more. On impulse my husband and I moved to Rome five years ago and I love it here. But I would say I'm so-so, and the reason is, what's happening in the world. I read the papers and follow the news. The environmental degradation has been getting to me for a long time. Overpopulation and of course, the pandemic. Now there's all the protesting. The injustices in the world. The abuse of power, the racism, sexism, all of it. I won't say I'm depressed but I get these kind of glum, dour days. I call it the 'Weltschmerz'. It's a German term. It means the pain of the world. I am world-weary.

∎

I don't think one should ever be totally content. I suppose I wouldn't be working if I didn't love my work. I've been working since I was 16. I am a workaholic. I should have given up 12 years ago but as the Chinese say, 'The older you get the more wisdom you get, therefore you don't have to run quite as fast.' That's what motivates me. I'm not particularly interested in money but obviously I need to pay the bills.

The 80s-plus

I've rather landed on my feet. I moved back to London after living on and off in Europe for 30 years. A lot of people said I was making a mistake moving back but I don't think so. You can't spend the day on the beach at my age, your body doesn't like it. That chapter is over. I decided to move back and downsize. I've worked for it. I planned it. I got rid of my car. Who is going to insure an 82 year old driver? I wanted to be back where my roots are. My friends from the '60s still live round here. I go out most evenings. This is the next chapter.

∎

I am diabetic. Hard of hearing. I have a prostate problem but it's benign. Oh, and I have a pacemaker. But apart from that I'm fine.

■

I'm very well for someone my age. I run my own business - a small chain of laundrettes. I've done it most of my life. It's very satisfying but physical work. It's just me. I don't have to supervise people and it's never the same day twice. I like to keep involved. If you don't, you become old and useless. Your senses and memory go. My wife doesn't like me to work too many days so I keep it to just half-days these days. If you give up altogether you can go backwards very quickly. There's never been a day I haven't wanted to go to work since I started my own business.

I was bought up in a family where working seven days a week was the norm. It was normal for me when I started my first job as a mechanic to work 12 hours a day. As time went on I got married and had a young family, there was no time for family life. I'd come home grumpy. It was very bad. My wife nearly left me. That was back in 1972. I knew I had to change things. I needed to get out of garage work. I started another job in my spare time. I bought a laundrette and every spare minute I'd work on it. We made a lot of mistakes but five months later I opened my first laundrette. Gradually I started a chain. It took me eight years and three laundrettes before I could leave my job as a mechanic. We now have nine laundrettes. I get to know all my customers and the home/work life balance has been much better. The garage depressed me but the laundrettes make me laugh.

■

I am 91 and a half and I feel it. I've got my marbles and I walk with a stick. I've had enough. There's not much to look forward to. I've got aches and pains but I can't do anything about it. I'm just growing old.

■

I'm a reasonably happy bloke. Obviously I've retired so the day job doesn't come into it any more. I have time. I am ineffective in many ways, not terribly important. I'm just simply one of billions of people. I am a bit of a Pollyanna. Never saw worry or danger. And I'm pleased by pretty things, simple things, music, a piece of poetry or a good-looking woman. The sheer loveliness of everything around us.

A longer conversation...

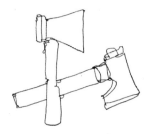

Nick 71

from South London, living in California

For five decades I've been rebuilding the world all the goddamn time. Physically, as well as emotionally. I've built several cabins, Japanese fences and of course I like working on boats. My tools have spa days. They're well looked after. My favourite axe is called a Freya! It's designed by an ex-special forces operator. Made from hickory, it's razor sharp and a beautiful piece of work. My axes are custom-made in French carbon steel. It's completely normal for a man to have several axes. My tool shed is like a secret salon.

Many years ago I would have described myself as a drug-crazed, brain-damaged cabin hippy. But I'm a much nicer person now as in, recovered! I don't work either, which helps. I live alone in a cabin but very close to another recluse, who's 78. We are wizened, sage-like hermits - in our minds.

I think I'm in pretty good shape. I arrived in America in 1974. I have a long relationship to everything here. I live in a bird reserve. I sit and watch the birds in the mornings. It's one gigantic seashore where I am. At the moment we are all living out of suitcases because of fire alerts. We live in wooden cabins and you only get 10 minutes to get out. The fires have been terrible.

I'm on a hilarious regime of painkillers and various other drugs. So I sleep at odd hours. A good nap in the afternoon helps. I might wake at 1am, write a fairy story, go back to sleep, then wake again at 4.30am. Writing fairy stories is how I express myself. Carl Jung wrote extensively about fairy tales. Then I walk the dog on the beach every day. It's full of wealthy old people and digital nouveau riche.

In 2007 my life was a disaster. My business was a disaster. Then I lost a lot of money in the 2008 financial crash. I was deeply depressed. A good friend of mine said to me, 'I think you are suicidal.' She had a point. I'm a long-term meditator in the Buddhist tradition but something wasn't working. I went to a therapist using the family constellations approach which explores the hidden dynamics in family relationships. Then something happened. I was on my way back from seeing this therapist and stopped off at a very nice Austrian coffee shop. I sat at the table and I went off into a very odd mental space. It's hard to explain but everything rearranged itself. Massive pieces of architecture were moving around. I was 'gone', and it felt as though I'd been away for very long time, but my coffee was still warm when I 'came back'. I went home and I felt completely better. I knew I'd never be depressed again and I haven't been. Depression never crosses my mind. It felt as though everything was realigned. All the tensions between old memories and experiences came together and settled. I practise Dzogchen daily (traditional Tibetan teachings) and have done for many years, which might also have had something to do with it.

I grew up playing on bomb sites in Mitcham, the haemorrhoid of South London's arse, with a Welsh dad who was very frustrated, deeply depressed, and listened to opera. He was a broken-hearted child who couldn't go to university to do his beloved mathematics. He was awarded a scholarship at 14, unusual for a Welsh boy at the time. Mum made cakes for a confectioners to the Queen. She was from Tooting but took up elocution and sounded like the Queen herself, and my father sounded like Dylan Thomas. So I grew up in a linguistically ridiculous house.

I was a scoundrel. I blew shit up. I set fire to shit. I knocked houses down with stolen bulldozers. I was one of those bad children. Those who smoked, took blue pills, had sex in the cemetery. I had to get away from my father so I joined the Air Force. At 17, I was in combat boots running though rain in Lincolnshire preparing bombers to blow up Russia! I lived in a caravan out in the field, took LSD and talked to the bomb, then lost my mind.

On the advice of a friend, I decamped to Sweden to run rock and roll clubs and take drugs with attractive blondes. Eventually I came back to the UK where I ended up in a Tibetan monastery in Dumfriesshire. I met a young guy recently crippled in a car accident, a Tibetan reincarnate llama, and we became the best of friends.

Some time later, after a good deal of bad behaviour, I ended up in India in a Tibetan monastery. I took my vows, then hitchhiked home. It was a very long way to hitchhike. I went through Nepal, India, Pakistan, Afghanistan, Iran, Iraq, Turkey, Greece. I weighed 120 pounds when I got back.

I die regularly. The number of times I've been doing something or other and have been knocked unconscious. I'm dead in that moment. At 14, I was in a bike race and went over the handlebars and there was a tree in the way. Knocked unconscious with a broken nose, I had a fracture here and a fracture there. Four years ago I was on a snow hike in the Brecon Beacons. I fell because it was icy. I had a backpack on. I was in a lot of pain. I laid there in this complete white out. It was very cold. I knew I'd broken something. I thought it was my leg. My thoughts were, 'I'll be dead in 15 minutes. I'm going to die here, on a Welsh mountain.' I did some further investigations and realised it was my forearm that was broken. It took some days to get off the mountains, being snowy and all. I walked down the mountain holding my arm to an abbey and a wonderful little pub. I proceeded to get raucously drunk with five French men I met.

Recently I had a heart attack. The more you hang on to who you think you are, the worse it is. I'd like to leave the world as quietly as possible. I'd get a kayak and go for one last paddle towards the North Pole. Drinking, and just capsize.

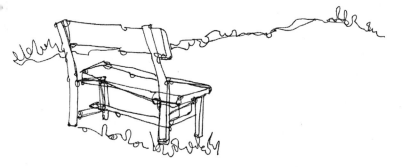

How do
you see yourself?

'As a quintessential enthusiast'

In my first book, 'Collecting Conversations', where I asked 100 women the same question, I found most women went straight into self- sabotage negatives with an emphasis on their physical side, but interviewing the men was quite a different tale.

The 20s

Pretty confident. Extrovert at the best of times but often I want to be by myself and shut everything in the world away. I find my self-worth when I'm being creative, especially when I'm on a stage. No matter how much I might feel pressured by the idea of going to work behind a desk, doing something with more structure, I don't think I ever would. I'm drawn to performance and being creative.

I'm someone who on the inside is calling out for his mother. My inner child is calling out for her. I seem to find her in everyone. I think people find mothers in all sorts of places - in idols, in friends, in fathers. I've been finding a mother in my partners. I want someone to tell me I'm doing okay. Tell me I'm on the right path. I'm constantly wondering if my life path is the right one. I've always been a pleaser. I've always been a yes-man. I'm so positive I'll say yes to everything even if I know I can't make it. It's ended up being a problem in the past. My logic is, if I say yes to everyone then they won't go away like my Mum did. It's as though I didn't please her enough so she had to leave, which is awful because it's just not true.

∎

As a disability activist, I've got a YouTube channel, about raising awareness for disability and the different challenges people face. It's what I believe in most, but what I'm known for is football. I'm about to start my university degree in football coaching. Football is my life. I have two teams, West Ham United and Luton. In 2019 I went to 73 games between the two clubs and spent more than £4,500 watching them. I have two nicknames - 'Stato' because I memorise football statistic, and 'Wheels' because of my wheelchair.

∎

As someone who is trying to enjoy the small things. Recently I picked up my brother's guitar and started strumming. I loved it. I can only do the basics but it relaxes me. I don't have ambition to get good at it. In everything else I do, I'm always striving to be better but with the guitar I'm not.

.

When I was younger I wasn't confident. I used to follow the herd. Joining the Royal Marines gave me a focus and purpose. As I get older life starts to get complicated. When you're young things were clear and simple. Now I realize there are limitations.

.

Independent - I've lived on my own since I left uni. I like not being reliant on other people. I have a keen interest in the mundane aspects of life, like walking in nature and not being materialistic. I drive a shit car and I don't have any money. I don't have nice clothes. Fundamentally I have wholesome beliefs, I like that.

.

I stop doing things! My Dad was very big on us having hobbies. 'You have a hobby, you set yourself up for life'. I used to do all sorts of creative things. I used to do performing arts, act, dance, sing. I used to play the piano. I got to grade 4 piano and stopped. I got to grade 3 saxophone and stopped. I got to competitive swimming level and stopped. I did lifesaving and stopped, martial arts and stopped!

The 30s

A little bit jaded. I can be cynical but at the same time I am a very optimistic person. Quietly confident. A huge football fan. I support Tottenham Hotspur. The way I talk and represent myself is an accurate expression of who I am. This is me, there is no facade.

.

I see myself as a bit of a failure. I don't think I've succeeded at many goals. I wasn't a particularly good solicitor. I don't see myself as a good brother or son. I tried my hand at writing. Starting things and not finishing them is a common thread. I was in therapy for most of last year, then ran out of money. My therapist tried to re-enforce my achievements but I don't see it that way. Once things are internalised it's difficult to break the pattern.

■

I come across as confident but I'm not really. I am trying to do the best I can with what I've been given. I put a lot of pressure on myself. I don't know where my need to be perfect comes from. My counsellor has been trying to work it out. For some reason I feel I have to be the best. I'm learning there's a lot to be said for imperfection.

■

I'm super competitive. I think it might be the product of living with my old man and growing up with three brothers. It's been instilled in me. I even compete in yoga, I can't help it. I want to keep achieving. I went back to studying and started a PhD. It was a real struggle juggling coaching with academia. After a massive tussle I parked the PhD and focused entirely on my coaching. Luckily that's worked out because I got my dream job. Initially I took a 100 per cent pay cut to get an internship. I consider myself pretty lucky. I've just started this role but I'm thinking, 'What's next? How can I get better?'

■

I got a promotion, which is great, but then all of a sudden I'm the boss who has to lead meetings. I can't turn up with a hangover any more. If I'm not prepared, I'm fucked. What I'm trying to say is, in your early 20s you can be ambitious. You can push, push, push for a bigger car, better house, nicer clothes. Then you get to a point when you move up in your job, your relationship becomes serious and you have a baby, all your freedoms are taken away. I think a lot of men find that transition hard.

■

I am a very literal person. I was always a bit shy. My sister used to talk for me. People used to ask me how I was and my sister would say, 'He's fine!' A lot of Asian parents push their kids into doing specialties. With me and my sister both being doctors, people assume my parents pushed us into medicine. It's not the case. I fell into medicine. My mates were doing it so I followed them. It wasn't a passion to begin with. I did what I needed to do to become a doctor. One time I was on a training shift, I came home and my Mum asked me what speciality I wanted to do. I didn't know. She said, 'I think you need to have a bit more ambition. You need to think about want to do with your life. You need to go and find it.' She was right.

The 40s

A person trying to live life purposefully. I'm balanced by nature. I give myself a hard time when it comes to creative deadlines. The rest of the time I procrastinate. The truth about creativity is the person who carries the vision is always the hardest worker and it causes stress.

.

I've just started the fourth decade of my life. I now have clarity of what I want and what I don't. I don't want to do my current job for another 10 years. I am constantly looking for a change of career.

I see myself as average. I'm a nice guy. I've a good marriage. I'm a good Dad. I could probably work a bit harder on things and that's why I feel average. I don't see myself as a particularly remarkable but I don't see myself as a failure either. I'm content. I'm not going to change the world and I'm okay with that.

Being in the army is a big part of my sense of identity and worth. When I was made a captain I couldn't fit into my parade uniform. I've put on 20 kilos since I got married, so I squeezed into my wife's Spanx in the vain attempt to get the trousers to do up. THAT was a particularly low point.

.

I see myself as realistic, bordering on negative although I don't like negative people. My day-to-day job as a postman is a mundane job. Every morning at 5am I put on my uniform. It took me a long time to feel comfortable that I am 'trade', that's not what I wanted to be in life. Oddly enough, I feel comfortable with it now. There is a frustration in me. There's something I want to do but don't apply myself. I didn't go to university. I used to have a chip on my shoulder about that. In our society people prove they're clever by going to uni. I don't have proof. As I've gotten older I've realised intelligence shows in what I say and how I say it. People see a postman's uniform and have their assumptions. When I start a conversation, they're quite surprised. People say, 'Oh, that was very eloquent'! My chip has gone. I see myself as funny, melancholic at times. On a bad day I think I am completely useless and selfish. But on a good day I can say I've bought my own home in a time when that's a really hard thing to do.

My academic and work achievements aren't great. If I look at my CV I'm appalled. Society measures success by how clever you are, how well off you are. Why doesn't anyone measure success by how many friends would be back and forth to your home every day if you only had a month to live? It's about having something solid around you. I was brought up to be told you can't trust anyone. My sister took that on, I didn't. I have total trust with my friends. I measure myself as a huge success by that. My Mum is 82. She has lifelong friends who visit her regularly. She's in a home and has no idea who anyone is. That's what I call success. She's won the prize.

■

I am really proud of being Tongan, it's at the forefront of what I bring. I organise community events - it's about cooking, bringing people together. I feel part of the community.

■

Inherently contradictory! I have always seen myself as pretty decent at some things but not exceptional at anything. 'Always representing the school but will never make the County team.' The feeling that I am being ignored - both professionally and personally - I hate it!

■

I see myself as a human being who is determined to learn, evolve and overcome my shortcomings. I'm in awe. I marvel at humanity. I think life is wonderful. It's so precious.

■

I'm a bit dizzy. Not a lot of men use that word to describe themselves. I don't have a problem with that. For years I didn't like myself. I used to be everyone and everything apart from the real me. It's been a painful journey. I like me now. I'm very self-aware. I'm conscious of when I'm being annoying. I'm not as erratic as I used to be. Medication helps.

■

I don't hate the idea of being fat. I don't hate the idea of having yellow teeth. None of those things matter to me. Left to my own devices I would gleefully be drunk every day. There are reasons and consequences for doing that, though. There is this looming reality that if I want to get to 80 that maybe I have to do something about it.

The 50s

The first question they ask you when training to be a counsellor is, 'Who are you?' You think, 'What a silly question,' but then realize you don't know yourself that well until you start working on yourself. I'm happy within myself but I'm a bit of a perfectionist. I feel it's never quite good enough. Self-doubt creeps in. I sometimes have imposter syndrome but I think that can be healthy. I didn't have much confidence when I was younger. I was good at most things but if an obstacle came up, I'd give up. From 11 to 16 years old I raced BMX bikes. I was seventh in the country but all of a sudden obstacles got in the way, so I gave up. To validate myself I had to be the best. When I wasn't getting that validation my inner critic would be really hard.

■

You move on from the size of your penis as a teenager to the size of your house as you get older. It's always about size of some description! I've been blessed growing up in a loving family, who are now old which gives you a certain viewpoint on life. I'm fortunate. I'm laid-back. I'm a relaxed man. It doesn't give me the drive that I 'should' have but when adversity has occurred I've been able, after some reflection, to keep going. For example, we got taken to the cleaners by a trusted person within our organisation. We lost a fortune. That could have made me incredibly bitter, but I learned from it. It wasn't a positive experience but I'm proud that my brother and I kept our company going. We were right royally taken for mugs! We were grown men and over-dependent on our father. He had trusted this person but a little voice said, 'This ain't right but Dad knows what he's doing.' After that we decided if we were going to make mistakes we had to make them ourselves.

•

When I catch myself in a reflection my hair can be like Boris' (Johnson). I should make more of an effort but I don't care what people think of me. I'm a nice person. I'm glad I'm the person I am. There's not a lot I want to change. I work on films, it can be stressful sometimes, people can go ballistic. I can get past that. I try to bring a mellow feel to my work. My wife says I don't overthink things. If that makes me a relaxed person then it's probably better for me.

•

Very self-centred - I feel like a person who's been dropped out of the sky and put in the wrong place. I'm happy in my own headspace. I'm quite introverted. I'm happy sitting, watching, observing and listening - just being. I suffer with a condition called common sense! I'm definitely a work in progress. I've suffered with severe mental health issues which put me in hospital. I'm still suffering from the effects of that. I'm actually pretty proud of myself and how I've kept going. My breakdown nearly broke me. It was after a bad road accident. I was on my motorbike and went through the windscreen of a car. I've been struggling for years with a nerve condition. It may well be a lifelong thing. I get up in the morning in agony. I can't walk long distances because of my feet. I shattered my foot and snapped my arm. I was told I'd never walk again. I'd had a premonition it was going to happen. The sensation was like putting my fingers in an electric socket and it reverberating through my brain. I had pain from the moment I woke up to the moment I went to sleep. I felt there was no way out. Everything shut down. I was left shaking like a leaf. It went on for months and months. I used to sit in a hot bath and think there was only one way out of this. That's why people take their lives, when you can't see a way out of it. It was relentless. Being in abject pain, you just want to die. Every fucking day I'd be lying in bed crying because I was in so much pain. Eventually I stopped taking the medication. I locked myself in my bedroom for two weeks and took control of it. A piece of advice I took on board was something Stephen Fry said, to the effect that when you do a task, you should aim to make it last five times longer than it would normally take. You slow everything right down.

■

I have the impression that I'm somehow less visible than others. I often wonder why. As a kid I was the weirdo in our family. Nobody really understood me. I didn't relate to the people around me. Three months ago I was at a gay discussion group. I was trying to describe the feeling of invisibility. The facilitator asked everybody in the room to cover their eyes, while I kept mine open. It was interesting. Suddenly being in a room where I could see everybody and they couldn't see me was exactly how it feels. I've realized I make myself invisible sometimes.

■

I'm judgemental, but not as much as I used to be. I like me now but there were times when I didn't. I've done things that weren't nice. Now I'm honest, I say what I think. I'm not scared any more.

■

I'm a slightly frustrated white, middle-class man who feels the world is changing around him. I'm lucky that I have good support around me - great kids, a brilliant wife, good friends, a lovely family and a good job in magazines. I see myself as someone who did okay but could have done better. Who didn't fulfil his potential. Occasionally I get frustrated with myself. I think we all think we're special at something. I'm straightforward, decent and slightly dull. I used to be fairly good-looking but now I'm a plain old bloke who's got an okay life. Could I have done something different? Could I have got more out of being a teacher? I like magazines but what's the point of them?

So what if I'm off to LA to shoot Taylor Swift! I am happy in my own space. I'm small-c conservative and old-fashioned. The 23-year old me would detest the way I see things now.

■

I function, maybe not to my full potential. I like myself. I have a wife and two kids I love, a small band of friends whom I trust. I have a house - yes it's a burden around my neck but it does the job. Without the cloud of my past hanging over my head (sexually abusive father) I would say life is good. I'm reasonably lucky. Lucky because I can verbalise what's gone on in my life. I don't bottle things up. I see myself as someone who could try harder.

■

I don't like arguing with people because in my head I'm thinking, 'Hit him, hit him.' If there's a fight going off I tend to head towards it. I see myself as a protector rather than a bully although I probably did some bullying in my time. I know I upset people sometimes. I don't mean to, but if I know I'm in the right I can't let it go. Me and my daughter butt heads quite a lot. We are very similar except she's a vegan feminist!

■

A little melancholy. I don't get depressed but I do get low and it's quite constant. Although I don't appear it, I can be angry and I'm not sure why. My Mum's side of my family are angry, it's in my genes - I think too much. I'm a dweller and a brooder.

■

I'm bad at relaxing. I have an ambivalent view about myself. The logical part of me says I'm a nice person. I do good things for people but the other side of me is, 'You're an arsehole!'

■

I see myself differently than if you'd asked me three weeks ago. I feel vulnerable at the moment.

■

I'm fairly cautious - a little conventional if anything. I'm a quiet bloke. Perfectly comfortable in my own company. I like reading, I like gardening. I'm really middle-aged. I'm content with my life, although I don't feel I've achieved very much.

•

I'm a reflective person. Probably on the spectrum of a procrastinator. I'm naturally curious, that's why I became a journalist. I'm motivated. I read about five books at a time, all at the same time. I play the piano, the guitar, then I burn out. I stop and do sweet fuck-all for ages, feel guilty about it - then the cycle starts all over again! I'm also an activist. I'm more left-wing now than I've ever been. If something fits with my values then I'm driven. My family think I'm going to end up in a cave in Tibet. I'm a Yogi. I read lots of spiritual texts. I see myself as someone who cares deeply about a lot of things and who loves life. Who wants the best of everything for everyone. I hate conflict. I prefer creation, openness and optimism. I live life like a musical. 'Gandhi on ice!'

•

I felt pressure to provide. I think men feel pressure to be the breadwinner. I know my Dad had a problem coping with that. He was a pharmacist, a bright person but he wasn't happy. He found it difficult to divorce himself from work and family life, that created a lot of frustration. He took his own life when I was 12.

•

There are no big thinkers in my family, we are simple sorts. Simple country bumpkins. I'm not a dweller. I'm a bit of a 'For God's sake, get a grip and get on with it' sort of person. I've mellowed as time's gone on. I've got a long fuse, it takes a lot for me blow but when I do - for a little fella, I could punch someone's lights out and end up in prison! I reckon in the last 10 years I've blown to that extent twice. (Thankfully he didn't end up in prison!)

•

I see myself as a very positive person with a good outlook. We're here once, so let's make an impression and if you can help change people's lives along the way, even better. When it's time to depart this planet you'll have achieved something and done a good job. I like to think I inspire people. I was awarded the Crest of Hartlepool for putting Hartlepool in a positive light with the work that I do.

■

I've grown to like me much more over the last few years. I was always hard on myself but I think that's what drives me. There's a drive to get things done. I won't take a day off sick, I've never done that. It comes from when I left university, I fucked up my degree and fell into law. It was a bit like, 'Come on. You've got to get on with this by yourself because no one else is going to do it for you.' When I started law, I was quite good at it. I was driven. My son recently asked me if I watched 'Live Aid' back in the '80s. I was so busy revising for my finals. I remember stopping for half an hour then going back to my work.

■

I'm conscious of my faults and don't correct them enough. I'm very comfortable in my own skin. The good parts of me outweigh the bad.

■

I like to do things on my own. I like to go salmon fishing. It's being at one with nature. I don't relax by doing nothing.

■

I see myself as an extraordinarily unfit, positive, a quintessential enthusiast, who is really interested in people and who gets things done. I'm a mixture of hard-working, perhaps a workaholic and good company. I tend to go from one extreme to the other.

■

I haven't been self aware enough to know the impact I've had on my wife or my children and those who are close to me. You don't always realise the impact you're having. Self-awareness is not something you naturally have. I think you can learn it, through coaching, perhaps? As soon as you give it a label people see it as remedial and therefore a bad thing. Ten years ago I would have thought coaching was for people who aren't performing properly. I would have taken up coaching early on if known about it. Back then, people didn't do it!

The 60s

Chirpy and positive. I don't want to be miserable unless I'm in pain. My first few years I lived with my Mum after my parents separated. She's Irish Catholic and my Dad was from Jamaica. When I was seven she said, 'I've looked after you for seven years, your Dad can look after you now.' I adjusted to my Dad's climate. He was strict. 'You must wash! You must learn to cook! You must learn to wash your clothes!' He tried. It was difficult because he worked nights. When I see all the mental health problems these days I think, 'If anyone should be down it should be me with what I've been through. Growing up with my Dad. Loneliness is a fucking killer.'

■

I work in security. I've got 64 drivers to get into their vehicles, load them up and get them off the premises, while sorting out their problems too. The work is as hard as you make it. It used to be dangerous. I had seven attacks in 18 years. Luckily attacks have gone out of the window because there are cameras everywhere and more plain clothes police. If we do see anything suspicious there's a number we call. It's much better than it was.

■

Imposter syndrome strikes everybody at some point. How did I get this far? It's not that I didn't have the brains, but I'm not terribly assertive. Recently I was made redundant (I now have another job). I didn't realize how ageist the world is. I applied for roles in similar organisations and didn't even get an interview. My face didn't fit. Diversity cuts both ways. My industry was dominated by women in their 30s and 40s. It wasn't diverse.

■

Skint, introverted and depressive. Maybe that's why I'm not married. I have an over-active imagination. I am interested in a lot of things. I get easily distracted. I have a very thin line between needing my privacy and feeling isolated. I am always negotiating. I can feel very quickly invaded and claustrophobic. Needing to go home to be on my own. I spend far more time on my own than most people but that's not lonely. I have had depression all my life. It's part of me. It's shaped everything. I'm wondering if there is a connection? I wouldn't be the person I am without it but there's a part of me that thinks, 'Is it worth it?'

∎

In my head I've been Peter Gabriel all my life. I've always enjoyed being the guy sitting at the piano, slavishly learning songs. I never had any intentions of doing it for a living. I have Tourette's (Syndrome) and OCD (obsessive compulsive disorder) and it has ruled my life. It's a terrible thing - it doesn't matter how clever I am, I can't concentrate for long and as a result I'm a very chatty, friendly person. I overcompensate. I don't like having Tourette's but it's part of me.

When people see me having brought up my three children on my own, they say, 'That's amazing.' That's not the way I see it. I saw it as ducking out of work. I felt I took a slightly easier option. I see myself as less exciting and active than I am seen. I'm actually quite lazy. I give myself things to do. I don't have any ambition. I'm not a guy that starts things. I try to be as giving as I can be. As a spirit I am pretty welcoming.

∎

Internally I spend a lot of time laughing about the bonkers nature of life. I hated my childhood. I was born and brought up in Yorkshire. As my father was a politician he and my mother spent all week in London and I was left with an elderly retainer and home-schooled until I was eight, then was sent off to a ghastly establishment in Berkshire – Sunningdale. It was awful. I didn't enjoy my childhood until I was 12. I was very lonely and insular, I had no friends. I was feeble and constantly in tears. It was a useful experience, though. I'd go off and sit in the lavatory thinking up things to say to the people I hated. I planned my answers, I became much more eloquent, honing my wit. Then I went to Eton. I loved it. I was completely free. It was an eccentric, bonkers place. If you had any ideas - say for example you wanted to set up a society for the breeding habits of Scottish lice, you'd find a Master to set up a society about it. They would celebrate your individuality. It was such a contrast of the utter horror of being a little boy. You see everything has a silver lining. That's why I think all the things you go through are immensely helpful to get you to the next stage. The steel goes into the fire and comes out tougher but hopefully more sensitive.

■

I'm not sure I see myself as other people see me. I'm always surprised why people want to be my friend. I don't see myself in a bad light but if I look in the mirror I think, 'Who the fuck is that?' I don't see what they see. My issue is my physical appearance. I would say I'm too fat and too old.

■

I am a tough task-master - I spend a lot of time on self improvement. I have this thing about becoming one per cent a day better every day - emotionally, spiritually, mentally and physically. I'm into affirmations and habits. I diarise my list of achievements. I have routine to my day, I write my diary, my ideas, my blog and I post on Instagram every day. I'm organised. It's a structure that makes me feel I've achieved something. Another belief I have is that I am merely a conduit. None of what I am doing is me, it's a product of the energy I am creating. I don't write the book, it writes itself. I am just a messenger. I don't know what name you give to that power but there's definitely an energy greater than you or me.

■

I see myself as a free spirit. I know I have been weak willed in my relationships so I don't think too much of myself about that. I'm gentle and a little out of my depth.

The 70s

Determined. If I decide to do something it doesn't matter how long it takes, I won't give up. I never give up. I am an identical twin. I used to hate being a twin. I wanted to be myself. People would come along and pat me on the head. 'Oh, you're one of the twins!' We made up our own language when we were little. When we started school, we used to walk on different sides of the road to establish our individuality. My brother died six months ago. He had leukaemia and died very quickly. He lived in New Zealand. I hadn't seen him in the flesh for 25 years. He'd say, 'If we don't see each other for 25 years, and bumped into each other in the pub, it would be like we've seen each other yesterday.' We've always had that kind of connection but we weren't clingy. His funeral was on Zoom. My sister said I frightened the life out of most people in the congregation. They thought my brother had pre-recorded his eulogy.

■

As somebody who's involved in community and cares about people, I have strong principles and get annoyed when I see injustices. A lot of people from my generation didn't go to university because there was a lot of industry around. The youth employment officer came into school saying there were plenty of opportunities down the pit. There were a lot of missed opportunities back then. The education system let us down. Luckily I didn't go down the pit, I went to college and got into engineering. I worked at Rolls Royce and was a trade unionist and shop steward.

■

There are times when I don't like myself but those times are rare. Without sounding conceited, I'm quite happy with myself. I'm certainly an optimist.

■

I'm as ordinary as can be. I get accused of being too laid-back. There's not much that stresses me out. I don't argue much - I don't see the point. I'm not the life and soul of the party either. I'm quiet but quietly competitive. I am a practical person - there's nothing much going on in my head.

I'm focused, self-disciplined and have determination. I even managed to get my blood sugar levels down. I am not emotional at all. Even when my brother died, I didn't cry. I feel guilty about it but you can't force it out. Someone said I have no empathy with anyone - and I probably don't.

■

I see myself as an older man who is content. I have a very loving husband. We live in a small but very comfortable apartment. I have a beautiful terrace strewn with a zillion plants, it lights me up.

■

As an alpha male, I'm quite outspoken. Political correctness never existed in my time. You should be able to debate and argue your point but you have to be so careful these days. People are very sensitive.

■

I see myself as a fish floating around without any specific attachments.

■

I'm committed, passionate and enthusiastic. Life has an order of priorities and family is obviously the first one. If you're managing to keep that afloat and they're doing as well as they can, then you can look at other things for a sense of fulfilment.

■

I'm a half-full person. I look on the bright side. I've had a lot to contend with. Luckily time is the greatest healer and you forget. If I have any problems this week, by next week I'll have completely forgotten what the problem was. I'm living in the present.

The 80s-plus

Not good enough. Not active enough. I hate mirrors. I appreciate you can't go backwards. I realise I'm slowing down but I live in hope that something nice is going to happen. I come from a Catholic background. My parents were very uninterested in me. I was shipped off to Catholic boarding school at the age of nine and progressed through school in a cloud of my own. I went through school waiting to leave. I was unsure of myself. Then the '60s came along, everything was becoming liberated. The invention of 'the pill' meant life was changing and I changed with it. It made being gay easier too. I'm creative, my mind is always coming up with ideas. Someone once said to me, 'The thing about you is, when anything goes wrong, you wake up the next morning with a new idea.' It's true. Forget the niggles and problems - in life you have to move on.

I like the life that I've led. I've survived and had some good times. Life is about resilience. Finding things you like and things you don't - I don't like failure. I don't like anything physical about myself. I'd like to be better-looking and have nicer clothes. I like the idea of wearing head to toe denim, looking like I've come off the ranch but that would require shopping - I hate shopping!

■

I have been a magician since I was 11 and a professional one since 1976. You never really retire in our game. I'm now 85. My father gave me my first box of tricks 74 years ago, that's what started me off. I built myself a magic act and by the time I was 14 I had a proper act. My first acts were turning water into wine, swallowing razor blades then pulling them back out of my mouth via a piece of thread. I am organised. I never stopped. My glass is half full. I'm positive. I like to see the funny side of things. I'm a nice guy.

■

I'm getting old but I don't want to admit it. Luckily I've only had one incident and that was seven years ago - I got prostate cancer. Thankfully it was caught early and completely cured. I feel I am a very lucky person.

■

I'm reasonably proud of myself. I don't think I've made many mistakes. I left school two weeks before my 17th birthday, in 1946. The war had just ended. There were no careers advisors then. I couldn't think what to do, so I went to work for the Inland Revenue. I was an assistant filing clerk. I didn't like it. It was boring. So I left and joined the Army. I spent six months in Northern Ireland. Eventually I went to Sandhurst. I liked the structure. Everyone knew what they were doing. You were all in it together. We formed a bond.

We looked out for each other. I was in the Army for 16 years. If you hadn't reached the rank of Lieutenant Colonel by the age of 40 you had to leave. I was invited to retire early. I left but needed some qualifications because I had three children, a wife and a dog to support. I didn't expect my wife to work. I expected to be a provider. I re-trained to be a solicitor.

A longer conversation…

Alex, 28

*author and wellbeing consultant
from North London*

I'm pretty much in a state of wonder. I've no idea whether I'm coming or going. I've been working very hard - I've just finished writing my first book and I have a weekly podcast. Once my book was finished, I was like, 'What do I do now?' I throw myself into more projects to keep feeling useful. I understand it's a toxic, masculine energy. I don't know how to rest. I'm trying to slow down. I don't understand a life that isn't a disciplined one, but there's a point where the discipline consumes me.

My day usually starts by 6.30am. I write for half an hour. Then shower. Then write again until 8am. Writing is a skill that needs to be strengthened. I read. Meditate and get my thoughts out. I think through a lot of what I say. I do slow thinking. I like to be clear about things. I don't want to be misunderstood. I do my podcast each week so I talk a lot. I write a lot. I am consistently communicating.

You've caught me at an age and in a phase of transition. I used to care a lot about how people saw me. What did they think? Was I caring? Strong? Talented? I used to want to be seen as interesting, now I'm like, 'If you like what I do, great.' How people see me is not my problem.

When I left uni, I joined the 'Daily Mail' as part of their Stephen Lawrence Scholarship Training Scheme. A scheme for training minority and ethnic people, but what they really meant was, black. I hated it. The energy was oppressing. I was a young Black man in a predominantly white industry. I had nothing in common with many of my colleagues, and they had no time for me. I had a lot of questions that they didn't have the answers to. I felt alienated. It became a well of toxicity. I was young. I didn't know enough. If I was working on the paper now, I know exactly what kind of stories I'd want to report on. I'd know what tone the paper has and the stories they want to cover. I'd just do my job and leave. But I had all these ideals, I thought a lot more of it than it actually was. It became a struggle for me. That's when I had my first panic attack.

I'm in therapy now. I'm not perfect. I make mistakes. A previous version of me would lambaste myself for making mistakes. I've grown and taken time to care for myself, and I've come to understand that compassion is something I need to give myself. I'm an advocate for compassionate thinking but, to be honest, there are days when I'm not very compassionate. I'm not trying to present myself as a perfect person I'm just trying to just be a decent, wholeheartedly compassionate person. Maybe I'm trying to save myself?

I feel very compassionate towards other people. I want to help and support as many people as I can, but when you can't do that for yourself, what does it all mean? I'm getting there. It's revolutionary because previously I didn't even understand what liking myself meant.

Life is a joyful thing. When we are in the moment, we sometimes don't see the joy of what's happening because the bigger picture is not clear to us. You have to trust the process. As you gain perspective you move through it. I'm big on souls and the understanding of what soul work means. I find it hard to believe that some people don't believe in that. My understanding has always been that there is something wider than ourselves. When we start to consider a wider perception, life becomes more manageable because there's more room to breathe.

I remember at uni, my flat mate was struggling. I could see him trying to come to terms with 'self' and the realities of where we were all heading - into adulthood. He had to figure out what life was and that was combative for him. When we had discussions and he would say, 'This can't be right,' or, 'That's wrong.' Someone had to be wrong and somebody had to be right. There is no right or wrong. People believe differently and therefore experience life differently. It's the rigidity of masculinity. Masculinity by its nature is a rigid form of ideology. Masculinity looks at straight lines, not squiggles. If we look at most buildings made over the last few centuries they're all up, boxed and crossed. It's rigidity. There's no grey area.

When you start to add in 'what ifs,' colour, and fluidity then you start to move in different ways. When you start to feel, you start to express. Then you start to change and become malleable. That is understood as feminine energy.

I once read that feminine energy is the river and masculinity energy is the river bed. One contains and allows the other to flow in the way that it's supposed to. Men inhabit the rigidity of the masculine mindset, it's what they can control. It's what they understand. They're taught to understand, strengthen, be strong and stand firm and women can do the dancing and singing!

I think as we head into a more spiritually focused society, the reign of the patriarchal society is slowly coming to a very welcome end. There shouldn't be dominance. I feel like we've been led by masculine groups for so long and the only answer is violence. I'm not saying that women are passive, I'm just saying that violence has had its place. Time moves forward and things that were acceptable are no longer. In 50 or 60 years things we see now probably won't be the norm then. Change happens.

'To protect my emotional well being

NO ENTRY

I put up a lot of boundaries'

How do you think other people see you?

*'When you're sure about yourself,
you don't care what other people think'*

Abrasive ⚥ Humble ⚥ Calm ⚥ Interested ⚥ Positive ⚥ Inquisitive ⚥ Questioning ⚥ Shy ⚥ Reserved ⚥ Quiet ⚥ Inspiring ⚥ The boy in the wheelchair ⚥ Loyal ⚥ Kind ⚥ Self-centred ⚥ Boring ⚥ **FRIENDLY** ⚥ Lacking confidence. ⚥ Well-mannered ⚥ Gay ⚥ A bit of a dick ⚥ Paranoid ⚥ Generous ⚥ Dedicated ⚥ Approachable ⚥ Wise. ⚥ Responsible ⚥ Fun ⚥ Cocky ⚥ Spiteful ⚥ Lovely ⚥ Selfish ⚥ Spoiled ⚥ Entrepreneurial ⚥ Determined ⚥ **INTELLIGENT** ⚥ Stubborn ⚥ Impatient ⚥ Achiever ⚥ Sensitive ⚥ A leader ⚥ Forceful ⚥ Snowflakey ⚥ Reliable ⚥ Thoughtful ⚥ Encouraging ⚥ Funny ⚥ Outrageous ⚥ Balanced ⚥ Reasonable ⚥ A fumbling idiot ⚥ Charming ⚥ Interested ⚥

Relaxed ⚥ As a piss artist with high blood pressure ⚥ Nurturing ⚥ Grumpy ⚥ Reassuring ⚥ **ARROGANT** ⚥ Over-sensitive ⚥ Moody ⚥ Aggressive ⚥ Stable ⚥ Centred ⚥ Nasty-tempered ⚥ Dependable ⚥ Solitary ⚥ **SERIOUS** ⚥ A worrier ⚥ Aloof ⚥ Loud ⚥ Enthusiastic ⚥ Hopeless ⚥ Easy-going ⚥ Too nice ⚥ Stuck ⚥ Political ⚥ Passionate ⚥ Ordinary ⚥ Dodges responsibility ⚥ Quick thinking ⚥ Lacks patience ⚥ Defensive ⚥ Shut off ⚥ Guarded ⚥ Unable to make decisions ⚥ **SOCIALLY AWKWARD** ⚥ Unselfish ⚥ Energetic ⚥ Warm ⚥ A breath of fresh air ⚥ Show-off ⚥ Snappy dresser ⚥ Rude ⚥ Accepted ⚥ Well-liked ⚥ Pompous ⚥ Pleased with myself ⚥

A longer conversation...

Karl 55

from Nottingham, works in analytics

I consider myself very fortunate at this time in my life. A few years ago I wasn't in a good place. I had a few mental health issues that I was ignoring. As a family we went through some very bad times. In six years we lost four family members. I pushed everything to the back of my mind in order to cope. I didn't think about my own health, I was too busy organising funerals.

Men cocoon themselves. We use vices to dull our emotions. For me, it was beer - I drank a lot of beer. I ignored it and I shouldn't have. 'I'll be fine, I'll deal with it, I'm a coper. Whatever you throw at me I'll manage'. But there's always a price to pay. Not only your physical health but your mental health too. If you don't deal with it - it will get you. We don't seek help soon enough. I cannot recommend enough, getting support as soon as you know something is wrong. Boys aren't taught to cry. You've gotta cry - get it out. If you're still crying after a year, that's fine - it has to come out.

I had a tendency to shut off. I was quite happy to sit in a corner on my own, that is the worst thing to do. My Mum helped me immensely. Me and Mum would go out for drives in the car and just talk. My Mum has an amazing ability to communicate. She's like a magnet. People flock to her. She is a defining part of my life. Not just because she's my Mum. She doesn't have a negative bone in her body.

It's finding someone who you're comfortable to talk with. If you sit in your aloneness for long enough, you don't know the decisions you're making. You have no one to bounce off and that's when things start to go awry! The problems with most of the world are because there aren't enough women in power. Women are better communicators.

I eventually got diagnosed with bipolar disorder. If you say you've been diagnosed with bipolar, you might as well say you have smallpox. Mentally and physically, I was a mess. My blood pressure was so high. I got pancreatitis and had to have my gall bladder removed. When you become ill with a psychiatric problem you know who your friends are. There's a pressure. Society expects everyone to be fit and healthy and if you're not, you're seen as 'lazy'.

The worst thing you can say to someone who is down is, 'Cheer up!' If I come across anyone who might need help I'll say, 'Is there anything I can do to help?' or, 'If you need to talk, let me know.' The best thing you can do with anyone is look them straight in the eye and be non-judgemental.

When I lost my Dad, I fell apart. He was the glue that held everyone together. I made the same fatal mistake that all males in our family make - we fell out and didn't speak, and exactly the same thing has happened with my son.

One time when I was still ill, I had a dream. I was in bed. The curtains morphed into a headless, moving snake. Then my Dad started talking to me, he'd been dead for six years at the time. There was no shaft of light or anything but his voice was crystal clear. It felt like a couple of hours. He said to me, 'I don't like you being unhappy, be happy, learn to like yourself - come on, you're better than that. I am all right - you have to let me go'. I was talking back to him. I was having a conversation with him. My Dad's 'visit' will never leave me.

I'm okay now but I wasn't then. It's taken four or five years. Now I feel the best and most positive I've felt in 30 years. I am a lot happier. Part of having a creative mind means I'm not very good at following rules, I'm too free-spirited. It has its pros and cons. I don't seem to be able to form any relationships with women. I haven't had a relationship for a very long time. Will I get married again? NO!

Although you should never say never.

I like poetry. I remember a poem by Gill Scott Heron. 'Whitey's on the moon'. It's about black culture in Washington. I loved it. There's a three-piece track called 'Home is where the hatred is', about his drug and alcohol addiction and how it's torn him apart. I think poetry is a powerful skill that we've forgotten. We should teach it again. If you can get your heart and mind to talk to each other you'll be okay.

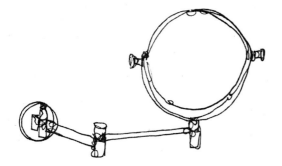

What do you like about yourself?

'Do I like myself? Yes, I do'

Previously I asked 100 women this question and most of their answers started with a negative: 'I can tell you what I don't like.' Which was interesting but didn't answer the question. When I asked a 100 men, most just told me. No ifs or buts or self-deprecation, just the answer. When I told women what I heard, some said, 'They would say that! They're so arrogant, so full of themselves, it's all about them and their egos!' I don't think so. They simply answered the question. They were literal. Some felt awkward but still answered. I think there's something in this. Men, I think are much more direct, black and white. That's not to say there aren't grey areas but when questions are asked, they are often quite literal in their answers!

Do we learn self-awareness or does it come naturally? Can you read the room? One man said, 'These aren't necessarily my natural characteristics, I've worked hard at some of these. I've taught myself not to rush in, not to respond when I'm upset, or press 'Send' when I'm angry. I've had to take a deep breath to curb some of my natural instincts.' I would say this man has self-awareness oozing out of him and the humility to try and change his natural default setting. Another said, 'I have no idea what it means to have self-awareness - I think it's something you need to be shown or taught.'

This question gave time for self-reflection. Taking the opportunity to say what you really think and feel about YOU! 'Do I like myself? Yes I do!' How refreshing.

The 20s

I'm caring. That's something that has never changed, it's one of my most consistent traits. I'm relatively interesting, or at least I have interesting stories to tell. I like that I've managed to get through so much in the last year - my father took his own life and, I found out that my Aunt is my actual birth mother.

■

I like my height. I used to be terribly insecure about being 6 feet 4.5 inches. I was this height when I was 16. I had size 13 feet when I was 13 years old. There's something quite ridiculous about being that height when you're 16. Your nose is too small, your ears are too big and you haven't grown into your body yet. I felt socially awkward. I like my red hair. It's something my Mum gave me. I love my positivity. I really value that in myself. It's a lot easier to feel sad than it is to feel good. There's nothing wrong with feeling down but I prefer being happy than sad although it can feel like a burden. I sometimes feel responsible for keeping the room bright and the mood right.

∎

My individuality. I'm very aware of how pretentious that sounds! I am a drag artist and love doing drag because it is authentically me. I've got about a dozen gigs coming up with the WI (Women's Institute) who are absolutely amazing. I'd never heard of them before lockdown, they're wonderful.

∎

The inability to not give up. More often than not I'll find a solution to something. If we go to West Ham for example, and the lifts are broken, (I'm a wheelchair user) my Dad will get quite angry, where I calmly say, 'Okay, what's the alternative route?' I like problem-solving.

∎

I like that I have grown and developed into someone who isn't as worried about what other people think. I like me most of the time. I like that I am trying to better myself and I can't see myself ever stopping. One of the biggest things I'm proud of is how family-orientated I am. I am a bit mushy - people say I'm a bit of a mummy's boy. One of my best friends is my brother. It frustrates me when people don't respect their families or acknowledge how important they are. I like to think I maintain my friendships very well. I can spread myself a bit too thin sometimes.

∎

I am very organised. Ever since I can remember, I've written down my goals. For example, if there was a specific fitness standard I'd have to meet for the Royal Marines, I'd write it down. Or saving money, stuff like that. I am goal orientated. I plan to buy as many properties as I can. I'm about to buy my second home. If I do become wealthy, I don't know what I'd do with all the money.

∎

I like my independence. I've got good social skills. I can talk to people from all walks of life. I like my interest in things. I'm curious. I'm fairly level-headed. I know what's good for me and I can call it a day at the right time - I have self-preservation.

The 30s

I like myself although it's always easier to go to the negative. I'm glad I've never been the typical alpha male and I'm not ignorant. I am very self-aware. I'm not bigoted. I believe in equality across the board. I'm glad I'm intelligent enough to listen to all points of view.

∎

I like my beard! I started growing thick facial hair when I was about 13. I'm thinking about dyeing it orange or red. I'm out of work at the moment, so why not?

∎

I definitely like my work ethic. It's been instilled in me from a very young age. My generosity, probably to the detriment of myself sometimes. If someone needs money or whatever, I'll help. I'm there for my mates if they need me.

∎

I've got a strong sense of self. I care about people. I like that about myself. I think the sound bites are different from the reality though. It's easy to be honest with yourself, but it's something different to be genuinely honest and live by it. I'm happy to give people my opinions. I'm strongly led by morals. I prefer people that say it as it is. The amount of people that will appease you and say what they think you want to hear.

∎

I like how accepting I am of people. I'm quite confident in my own little way. I've been brought up well. I'm set up for what life throws at me because I've had a good grounding. I was born in Muscat, my Dad worked there in the '80s as an ecologist. Then we lived in Somalia for two years. I've always been quite worldly, I think it's because I've always travelled. I'm not scared to try things. I'm up for challenges. I'm very resilient, ambitious, strong, capable and up for life. I love life. I never big myself up and my Dad doesn't either; he's done so much in his life and he's the most modest person in the world. I like to think I am. When I first heard the question I thought, 'Shit, what do I say without sounding big-headed?'

The 40s

I'm quite willing to chuck it all in and do something different. I'm inert but adaptable. For example, moving to a new country, which I've recently done. I'm talking about changing my entire approach to everything.

.

I'm good at forgiving myself. It's a Caribbean, laid-back thing. I can let things go. When you see the water coming up on to the shore, it's cleansing, the stress disappears. I've seen a lot growing up. My Dad would hit my Mum. It's left me with a certain sensibility. I can take a lot but remain calm. I like myself but I don't! I have some failings. There are some things I wish I didn't do. I'd like a bit more time on earth to do a better job.

.

If we'd been having this conversation six months ago, I'd tell you I didn't like myself. Everything was going wrong. I hated everything about myself. Now I realise I'm a pretty easy-going person and am able to adapt to different circumstances. I was in a bad situation with my wife. There was a lot of screaming and arguing. I didn't have the experience to deal with what's happening. Nobody tells you what to do - you have to figure things out by yourself. There's been a lot of self searching. I didn't know what to do. We've had some very difficult times. There were weeks where we were talking about divorce. The situation was unbearable. Men don't seek help. I had faith that things would get better between us. I was more attentive to her.

∎

Automatically I was thinking what I don't like about myself. That's another thing I'm going to have to look at. I think I like myself. I am very comfortable with myself. I don't know how to answer this question. I like my friendliness - I'm cringing!

∎

I've worked hard to treat people as I would like to be treated myself. Be nice to people. Be generous. I don't take myself very seriously - I don't like people who do. I have a good sense of humour. I understand myself - although not fully. When I was younger I would react impulsively, making a bad situation much worse and failing to understand that my reaction wasn't the most important aspect of whatever was happening. Why is you being offended the most important thing - no one cares! I try to take a more measured approach, it's my medicine - it takes away the agro. How much time and energy does it take to have an argument? Sleep on it! I see these tendencies in my children. They'll get it in 30 years time.

∎

That's a hard question. I like that I like to help people, especially children, it's who I am. I always treat people's kids as I want them to treat my kids. I'm patient. People say, 'I don't know how you do it.' I like that I can work right across the board, working 20 years in primary schools, then transitioning into secondary - that's a skill in itself. Secondary school can be intimidating. Kids can be weird, I like helping them.

∎

I'm honestly happy with my seriousness. I think in a way it makes me who I am. I like my sharp mind for understanding things and people. I think that's probably my most precious gift.

∎

I like that I can start up a conversation and come up with completely random facts like talking about François Truffaut meeting Graham Greene for the first time in 1973. I like that sort of knowledge. It certainly gets you through any social event. I'm relatively cultural. Culture is very broad. It stung me once when someone I knew at uni said, 'The only culture you have is pub culture!' People are very quick to judge. You learn from that. Don't judge people.

The 50s

Do I like myself? Yes, I do. I look at my kids. They seem well-adjusted, likeable. They do the right thing. That's a reflection of us parents. In the majority of my life I try and do right. It comes from the heart. I talk too much. Sometimes I blather on. I have been known to boast occasionally. But the good news is, you get older and you stop yourself. You start to think, 'SHUT UP! You don't need to say any more! BE QUIET!'

■

My humility. I'm happy and comfortable in myself. If I didn't like a certain element of myself, my common sense would kick in and I'd have to do something about. I'm always self-checking. I'm in my flow.

■

I have a positive attitude. I like to get things done. I am a bit of a control freak. I don't linger on things. I like that quality in me.

■

I spend my working life listening to other people. I am the sort of person that loves thinking about the world and relationships. I like that about me. My own analyst has taught me in a profound way to be kind, calm and nurturing to myself. One thing she's taught me is that I love change and I should nourish and nurture it. To actually make sure that I've always got change in my life. Sometimes that might mean I'm not the ideal partner. It might mean it takes a long time to accept somebody new coming into my life. I have to respect that because that's part of my soul and my spirit.

■

I'm very passionate and committed. If I'm going to do something that I really believe in, then I give it everything I've got. I spend too much time doing things I don't really believe in, in a half-arsed way. I need to shift the balance. I've lost a bit of energy and spark and I need to find it again.

■

I like that I am a good son to my Mum and Dad. I hope I've been good to my family. I like that I say what I think. I don't play politics. I've never been taken in by all the crap side of the business. I come from working-class, Cockney geezer roots, I hope I'm untainted by what I've been doing for the past 30 years, working in magazines. It's a game - I am lucky. I've loved what I've done. I work with good people. What I like about myself is what my Mum and Dad gave me.

■

I like that I'm confident. I love making people laugh. I've been told I'd make a good comedian. I lie in bed sometimes and make up comedy routines. But I don't think I've got the balls to do it.

■

There is something very egotistical about this question and I am sure my wife would say I am very egotistical. You've found the one question that I find difficult to answer. I can tell you everything I don't like. I don't know why I find this question very hard to answer.

■

I am really comfortable in my own company - I always have been. I'm loyal. I suppose I spend a lot of time being negative. I like being current and open to new things.

■

I like being generous. That is really important to me. Instilled in me is this thing of being an Asian-European man where you take responsibility for everything. I have to be careful not to overdo it. I am considerate. I can over-worry about people, and if I can't read someone that bugs me.

■

I like my sense of humour. I can make myself laugh. If you can't laugh at yourself then there's no hope.

■

I'm kind. I'll do anything for anyone. I generally have good thoughts about people. I love animals and I hate cruelty to animals more than anything. I'm a vegetarian and have been for 30 years.

■

I like my curiosity. I like my enthusiasm. I like my love of people and of life. I love my reflective qualities. My reflective quality has kept my enthusiasm in check from being too foolish and I like that. I love the magic of life. The chance, coincidences, fate, all sorts of stuff. The mystery and magicalness of life. It's led me to meet some great people and go to great places. I get caught up in duties and obligations like the rest of the world but there is an inherent mystery in life - and I know that!

■

I think I'm a relatively stable human being with a good moral radar. I've never had that killer desire to trample on people to get to where I want but I won't be mugged over either. One thing I decided a long time ago is to avoid people who moan and who are full of negativity. It's just fucking draining. Some people latch on and suck the life force out of you. I refuse to have those conversations any more. Empathy is kind of understanding and knowing personality types. I don't see my actions as selfish. It's a choice to unplug. I don't want to spend time labouring under a false intent. It's not about being a shit, it's just saying, 'This is going nowhere, why bother?'

■

I like my compassionate side. I like my humour. I like helping people. I'm a Leo, we like being entertaining. I like to make people laugh, in some cases it can be a bit of a deflection!

■

I like most things about myself. I was the village idiot before I met my wife. I'm always the one dancing. I can get a bit crammed sometimes. I'm a little less tolerant than I used to be. I used to think, give people the benefit of the doubt but now I'm like - 'stuff them, as long as we're all right.'

■

I do like me. Not in a big-headed way. I didn't like myself for a long time. I had weight problems. I used to battle with myself. I'm the most positive person out there but then for some reason I used to get very critical of myself. I'd be doing a marathon and think people were looking and judging me. It felt like imposter syndrome.

■

That's a tough question. You've stumped me. I liked the fact that I have a lovely family, that I cry at almost anything sad on the TV. I like that I'm a lawyer and that means I can help people. I like helping people. I like that I am changing and learning to enjoy change.

The 60s

I am quite a perfectionist. I'm very fussy about presentation. Whether it's me or my children, my grandchildren, my home, their cars, our car, everything must be clean and tidy and well presented. I think I got that from my father, he was definitely a perfectionist in everything we did.

■

I still think I'm much younger than I am. I look in the mirror and see a few wrinkles and no hair - was I ever attractive?

■

I have a positive restlessness. I am curious.

■

I don't follow people's expectations. I live the way that I think I should live my life.

■

I have a residual remaining vigour that is still there but I have to say, looming is this feeling that I'm becoming more and more unhappy and therefore prone to be impatient, nasty and sarcastic. There's an element of malleability, flexibility, and resilience.

I like my enthusiasm for people. I appreciate creativity, my openness and interest in other people. The channels can easily be blocked by circumstances; people, mortgages etc. I am quite determined and committed to creativity. I like that I feel young. The body's still chugging along. I am still amorous. I feel alive. I'm family-minded.

∎

I am physically fit. I am a good tennis player and proud that I'm in a high league. Thrilled that I can call myself a musician. I am good in a small party atmosphere. I'm quite funny. I'm loyal. I hate letting people down, that's why I say 'No' a lot. That would be my advice - say 'No' more often, that way you won't let people down. Having the money and education I've had has absolutely changed my life. Having a good education is essential.

∎

I like me probably better now than I was when I was a teenager. I was too loud back then. I didn't try at school, I wasn't interested. It wasn't until I went back to night school and tried a bit harder - I just wanted to go fishing. Once you're down by the river, you're just contemplating. I try and go every couple of weeks. Sometimes I can have a whole lake to myself – it's fantastic. Occasionally I catch a fish, gut it, have it for my tea. I have an allotment, I grow my own veg and catch my own fish!

∎

That I am curious. I have many more interests to come. For as long as I'm alive there will be new things that excite me - particularly books which is unusual being dyslexic. At school I had such a humiliating experience, I was asked by my teacher if I was lazy, stupid or insolent - it had a lasting effect on me. I can become quite stressed and stammer. It takes me right back to standing in front of the headmaster. There's a lot of cruel behaviour. Now of course I'd plead the Fifth Amendment.

∎

I've been true to my beliefs for the last 50 years. I've not wavered from my political beliefs. I've been a proactive member of the Labour Party. There's been a continuity and an honesty, and I'm proud of that. I've still got that passion. I like me now better than when I was younger. In my '20s and '30s I wasn't a nice person in terms of relationships. I wasn't trustworthy. I've got a lot of regrets in that I hurt people. I've changed and a lot of that is down to my partner. She made me realise you have to be reasonable, honest and trustworthy. I'm a big believer in lifelong learning. When I retire I'm going to go back to studying.

■

I'm actually a good teacher. I think kids like the fact that I'm upfront and honest. You can't fake it with kids. They see straight through you. If you're having a bad hair day and you tell them you're in a foul mood, they leave you alone. They like that kind of honesty. When I became head teacher I had to sit in an office and play God. I think that's why I retired early.

■

I like that I'm still healthy, positive and not ground down by life.

■

My Dad was really interested in astronomy. We bought telescopes together. I think once you start looking at the stars and consider your place in the world and universe, it puts a lot of the smaller things into perspective. Top tip - if you can't afford a reasonable telescope buy a very good pair of binoculars. Best stars so far: Yellowstone Park in Wyoming. The Andromeda Nebula. It's endlessly fascinating. Once you see the cloud bands on Jupiter and the rings of Saturn you're hooked. What must Galileo have thought?

The 70s

I don't look at myself and think, 'Yuck!' The only thing I've done in my life that I spent a long time working towards was joining the Navy. It's all I wanted to do. I joined at the same time as my twin brother. We were in the Navy five years and only met once during that whole time. It was a funny story. I was on a destroyer in the Atlantic doing exercises refuelling at sea and doing some Jackstay transfers (movement of goods or people from one shop to another via a cable.) I was the youngest officer on board so the captain said, 'Off you go!' I flew over to the other boat where I landed on the deck, and the first lieutenant looked at me and said, 'What are you doing here? I thought you were in the wardroom'. I said, 'It isn't my twin brother down there, by any chance, is it?' It was! The first lieutenant told me I'd better go and have a drink with him. That was great. I had about half an hour catch up and got back to my duties.

People say, 'Wow, you're lucky to have the opportunities you have.' The thing about opportunities is they are around all the time. If you keep your eyes open, you'll see them. The reason why people don't take the opportunities is that they arrive at inconvenient moments. Opportunities don't come knocking but when they do, you've got to decide whether to take them or not. You don't go looking for chances, you let things evolve. You see a chance and grab it. I like change. I don't like being in the same place very long.

■

You don't get to your early '70s without thinking that most of the time you're a fairly okay bloke. I'm pretty much getting towards the finished article.

■

There's nothing much I like. I am a bit down on myself. Other people think more of me than I do. I'm always worried what other people think of me and I'm quite often surprised when people like me.

■

I do like me. I'm honest and straightforward. I've no airs and graces. Currently I'm trying to get a public footpath re-opened. After the foot and mouth outbreak years ago, a lot of the footpaths were closed. Then the restrictions were lifted but there's this one fella that will not take his fence down, denying people access. It's a great big bone of contention. I've been pressing very hard to get it open. I'm very persistent in some things.

■

I'm very busy and involved in community life. I like to feel that people consider that I've got a natural charm and am friendly and approachable. I've been pretty constant throughout my life, even with my setbacks.

■

My patience and tolerance. I'm not short-fused at all. There have been occasions where I've been working out on the streets (policeman) and people have pushed me right to the limit but I'm tolerant with people. I've never been vindictive or abused my power.

■

I feel really good when I crossed the finish line after a race. (I took up marathon running at 62) I feel I've really achieved something.

■

I like that money and material things don't mean as much to me as connection, whether it's with people or animals. That's my source of spirituality. I'm not religious at all. I'm an atheist. My sense of spirituality comes from being connected. It comes in moments.

■

I don't dislike myself. I'm honest. One of the reasons I'm still working at my age is people trust me.

The 80s-plus

I try and see the best in most people. I am affable.

■

I like the image that I have of myself. I think I'm okay - there's always room for improvement. I try so hard to be a good person. One time a parcel was delivered to me. Two items came, I'd only ordered one. I just couldn't keep it - it's stealing. That was the way I was brought up. You only buy something when you can afford to pay for it. I wouldn't deliberately charge people more money than I should. Be fair and helpful. That's how I try to be.

■

At my age you don't care what people think about you. I'm going bald and I've got a pot belly, and I've lost a lot of teeth! I'd have worried about that when I was younger but not now. I can laugh at myself.

■

As I'm in my 90s, I wouldn't mind being a bit younger and I would have liked to have been a bit taller. I was five foot seven which was the average height for a man in the 1920s.

A longer conversation...

Peter 66

retired teacher and now a part-time London guide, from London

What will my legacy be? I've already left it in many respects. My long-term feeling is that I've given more to my pupils than I've given to my own kids. As a secondary school English teacher, I've dedicated so much energy and enthusiasm, so much of my life to my pupils. I've neglected my own kids to some extent. I've left a curiosity, enthusiasm and energy that still manages to prevail, despite my negativity.

I am judgemental, cantankerous and grumpy. I am a person who has limited horizons but is open and has a moral energy. I am very easily irritated by people showing their emotions. It spooks me. I like people to have a certain reserve.

I see myself as a person who despite everything manages to maintain a pretty good continuity with the person I was when I was younger. I'm amazed to find there's some inner being in me, some ancient throwback which is a great source of energy and that whatever happens, still manages to carry on and survive and be resilient. For other people - not for me – my negativity is eclipsed by a youthful energy and an inquiring zest.

I have three children. I am the second child of six. I ended up being an assistant parent to my siblings which was a good thing for my teaching career, but also led to a lack of professionalism. I never regarded teaching as a professional job. I saw it hedonistically, as fun and creative - looking after kids and getting them to play and do things. To be encouraged - but I was a bit of a tyrant as well.

The main thing I'd say is, look beyond yourself. It's not just your life - it's everyone else's life. I've always been an educator in the sense of drawing you out of yourself. I can't stand it when people are too concerned about their own past. If history is the history of 'your family' or 'your grandfather' or 'your childhood' and 'your evacuation' and 'your' time in Devon, or whatever, it annoys me because the evacuation was a phenomenon that affected so many. The Holocaust, the War, had an enormous context that demands respect and proper knowledge. You have to look beyond the personal.

I know my attitude is wrong because your own past does matter - but I do tend to say it doesn't matter. It matters only in the context of the broader life. I think life matters globally and we don't behave as if it does. There's a schizophrenia about us in England. We are bloody well all about ourselves, all the bloody time. It annoys me that the BBC, which is such a fantastic organization, is so phenomenally parochial. Life is so much bigger than that.

I like to speak to people from the old days. I can't see the place as it is, but want to see it as it was back in the day. I'll stop some wizened old lady carrying something, to chat with her. I like being with people who don't have modern prejudices. People who blurt out their prejudices I find refreshing. I'd like to be in a world where I'm not always irritated by political correctness and 'virtue-signalling' - which is a word I've decided not to use any more!

I like to meet people who are in touch with their heritage and background, while at the same time having the luxury of being really scornful of people who think in terms of 'their' heritage and create 'their' identity from 'their grand heritage'.

As a second generation immigrant I'm more English than the English. So when people talk about the stereotype of English people, I get very annoyed. I don't like imposing stereotypes on English people, When people talk about the cold English reserve, I think - YEP! Yet, I am a blabber mouth!

My father was an immigrant refugee. I liked his bluntness. He particularly despised the commonplace and people who just repeated some view that was in the air at the moment, tuning into some modish orthodoxy. They thought they were saying something but in fact were just a zit on the zeitgeist.

I'm more Polish than my family, in that I speak the language which no one else in my family does. I went to a Polish boarding school. In short, I don't consider myself Polish! There's a lot of phoney ethnic snobbery and one-upmanship in my family. It's pathetic. Pulling ethnic rank. I'm a true Londoner in that I'm the son of an immigrant and I've got a bit of Irish - who hasn't in London? My grandfather sold flowers in Covent Garden.

I was educated beyond my intelligence. I went to a private secondary school and by the skin of my teeth I got into Cambridge. It was overwhelming. I developed a negative attitude about my abilities and when I started teaching I wasn't confident. As time went on, I was bigged up as this fantastic teacher but actually I really struggled. There was an element of disappointment in my father that I became a school teacher instead of being an architect, for instance.

I am kinaesthetic. I love moving. I wish I were a dancer. I go a bit wild when I'm dancing, which is obviously embarrassing.

I used to do a lot of drawing. I like drawing because it's a form of meditation, of focus. I am sorry I gave up on my creative side because being creative means you don't get caught up in intellectualism. I am anti-academic. You don't want to be a bloody intellectual. Yet, what happens when you're not engaged intellectually? There are times when I give up on my mind - I become catatonic. I revert to hebetude. I am quite content in my own misery, yes - that definitely defines me!

I'm a person who creates background stress and damage! I have counselling every two weeks. I've got to say it isn't getting me anywhere. I am often crippled by anxiety. It's the Rev. Casaubon effect, in Middlemarch, who has a sense of being watched and judged. Fundamentally, Casaubon is crippled by an invisible audience and so am I. George Eliot is saying, 'Lighten up. Don't take yourself so bloody seriously.'

What do you think about marriage?

'Marriage becomes a strong friendship that is more than sex, thank God!'

Commitment. Staying power. Through thick and thin. Stability. Structure. Routine. Rhythm. I have come to the conclusion that all these things are good for the human psyche. Humans need to be grounded for safe passage through this life. That grounding can come in many forms. There will be ups and downs obviously but if there is an anchor of some sort, and it holds you steady, we might not get pulled too far away from our senses. Was that wishy-washy enough for me to stay firmly on the fence about marriage? I have heard every scenario of how marriages and long-term partnerships work and don't work. And having read all those comments, I think there is no right or wrong way. Just keep open, honest and listen.

A friend said, 'Our partners should bring out the best of ourselves, and protect us from the worst of ourselves.' That's a nice thought but having now had well over 200 conversations with people about marriage and partnership, I'm still not sure what I think. Most things in life get checked, assessed, upgraded. Licenses given to prove you're equipped to sell alcohol or drive a car. MOTs check annually to make sure you car is safe. Upgrades on products ensure we are up to date with the latest technology. Annual reviews take place in the workplace. So why don't our relationships get checked? Are they reaching their full potential? Are there things to improve upon? And are we bringing out the best in each other? Whether or not you're in a long-term relationship, married or not this question invites you to reflect upon your interactions with your relationships.

The 20s

My aunt and uncle recently split up. They'd been together since their early teens. They are still best friends. They fell out of love. They'd been together too long. That's terrifying.

∎

My Mum was married and divorced several times. My Mum is besotted with her husband now. I'll be very surprised if they're not together for the rest of their lives. He was a breath of fresh air when he came into our in our lives. He's my godfather.

■

I would like to get married. I see marriage as a manifestation of my undying love towards someone and commitment that I can't show or verbalise in any other way.

■

I love the romantic idea of marriage. The idea that you love someone to the point of getting the law involved. The idea of wanting to spend your life with someone. I heard this great monologue from the actor Andrew Scott, 'We're born with love. It's such a great burden to bear that we have to share it with someone else.'

■

Many people my age say they don't need or understand why they'd want to get married unless they were going to have kids. In a world of quick turnarounds, changing countries or jobs every few years, you can change partners every few years too. When you do find that special person, you want to hold onto them with everything you've got. Maybe marriage could be a way of keeping someone longer.

■

My friend's dad said, 'Anyone can do marriage from zero to five years. That's the bit everyone wants to do. It's the five to 100 is where the interesting stuff happens - the real stuff!'

■

I'm not sure if it's for me. I don't see a point in marriage outside of legal reasons. It's not on my to-do list at all, it just doesn't interest me.

■

I never really thought about it - I don't know enough to have an educated opinion about it.

■

One thing I get frustrated about with my disability is not having a relationship. A lot of girls, especially my age, don't want to be with someone with a disability as severe as mine. My best friend has a baby and I see how happy he is. I'm envious. I would love to have a relationship like that, to be with someone I can trust.

■

I have a positive view on marriage. I'd like to get married one day although I am slightly apprehensive seeing so many of my friends' parents getting divorced in their '40s. I wouldn't want to go into marriage and then 20 years down the line it breaks down. I like the idea of having that one person for your whole life.

■

Growing up watching my Mum and Dad, they appear to have it all - they've been married for 30 years. I would like a relationship like theirs. Marriage is daunting. You are committing yourself to one other person for the rest of your life. It's not easy and sometimes it doesn't work. I don't think it's selfish to leave if it's not working. I'd much rather people split up and try and find happiness somewhere else. My auntie got divorced and has met a new man, she's like a different person. If it's not right, it's not right.

■

Don't do it! It's an institution. My Dad talks about it like it's something to do, like a job. I understand people who get into long-term relationships but when it comes to marriage, why? Why does it have to be official and legal?

■

It's something I can see myself doing at some point. It's antiquated, though. It can set people up to be in a vulnerable position as far as money and breakups are concerned. I think it's easier to get divorced these days but I hate the idea of divorce. I'd consider getting divorced as a bit of a fuck up.

■

My Mum was married at 22 with two kids. I don't know what I was doing at 22 but nowhere near getting married. I'm single. I've just come out of a long-term relationship where I thought that would be the progression, but it wasn't.

■

Marriage is a construct, a sociological experiment that doesn't benefit women at all. The jury is out for me on marriage. If I get married, I'm getting married once and once only. Whatever happens - if there is a divorce, I'm unlikely to marry again. If I were to get married I'd want to sit down and talk about what it's going to take to make it work. Me and her working together for the common objective - happiness.

My parents have been together for almost 30 years. They're not married. When I was in primary school I remember a friend and I talking about my parents not being married. We were about eight at the time. He said, 'What are they?' It was an awkward revelation to me that they were different. I wondered if it was strange and why weren't my parents married?

The 30s

Marriage is a journey together. Marriage is important but if your marriage ends for whatever reason, you shouldn't judge. Love changes. We had been together for two years when my wife said, 'Why don't we get married?' so we did. Once you get married something changes; you feel more comfortable. I was more committed.

At the beginning, I thought my life was complete. I stopped meditating. All my problems came back. I started drinking more and we fought over money. My advice would be to give all your money to the women, they look after money so much better than men. A few years on and I would say we aren't as tightly bound but there is incredible trust. When we are together, we are together. When we are apart we are apart. In the beginning there was a lot of jealousy. We both went back to meditation. Our relationship is very different now. We give each other a lot of space.

∎

I was married for three years - legally we still are, but we parted company last year. We simply hadn't been in love and we couldn't reconcile. It was a very lonely time for a while. The initial mourning period was hard. I was overcome with grief and pain. I would cry myself to sleep. I've moved on a bit now. We've had time apart - maybe we could get back together? She will always love me and I will love her forever. When I was married I was so proud and happy to be married. When I went down the pub all I'd talked about was my wife.

.

We don't believe in it. We are going to have a civil partnership now they're legal. Whether we are married or not doesn't make any difference to us. Why should we go through all that when we are going to spend our lives together? We don't believe in wasting £30,000 on a day.

.

Women want a man who's got his shit together. That's not really me! I want someone to spend my life with but I'm equally terrified about screwing it up. I did a bit of divorce law when I was a solicitor - it gives you insight. It's a major taboo to get divorced in the South East Asian community. I've been speed dating recently. I couldn't handle it. A guy at the mosque said, 'If you feel shy I can approach these women on your behalf.' What does that say about me? My Mum has tried to arrange a marriage for me but most of the women weren't too impressed. My mates try and set me up. A non-Muslim would be tricky. I am going to need a woman that kicks me up the arse. I am open to possibilities.

.

I always thought I'd get married. I went on Tinder and matched with my now fiancée. We spoke for six months on and off before we actually met. Hopefully we will get married at the end of the year. I'm excited about it.

.

My partner wanted to get married and I was more than happy to. If I'd said no to marriage because it was outdated institution which came from ownership and the suppression of women, my partner, having sympathised with the sentiment, would likely have been upset. What a crazy world we live in when you're in a situation where to support the equality of women, you're maybe making women upset. The symbolism of marriage, the giving and receiving of rings, that infinite loop, a sense of togetherness. You're making those vows, for ever. It's very meaningful and powerful. The spiritual element of marriage stands the test of time. What on earth has lead us to be so attached to one person? From a scientific perspective it doesn't make sense but from a spiritual perspective - it's magical.

■

I've been a bit choosey with women. I've not had a lot of relationships, so meeting my wife was a big deal for me. I knew she was the one. We were together for five years before I proposed. She means the world to me, she's my soul mate.

■

My parents have been married for 40 years. I don't think my opinions on marriage are aligned with theirs. My Dad's a bit intimidating and there's no real closeness or warmth with him. He's very traditional. He's the man of the house. He's never worn a pair of jeans or a t-shirt. He's always in shirts and suit trousers. He's very reserved. My Mum, who we have a bit more connection with, was more of a helicopter parent. She judges her success as a mother and a human on her kids. You have to be married. You have to have kids. You have to own your own property. You have to do this. You have to do that. I think she's always struggled with me because I've been slow to do a lot of those things and I don't have a normal job. I don't look at my parents and think they're very happy. I don't see a lot of joy there.

■

Marriage is one of those things you do but you don't really know why. I think it means more to most women than it does to men. I want to get married because when you're married it somehow seems 'right'. Getting married is on my tick list. Marriage is a display to everyone else that you're committing to that one person but it's the display to your partner that matters.

■

I'm getting married in a few months. I always saw myself getting married. I hoped it would happen one day. It's a symbol - joining two people together. We are having a fusion wedding. An English and Indian ceremony. My culture is more important to me than the religious aspect. The values of my culture mean a lot to my family. Traditionally, I should only marry an Indian person from a certain caste. I am happy to say I'm marrying a girl from England and my parents are 100 per cent supportive.

The 40s

I think there is some legitimate value to at least having a crack at setting up something that could last for ever. Marriage is the standard way to mark that intention and I approve of it.

∎

Marriage is a good thing. I was married. She pushed for divorce. It wasn't the worst break-up but I didn't want it. We were together for seven years. We have a child together. It's a beautiful thing. I think you have to be ready for marriage. Marriage is a Christian thing. Based on the written word of God, you're supposed to stay together for ever. We don't live in that world any more. I think the question is, what is love? I don't think love is butterflies in the stomach but love needs butterflies in the stomach. Making love, sexual energy is great but that's not love. Love is a commitment in the end. An intention to take care of another person for life. That's love. The other part of love is infatuation. You have to work on that to keep a romantic relationship going. You need to keep working through, nurturing it like a garden. Keep watering it.

∎

We have been married six years but together for 14. We should have got married years ago before but it was never the right time. We were sure about it from the beginning. We can't be so bohemian and go with the flow any more. Things change, there are expectations. The modern world requires that you have a house, a car and everything is set up. So far I don't have everything set up but I'm still here. Is the 'set-up' that important?

■

If you're with the right person, it's the best thing. I absolutely love being married to my wife. It wasn't always like that. We came very close to breaking up and had marriage counselling. Both of us brought so much baggage into our marriage. We married quite quickly after meeting but I stand by my initial instinct that she was the one. After counselling I became much more self-aware. I'm blissfully happy being married. It gives me a real sense of security. I don't go off and withdraw from family life. I will say nobody can piss me off as much as she can and vice versa. Marriage gets a thumbs-up.

■

It's not for me. In a dream world I would have loved to fall in love with someone and be with them for the rest of my life. I don't have the ability to be in a relationship. I accepted that a while ago, although there are moments when I will never accept it. I'm not a machine but I just don't see it a possibility. I wish I could seal the box on the subject and not think about it anymore. If I wanted to be a nuclear physicist, for example, I'd immediately say, 'Don't be ridiculous, you're wasting you time.' That's how I see relationships. I don't see it as self-sabotage, I see it as self-protection. There again, if you want me to be honest…. (long silence). That silence speaks for itself, doesn't it?

There's a lot of luck in relationships. I think men see relationships very differently. I have a very female perspective. What goes through my mind from past relationships is, 'He doesn't understand me, he doesn't know what I want and he is not interested in finding out. He doesn't listen to me. He's quite content and that enrages me. How can he sit there, all contented while I'm going through torture in my mind?' The other side of the coin though is, 'If I tell them what's going on all hell will break loose and it will be over.' So what happens is, out of the blue, on a quiet, lovely afternoon, I sabotage the relationship by saying, 'I can't do this any more.' I can't do that any more, it's like going insane.

■

Our wedding day was amazing. It's good to have a day to look back on when you start out on your journey together. I always wanted to get married. I wanted that journey. I don't think it's for everyone. It's the ultimate submission.

■

Marriage is a very good thing, a stabiliser, a backdrop for having children. Some people stay married a lot longer than they ought to. People go on stag dos because it's a marker that life is going to be different but I think the difference between being married and single is inconsequential compared to being childless and having your first baby. Having children is the really big change in life.

■

I was always conscious of not being alone. My Mum and Dad separated when I was seven. My Dad had the stereotypical affair with his secretary. I think that had a lot to do with my emotional upheaval. I'll vividly remember him leaving because I tried to stop him going out the front door.

■

Disney made me believe that when you got married you'd be happy 'forever after'. I thought I would meet somebody and fall in love and that would never change. That feeling will be constant. It's just not the case. I believe in strong, profound, vulnerable, solid relationships but marriage is a structure that can be corrupted. In relationships there are stages; there's the physical attraction, the lust, then getting to know the person and then things change. My longest relationship is just three and a half years. I don't have the experience to know about long-term relationships but I'm learning that the word marriage scares me.

■

I married my best mate. We've been together 22 years. When we got married my father-in-law asked one thing - not to stand in her way professionally. That told me everything about how he saw his daughter. I was never going to disagree because that's how I see her too. You don't want to stifle the person you love the most. Marriage formalises a relationship. It doesn't change the relationship. It's a celebration, a ritual. I love marriage. It sounds really conservative and traditional, that's not a bad thing, is it? Marriage becomes a strong friendship that is more than sex, thank God! You get each other. The reason we work is because we are chalk and cheese. She's the ambitious, driven one. I'm the ambitiously relaxed one. She's the breadwinner, the most committed. It's taken me a long time to accept our life style and our roles. I struggled with the concept of traditional roles for years - part of it was guilt. Our relationship is different now. It's much more about emotion than physicality. If physicality is all you have in a relationship then that's not going to be enough. It's about having enough in common to tolerate each other. For most men it's someone else in their life that brings out the best in them. We are like naughty little boys and our partners tolerate it. I'm grateful for that because I don't always want to feel like the 47 year old I am, worrying about my body hurting, or whether I've done enough exercise, or if I'm eating the right things. Life is full of responsibility and burdens. It's nice to be daft from time to time.

The 50s

My first marriage lasted six years. We broke up, it was a shock. I felt terrible. It was gut-wrenchingly awful. The way she did it made me angry. In those times anger is quite important so you can start pulling yourself out of it. I had a few decent friends, they really were important. My first marriage taught me that the most important thing is, you can't float through life like a gorgeous butterfly. Grow up! Get yourself sorted out. Life is moving. You cannot be like you were. I was stoned for over a decade. I didn't go completely mad with anything stronger, which was fortunate. What a waste!

■

Since the boys left home my relationship with my wife has changed for the better. It feels like a new chapter in our lives which is exciting. In another way I'm wondering - is this it, just me, her, the cat and the dog? Our relationship is having to move on in a more grown up way. We've played Mummy and Daddy - what's next?

∎

I've always wanted to get married. I'm old-fashioned. I wanted kids. We've been married 29 years. We were good friends for five years before we went out. Obviously the danger is, if it goes wrong you lose one of your best friends. I suppose the flip side of that, 29 years later, it's probably like living with your sister. Getting a dog has made all the difference to our relationship. Before she came along we'd do our own thing at the weekend. But now, come rain or shine we are out for a walk. We stop at the pub and just talk. It's re-engaged us.

∎

Why do I need to be married? My partner would probably love to get married but for me it's a non-essential thing that's going to change what, exactly? If I was the sort of person who couldn't be on my own and was unsure of myself then marriage would be the perfect thing. It would give me that reassurance. I haven't got those insecurities. I have my partner, two dogs and a house. Marriage isn't going to change any of that. People look outside of themselves for contentment, not inside.

∎

Marriage is pointless and unnecessary. I wouldn't do it again. I got divorced in 2015. I spent 19 years of my life with that person and we have two wonderful children. I put a huge amount into what effectively was a loveless relationship. I did the right thing by leaving. I didn't do it well but I'm glad I made the move. I was so bored in my marriage. The only ray of sunshine are my kids. I would like to have a good relationship with her when the dust settles. I care about her. I am annoyed and hugely disappointed in her. I think our kids have handled our divorce really well.

∎

It would be interesting to know what it's like to make that commitment. When I see my son's mums, they're such a unit, they're so committed to each other. I'd love to get married. To make a commitment feels incredibly powerful. I like the idea of signing up to be a team.

∎

My Mum and Dad's marriage is not a great example. It's not violent but it is in its disdain. How terribly unmatched they are and how unspoken everything is. They've never had an easy relationship. They're amazing in their own way but they're so different, they don't seem to enjoy each other's differences.

∎

I am a firm believer in marriage and if you get married you stay married. I'm Jewish and come from a really close extended family - it's that East End Jewish thing. I was brought up in a very dull family (laughing), we all got on with each other – imagine that. There are no skeletons (hopefully). I'm spoiled - my parents are alive and kicking and still together. Mum and Dad are salt of the earth types. I was lucky. I think one of the worst things about how we live now is leaving the extended family network. I love our house and our street. I walk down my street in the mornings and people say 'Hi'. I feel part of our community.

∎

Marriage isn't for everyone. I'm lucky. I'm in a happy marriage. It's not always been - we've had our ups and downs. We've been married for 28 years - it's a long time. How many kids would be in a better place if their parents had spent time listening to each other? Marriage gives stability to your children.

∎

I like being married. I've been married for 25 years. A lot of people don't marry for the right reasons. When I asked my now wife if she'd marry me, I said, 'I am being serious – don't say yes unless it's a lifelong commitment.' Marriage is for life. It's not easy.

∎

I don't like it. Marriage is suffocating. Being with someone all the time. There are two things I needed to change, my job and my marriage. I've known for a while that we are going to split up. I was uncomfortable at home. I felt I was being crushed. Neither of us is having an affair but there is this tension. I don't want to fall out with her - I like her. We still live together. When I told her, I felt a bit freer. I came from a broken home. Both my parents were repressed. Dad would go quiet, go to the pub and get drunk. My Mum was just angry. When they split up it wasn't a shock, it was a relief.

∎

We've been together 26 years, we're not married. I'd love it if her idea of heaven was taking a campervan and going off for a week camping by a lonely loch, fishing - that would be amazing. But that's not her idea of fun. I've got over it but by the same token if she said, 'I love football, I want to come to the World Cup with you,' I'd be, 'Do you really, why?' That would ruin it. I love her dearly but I like to get away, have fun with my mates then come back. I'd never go after other women, would I look at other women? Yes - apologies. I don't go into strip clubs. I like eating, drinking, laughing and acting like a schoolboy with my mates. That's all I want to do. I just want to giggle having drunk too much vodka in a bar in Lithuania. I just want to be laughing and laughing and laughing. Filming my mate, who's a big fat bloke, getting into a little police car putting a euro in the slot so it wobbles back and forth. It's cramped in there and tears are streaming down our faces. It's completely immature and so what - it doesn't matter. It's not all laughing and joking though, we talk about our feelings and where we are at and where we're going. We are very honest with each other.

∎

Marriage is fucking hard. I've been married for 22 years. It's a good thing. It's brought out the best and the worst in me. If you don't have a base of commitment you'd be all over the place wouldn't you?

∎

It's a good thing. I've been married twice. The first time I was 28. We went off to Gretna Green. Marriage is one of those things you do because everyone does it. Going to Gretna made it a bit more special. We were married for 10 years. Then she started taking the dog out for a walk in the rain which she never did. I thought, 'That's a bit odd.' Things started to fall apart. The second time I got married was nine years ago in a registry office in Bangkok. If this marriage goes wrong I won't do it again!

■

I've been married twice and they were the two best days of my life. I think it's a great institution. All I ever wanted was a wife and two kids. My first wife left me. I know exactly why. I used to play a lot of high level cricket and football. I'd work all day and come home looking like a dust bomb. She was wooed by some suited and booted, 6 foot bloke. Time over again I would have been a better husband. Better hygiene. No, seriously. Being a decorator I would come home covered in dust and paint. I could have made more of an effort; cleaned up, put aftershave on. It was tough, paying the mortgage, making sure I had work coming in. I had ten decorators working for me. It was stressful. I was miserable. We didn't grow apart. She just had her head turned.

■

I love marriage. One thing I do recognize when I feel down is how much of a rock my wife is. I couldn't have done my career without her.

■

A work mate was telling me that his parents, who are in their 70s, are thinking about getting divorced. I was like, 'Well, that's just fucking ridiculous.' Why would you, at 70, think about getting divorced? You've got stability, you know each other. What grass could possibly be greener?

■

Any relationship should have some kind of debate within it. My wife, when she's fed up might say to me, 'Oh, you can leave'. My response is, 'I'm going nowhere, baby!' I'm 53. I've worked, bought a house, there's no way I'm sitting in a bedsit - I'm not going back to all that shit. We've been married for 24 years. Marriage is not sticking together for the sake of it - it's about working things through. If I look at my extended family and see the happiness level and the split-ups, I say to my wife, 'We ain't doing that bad.' I'm still in love, but now there's a respect for each other. There's always peaks and troughs. Anyone is a fool to think marriage is all rosy.

■

Before we were married I never slept in the same bedroom at my wife's house. Her family are very Catholic. It's been a good marriage. I've never strayed or looked at anyone else. I've been married for 28 years.

■

I was 28 when I first got married. You have to think very carefully about it and I didn't think about it carefully enough. She was lovely, a brilliant mother and although I was very upset when she decided she didn't want to be married to me any more. I look back and realise I've been much, much happier in my second marriage. I'm not even sure I realized what really marriage was all about. Having said that, my first marriage coincided with that critical period where I was trying to earn a living and do the right thing and protect our family. I was genuinely shocked when she left, which goes to show how un-observant, hardworking and distracted I was the time.

Marriage is a wonderful thing. I'm not sure that we are mono-gamous as a race. You're exceptionally lucky if you stay married to the same person because everybody evolves, grows up and interests change. Characteristics can become hardened.

■

My wife is my best friend. Recently she had to go into hospital. I just sat there and waited.

■

It's not the institution of marriage, it's the person that's worth fighting for. Most of the people we socialise with are like us. Married for 20 years or more which is quite strange as our parents' generation flipped it around a bit more than we'd perhaps appreciate. Jumping in and out of each other's beds, they had these weird parties! Lots of divorces. I'm not going to do that. Divorce is a seismic event.

■

When we told my parents we were getting married my Dad said, 'I am very happy for you, I think it's the right thing to do. Make sure you get a pre-nup but we're not coming to the wedding.' It was bizarre behaviour. They just couldn't handle the public shame - me being gay and being married!

■

I find my partner frustrating sometimes. I have a tendency to be happy and content. A half-full glass. I'm broadly positive but she is, 'If only this happened, then life would be good.'

The 60s

We were very young - we got married at 18. She was a lovely girl from a lovely family. It was the next progression. We got our own flat, had a kid, and I worked in various jobs. Marriage is good for men, it stabilises them. Once you live with your partner you get to know the ins and outs and I think that's the problem. People dive into marriage, it's all rose-tinted specs, everything's happy, and then a few years in, you're looking at each other thinking, 'What's this about? What shall we talk about now?'

■

I met my wife at the laundry where we both worked. She was only 16. I was 20. We were good friends. She was my best friend so I didn't expect to end up with her. I'd be lost without her.

■

I'm about to celebrate 38 years. To this day my wife still says the only reason I got married was because my father told me to. The story goes: one afternoon, my father gets me a strong drink, sits me down and says, 'It's about time you married this girl and if you do the wrong thing, I'm on her side.' I hadn't given it any thought. That was about as romantic as it got. I can't believe I was as unfeeling as that but that's how she remembers it. I'm a bit ashamed of that.

■

I was married for 25 years. My parents bickered throughout theirs. I'm not sure they would have stayed married if they lived in our time now. I don't have any friends that have stayed married. I think marriage has a built-in expiry date.

■

I won't be doing it again in the next life, that's for sure. I allowed her to take away some of my freedom. I don't care any more. I do what I want. If she's not happy then she can always leave. I've done the best I can. I won't leave her, there's no need. I'm not looking for anything better, everything comes with its own bullshit. Two of my kids have said they'll never marry, having seen the shit time I've had. I think they'd say my wife was very controlling. I've not been allowed to be me in lots of ways. We were going to split up 20 years ago but I wouldn't leave because of my kids. It's always been about the kids but now the kids have left and it's just me and her. There's no point in getting divorced. I don't think she's a nasty person, she's just insecure. If you're going to make the commitment, make the commitment.

■

My wife and I are separated but still married. We've kept up a very close friendship. I go on holiday with her. This is the number one issue in my life at the moment, in that I've got another partner and have had for the last two years. This is a typical example of my lack of resolve, not sorting things out. I'm not divorced from my wife, who I have three kids with yet I live with my girlfriend. Does it matter? Yes it does, because I haven't absolutely committed to my girlfriend. That is the elephant in the room. I fundamentally believe in 'Till death us do part'. Life is short therefore a marriage is for life. My wife loves me, she doesn't want to get divorced. And I love her!

■

I suppose my model of marriage is that the man rants and the woman just has to sit back and take it, and where the woman is in effect an unpaid whore - the sexually available woman. Men stay younger and have the sexual hunger longer than women do. That's my very negative view of marriage. I've got a misogynistic, old-fashioned view.

■

People will always want to live together. Marriage leaves me cold. If my children don't get married it wouldn't bother me one little bit. My marriage was cut short. I have no idea if I would still be with my wife had she lived.

·

We got married 18 months ago. We had to re-do the will. The solicitor said that if one of us were to die, there would be a good deal of inheritance tax to pay. So we got two witnesses and went along to the registry office. It was fun. We didn't take it seriously.

·

There's a lot of male pride about coping and managing. Sometimes you need other people to give you a shove in the right direction and to stop you doing things like smoking or indulging in bad habits. We all need some kind of regulator there. I am not too proud to say I can't do it all by myself.

·

My parents' marriage broke up and it had an impact. There was no way I was getting married. Back in the '60s there was this view that marriage was some sort of bourgeois concept. My Dad was verging on alcoholic and a domestic abuser. My mother left him. It was difficult. As a single parent on her own in the early '70s, I remember fingers pointing at her - how could she leave her marriage? Because you don't know what the bloody hell was going on, that's why! She absolutely made the right decision.

·

I was always scared of getting married. It worried me as a kid. My first partner with whom I was with for 26 years wasn't into marriage so we never did it. I'd like to get married to my current partner but she won't have me! The thought of standing up in church, I would find very embarrassing. I'm quite the romantic. One of my favourite songs is 'Soho Square' by Kirsty MacColl. It's a sad song. I arranged to meet my partner when we first met at that bench in Soho Square. I do think we will get married when the time is right.

The 70s

I'm on my third marriage so I'm not very good at it. My first marriage lasted 25 years and produced my four children. My second marriage was probably on the rebound. It lasted 10 years. We spent six or seven years sailing around Britain. It was very nice. When we got home and I suggested France next, she didn't want to go. She decided to be old, live in a flat and go to the library every day. I couldn't cope with that. Life's too short.

∎

We've been married for 55 years. We grew up in the same village. As teenagers we were always off in the car! She trapped me into marriage and took advantage of my sensibilities, stroked me inappropriately and nine months later my daughter was born! (laughing.) I always said it was the best mistake I'd ever made because it calmed me down. I was a bit of a wild youth, an idiot. I was 19. We were lucky. We got a lot of help from both sets of parents. Girls at that time who got pregnant often got their kids taken from them.

∎

It sounds really old-fashioned but I think marriage is the basis for good family life. I was glad when my kids got married. It's one of the best institutions there is. Marriage is a good sounding board for your kids to grow up in. You hear such horror stories of blokes having four or five kids with four or five different women. What sort of way is that for kids to grow up?

∎

My Mum married my Dad when she was 17. They used to argue like billy-o. They had five kids. Seven of us all together in a two bed house. When the twins were born the council moved us to a four bedroom house. Mum and Dad stayed together for the kids but when we grew up they split up. My Mum walked out. It didn't really affect any of us, to be honest.

I got married at 23. I've known my wife since we were tiny. We were childhood family friends. Marriage is a thing you have to work at. We are committed. You have your problems but you have to work at them. We've been married 48 years so far. We probably take each other for granted. We try not to but I don't think you can help it. Me and my wife are football mad. Seasoned Chelsea supporters. She's the one shouting at the telly. We go to a lot of football. We do a lot together but we also have separate interests.

■

I feel a bit terrified about it actually. I've been with my partner longer than most people have been married. Why get married and spoil the relationship we have? Marriage does change people. My parents were very secretive, they weren't married. It was only in their later years they decided to do it and even then they didn't tell us. We found out.

■

It's a good institution. I don't think it's always essential. As soon as you even suggest it to someone that's a compromise because you've got two people whose views of marriage are never going to be identical. Compromise will be from what you want to wear, to being able to get on with mother-in-law, father-in-law. It's a big step. In any long term or meaningful relationship it means you want to go deeper into that person. You really want to know them as well as you possibly can. Where they came from, their influences, to how much they like polycotton or Egyptian cotton sheets. (laughing.)

■

I was married six years to my first wife. It was drink that did it. She eventually decided she would go into a drying-out clinic. I looked after the kids. The person she became was not the person I married. That is my definition of someone with a drink problem - when they start trying to change everyone else's life. She was changing all our lives. It would have been worse had I left and taken the children but the state she was in, that would've been the end of her because she would have had nothing to fight for. It transpired those were the most difficult times of my life. My older children still have some bruises. It was very difficult.

■

A great many people get married based on their own psychological trauma rather than any good sense. People represent a long-term thread - their relationships, and the relationships between their ancestors. All these stories come together so we end up meeting people who fill in some kind of niche. It's a pretty tenuous construct.

∎

A balanced relationship is important for a good home life. I haven't got that.

The 80s-plus

I think if you choose to get married then you should stay with your partner but I can see that's not easy. I never wanted to get married. All my friends who have been married seem to have done it twice - that seems to be the norm.

∎

I've been married 57 years. It's an extraordinary thing. The main objective in my life is keeping my wife happy. My Mum and Dad didn't approve at first because she was Catholic. At the beginning I wasn't giving my marriage 100 per cent and she nearly left me. That gave me a right kicking. Since then I've always wanted to be a nice person and I think I am. Whatever she wants, she gets. We still don't do enough together. The man has to be the earner - I didn't expect my wife to earn. If you're an earner and a miserable bugger then that's no good. You're dammed if you work too hard and dammed if you don't work hard enough. I would never dream of pestering my wife for sex – it's up to her. It's got to be when you both want it. You have to be patient - be kind and helpful to each other. I listen to her. Listen to each other and do your best for each other. I should have done more to help with the kids. It's all a matter of consideration for other people. I always tell the lads around me - you must put your family first. My son has married a woman that doesn't love him - I think young women get bored.

∎

It's a wonderful institution providing you have the right person. I was married for 56 years. She died 9 years ago. She'd been by my side for so long, I'd grown used to it. She was part of me. I was sorry when she died, I missed the companionship but for the last couple of years she had dementia and was in a wheelchair. Eventually I put her into a home which I didn't like doing.

.

I saw a couple on the television the other night and their love for each other was marvellous and absolutely genuine. It was like a beautiful poem. What is marriage? At best, it's a wonderful thing. Is it necessary? Of course it is. I'm very cavalier about life. I think marriage as a state is essential. It's the only thing that offers stability to the children and the women, less so these days. I've been married since 1963. I know people who are in marriages that are made in heaven and they simply can't imagine a life without each other. I am always very moved by that. It's wonderful to see. Equally I have mates who've told me stories which their wives wouldn't want to hear. What they tell you, you take to the grave. Often, all is not what as its seems.

A longer conversation...

John 58,

freelance journalist from Canada,
lives in London with his wife and three children

Recently I went on a trip with an old mate - we were looking back at our lives and laughing until we were almost sick. Of course there's an ageing process but you get more comfortable in your own skin as you age. It's taken me a long time to get to this point. I've accumulated a lot more experience. I'm feeling pretty strong. I was a late bloomer, constantly measuring and checking what I was doing. Never really letting go. I'm a good self regulator now. I used to worry what people thought about me - not any more.

I like spending energy on things that matter. Music, getting out into the woods. When everything is going shit, I listen to Joni Mitchell - it's like being with a friend. She's talking to me in that moment - it's devastating. I listen to music on my sound system and the backing vocals are like angels. It's communication that transcends time. I talk a lot about music, feeling something deep - it's a good release for me.

There's a new sound system I've been shown, the speakers are special, they blow your mind. I've never heard anything like it - there's all the listening I've ever done in the world and then there's the few seconds I've listened to on these new ones. I didn't know there was such sound. I can't afford them - they are £15,000 – but they deliver music in a way where you can see the artist on the stage. Close your eyes, put on a Billy Holiday album and I'm there in a club watching her. Those kinds of things are all that really matter.

I read once how important it is to feel AWE and how good it is for your mental health. Ever since I was a kid, we used to go to camp. Sometimes 40 days at a time. They had nothing to do with the rest of my year - a complete change and that makes you realise it's a big wide world out there. There are things more important than me. Bigger than me. All the egotistical stuff is dislodged in the face of big weather, big storms, big challenges, being hungry and cold all the time - you learn a lot. You definitely find out exactly who you are. Throwing yourself into a situation and getting on with it. There was time to pause. Nature is physically and psychologically good for your mental health. Camp was more important than my college education.

I remember sitting on a lake in northern Canada. There's a quiet that comes over at certain moments - no wind, perfectly still, it's like glass. There's a name for it - 'the great silence' - it's a phenomenon. It's sensory deprivation. You're in the middle of this vast open space. That moment is indescribable, literally nothing, no sound. For hundreds of miles in every direction - then the storm comes. That's what you go there for. That spiritual connection can only come from your connection with nature.

The Hawaiians, their eye is more on nature, they're connected to the land and the spirits, yet they're fully westernised. It's a cool blend. The usual American way leads to antidepressants and therapy, it's a generalisation but true. We're tiny compared to the next galaxy. Trying to describe the world is a waste of time - just experience it. Nothing else out there needs to document life, you don't see an elk painting!

The sum total of all your decisions on your death bed - did you make good choices? Did you leave the world a better place? There has to be personal responsibility. Does it make me more moral and better? No, I don't think so.

I'm not always so positive - I get angry and frustrated because the world isn't perfect and it could be more so. When you see people flicking a cigarette butt on the ground, I'm like, 'What the heck?' It's so unnecessary. There is so much unnecessary waste - we all consume too much.

I'm pretty self-aware – however, my wife would say not. She'd say that I avoid confrontation. I might be seen as easy going, but I have a nasty temper. Marriage is hard. I've been married twice. I don't have much faith in it. I don't see it as necessary. As an institution it isn't as useful as it used to be. The western world is the last place where the romantic notion survives but in the majority of the world, marriage is about convenience.

Are humans supposed to be monogamous? I'm not trying to get out of it but I've been divorced once. If it's not going well and the bond has broken then there's no point.

I wrecked my parents car at high school - we hit a tree head on, an immovable object at 40 mph. If you've ever been in a car crash and you've heard what that sounds like it's a really weird instantaneous sound almost like an explosion. The waves of realisation come over you. You feel sick - divorce is like that. Once you know what that feels like - the next time you get in a car you drive differently.

Nobody tells you how to be married. You have to keep a marriage going by having open communication. We've been together a long time. A lot of things aren't going to change - this smacks a little bit of inflexibility as I hear it coming out of my mouth.

I have admiration where there is respect and a bond. Where couples still have fun together. Are we admiring from afar the old couple sat in a restaurant bickering in between the silences? I'm not sure if there is something to admire there. I think opposites attract but same tribes are probably best for longevity. I definitely wouldn't get married a third time. My relationship isn't going as well as it should be, we've grown apart. I need an emotional release. I gotta get this bad energy out of me.

I've done things that have repulsed her. The song by The Foo Fighters 'The Best of You' - are you getting the best of somebody and are they getting the best of you? Someone else was getting the best of me and someone at home wasn't. Have I screwed up at some point in my life? I have in my marriage.

You've gotta keep curious - if you stop being curious, you get old.

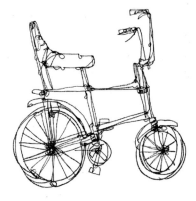

What do you think about children?

'I feel pressure to have kids'

There's a growing trend not to have children - for the sake of the carbon footprint perhaps? Statistics show the birth rate is declining. Maybe we will naturally wipe ourselves out sooner rather than later and that's how we will save our planet.

My Dad used to encourage people to have kids, like it was the 'right thing' to do. Young lads would come round for a chat he'd say things like, 'Have a couple of kids. That'll sort it'. I'm not sure much thought went into his counsel but my interpretation was that he was trying to emphasise the need not to be solitary, alone in your thoughts and your whole life being centred around YOU, because you can get stuck there.

Historically, child rearing has always being a women's issue but things are changing. Nothing is as it was. Men are certainly more visible in the parental role. I don't know if my small study of 100 men is reflective of how society is today or if I just got lucky, but I heard such a wide range of experiences that I think we can no longer make assumptions about women being the main parent anymore. Many men have strong feelings about raising their children and actively wanting to be part of the day-to-day detail. It's refreshing. Those who don't have children often like the idea of being involved in some way - as a mentor or role model.

Several of the men I spoke to had raised their children because the mum had left. I don't know why, but that still seems more shocking to me than if the man left! I was also concerned to hear how many of these men when they were children themselves had been abused physically, verbally or sexually by a parent, and were having to actively make a choice that they wouldn't repeat this with their own children. Someone said, 'I made a choice - I won't be doing this to my children.' Imagine having to have that thought? It wouldn't even cross the majority of our minds, but those who have been abused make a decision – not to do to their children what was done to them.

The 20s

Children are wonderful. The next generation, full of curiosity. I'm desperate to raise a child.

.

I'm a nanny. People say it's just a job that I'm doing until a big film comes along but I really do care about these kids. I see it much more than just looking after them. I never wanted kids because I thought you needed to have the right amount of money to raise them and the time should be right, but what is the proper amount of money and when is the right time? I would like children. As a parent, you perhaps give your children what you weren't given. My Dad always tells me how he was never hugged by his father. My Dad is a very tactile father.

.

Having kids is probably the worst thing that could happen to me. I'm not a fan of kids in any sense of the word.

.

Being a father is something I know I want to do. I don't think I am ready now - I don't think I've reached full maturity to give children what they deserve. I'm still going through rocky bits in my own psyche. When I have a family I want to be able to provide. Call me part of the patriarchy but I see that as my role.

.

I have been broody since I was a child. I can't wait to be a dad. It's the one thing I do want out of life. It's beautiful that you can make a child and it's half you. It's the biggest gift you can get from life.

.

I don't want any. I don't see myself having any. I don't see what the draw is to having them. There are people my age from school who started having them at 16. Children are a constraint.

The 30s

If I have them, fine, if I don't that's fine too. There are plenty of kids in the world. People worry that kids are expensive but I feel once a child is born the world accommodates them. We take the onus on ourselves to carry the weight of everything but the world gives you what you need. I remember when I was young I wanted this particular games console but my Mum and Dad bought me a different one. That's when I realised how much of a brat I was. On my 21st birthday they showed up. I was so embarrassed and disrespectful - they'd only come to help. It's amazing how your brain works. You can be a slave to your own mind.

■

I'd like to have been a dad in my '20s but let's face it, you're not thinking much more than sex, booze and work at that age. For all I know I might have a child out there somewhere.

■

Both my older brother and younger brother are married with kids. I live with one of my brothers, his wife, their kids and my Mum. I feel pressure to have kids.

■

We are at the age where all our friends are having kids. We all say the same things. Everyone pretends it's nice all the time but it's not. There's a large proportion that isn't actually fun. It's nice for a small percentage of time. The rest of the time it's shite. It's starting to get a bit easier. Most things are temporary but having children is permanent. I want to be fiercely ambitious for my children, pushing them to be the best they can be.

■

I don't feel negative about children in terms of responsibility. They're worth every ounce of your energy. It's lovely watching my son develop. The whole sleep thing is a pain but I wouldn't change it. It's one of the best things I've ever done in my life.

■

My wife's parents are the sort of people who think you get married and have kids or there's something wrong with you. They have strong feelings about it. It got to a stage where we were a fed up with being judged. We told them we were trying but it's not working. They've removed some of their expectations now. With my parents, we had to tell them. My Dad's reaction was to ask a lot of questions. Taking an academic interest, which I suppose is his way of showing love. My Mum just said, 'That's very brave of you to say this, because I could never have this sort of conversation with my parents.'

∎

I always thought I wanted two, being one of three. There was always a fight: who sat in the back of a seven-seater taxi, or who got to sleep on the put-up bed in the hotel. I remember being interested in holding babies but never got the chance because my Mum or sister would be very much the ones doing the holding. As a young lad I wasn't used to doing the embarrassing things you have to do to interact with young children - you have to talk like a baby, always look really surprised and take sharp intakes of breath whenever they do anything!

∎

There's been a lot of soul-searching. Trying to understand how to cope with my partner, especially after she had our child. In the beginning she turned into a completely different person. Men need attention. I tell my wife - guys need attention, too. Having the attention shift away from you is difficult. Men need to feel good about themselves. A lot of men get into a tunnel. There's a lot of expectation. I'm not going to blame it on the women, but they're expecting you to be a good dad, bring money home and take care of the kid. This is expected of fathers. Can you deliver all that? Some people don't have the capacity. I was trying to find my place within our family circle. I didn't know what to do. We had some very difficult times. There were weeks where we were talking about divorce. The situation was unbearable. Men don't seek help. Talking helped. It's good to talk to people. Some of my friends were experiencing the exact same thing. Some got divorced. You need someone to lean on. Sometimes you are lost in the forest and you're with the one person who is lost too. You're asking them the way and they don't know either. You're pulling in different directions. It's good to have a common road. Sometimes it's not possible, things don't always go to plan. I didn't change what I was doing but I observed myself and became more positive. I had faith that things would get better between us. You need to learn how to react to different situations. Exercise helps. Maybe professional advice too. You need support. If you're alone, you can die a little every day just by thinking. You need to de-stress. Everything is reversible.

The 40s

I love my son. I was quite overwhelmed when he came along. A lot of my family are in Barbados so it was just me. I wasn't financially ready to have a child.

■

I have two step-kids and the 'step' has lost this distinction. They've yet to turn around in a fit of rage and say, 'You're not my real Dad.' I became their step-father when they were at an age when they were all lovely and cute. We were the centre of their world. Now they've entered the teenage years and boy they piss me off. We've become their doormats!

■

A child's imagination is utterly magical. Why do we stop? Why do we grow out of telling stories? It's psychologically good to hang out with kids. I adore children so long as they're someone else's – I've no desire to have them.

■

I would have liked children. They're engaged and they don't judge you. They just want you to join in. They don't think, 'Oh, there's a 45-year old, should he really be playing with Lego?' Everything is acceptable to them.

I thought I understood about life before I had children then when my son was born I was overcome with the feeling of, 'Oh my God, now I get what it's all about!' I've tried to pick and choose from the parenting that I observed as a child, taking the best bits, leaving the rest behind, and adding on some new bits too. My son once said to me, 'You're quite tough on us but you're fair.' I'm happy with that.

Having children is a great way of understanding yourself. It's like when you learn a foreign language you suddenly understand English a lot better. Seeing their impulsiveness has helped me recognise it in myself and to try to do something about mine.

∎

I'm a proud father. I always wanted to be a dad from a young age. I wanted five - I have three. I am deeply grateful for those early years, they were really hard but character building. I hate most children which is ironic as I work with them. I find them frustrating and quite irritating. Spending a lot of time with damaged children has had an adverse affect on my relationship with children. I have an intolerance to spoilt kids. There are certain parents who choose not to set appropriate boundaries for their children.

I know the way I parent is how my Mum did it. She had a profound effect on me. It's only when you have your own kids that you appreciate what your parents did. My Dad died when we were young so she did both roles. She tried to be everything for us.

∎

We had three miscarriages. I was told to be strong. I struggled with my eldest, we clash. We are very similar. My biggest regret as a parent is not being the adult at times. You never stop worrying about your kids. You learn a lot about yourself having kids. I want my kids to go out there and know right from wrong. If you can make thoughtful young people, then you're doing okay.

∎

I think people are fun when they don't know everything. I like my one child, that's enough. It's significantly more expensive to have more than one. Me and my wife are not very well organised people. What we have is a free and easy life. I think our daughter will have a really nice time living with us, whereas two kids would be a fucking shit show.

The 50s

I'm blessed with two absolute crackers. I think they are fantastic little creatures. Short years, long hours, but when you're in it, it takes for ever! They've had some difficult times. When they're not very sure about themselves you have to build them up without talking bullshit but give them confidence about their talents. And try not to get angry when they waste their talents. Having two daughters is an education. I came from a long line of males. My sister-in-law said, 'I do hope you have daughters.' I laughed and said, 'There's no way. We will be having boys.' God laughed and I got daughters. I have acquiesced in every way. I am a pushover.

■

I had my first child at 23. Having him young was great and I don't regret it. I felt grown up. I played Dad. We were so young. When the relationship with his Mum started to go wrong, I could have walked away but I didn't want him to be in a single parent family. He kept us together longer than we were meant to be. Thankfully in the end, she had the balls to leave. I came home from work and the house was empty. We could all get on with our lives without me feeling guilty.

■

I was never great with babies, that's why we stopped at two. My wife had a bit of postnatal depression with the second so that sealed the deal. I was working so hard in those days. I missed large parts of it. We reaped the rewards later, as have the kids. I don't think they missed out on much. I don't think the kids notice that Dad's not in the house when they're having a bath. I used to take them to swimming lessons and weekend rugby.

■

A lot of people go along with marriage and children without thinking about the consequences. How many children are out there who have been abused, purely because their parents shouldn't have had kids? I'm a selfish fucker, I don't want kids. I've had three dogs. They have a brilliant life.

∎

We have one child and we tried for more but it didn't happen. All I ever wanted was to be a Dad. I never really questioned I wouldn't be. You become an adult, you have kids. It was always part of my thinking. I'd love to have had a bigger family. I live in a different country to my son and his mums, it's complicated trying for kids. It's difficult enough when you're in a standard heterosexual relationship living together, let alone gay, trying at a distance!

∎

It's relentless. The past 20 years have been a blur. I don't regret it. Time again, I would be less cynical in their earshot, less judgemental of others. It was one of the last things my Dad said to me before he died, 'Don't be so judgemental.' He was right. Who am I to judge? First impressions can be so wrong. I spent too much time judging, being sarcastic about other parents in the playground. I'd bitch about them in earshot of my kids.

∎

We always took the kids to Glastonbury. I loved being the 'cool parents', smoking the 'special festival cigarettes', then wondering why 15 years later my kids take drugs and are really hammering it!

∎

They drive you bloody mad. People don't tell you how shit it can be. There are times when it's bloody horrible - when you're shouting and we're all in bad moods. It's a tough world for kids. I try and ban my kids from going on their iPads and phones during the week.

∎

I am so proud of my kids. I would do prison time to protect my children. But not everyone can have kids and I appreciate that - some people are here to further our knowledge and are not intended to have kids.

∎

I always wanted kids and to have them young too. My wife wasn't that bothered - it was me that wanted kids. Once they left home, my wife wanted to do fostering. I didn't! Although I said I'd give it a go. We went through the selection process and now we do respite. The system palms these kids off. We have a teenage girl, she's been in foster care and children's homes all over the country. She's a nice kid. I feel sorry for her.

.

We knew if we were going to have kids together it would have to be through IVF as my wife had ovarian cancer 20 years previously. She told me early on in our relationship that she was going to put herself on the IVF list as it was a two to three year wait. It put me in a difficult position. She was going to go ahead with or without me. If my partner had to have kids this way and was asking me to commit, she'd changed the conversation. The process didn't have any spontaneity, it was clinical. I wasn't ready but once I was in the process, I was in it. It took a while for me to get used to the idea. She wanted it more than anything else. Women's bodies rule their minds - biology rules.

.

I always wanted children. They are a huge strain but I wouldn't have it any other way. There's a six year gap between our two kids. Secondary infertility is quite a big thing. Our second child is the most expensive baby ever. We went to four fertility clinics. It was a huge process; interviews, taking drugs, wanking in sleazy rooms. It was a pretty hideous time. The 'wanking' room is different in every clinic. Everyone knows what you're doing in there. It's the walk of shame. Think about it; there's a big lazy boy chair covered in cellophane. Porn mags and videos. It's humiliating. But hey, my wife had to inject hormones into her bum everyday. Sex became a job. It puts a strain on your relationship. Eventually we went to America. The doctor told us he was confident he could get us pregnant and he did. The conceiving process had a big hangover. You get tired of each other. But over time your relationship freshens and changes again.

.

I'm a great believer that children get on with their own lives and we don't mollycoddle them. All my kids still talk to me! When I moved in with my now wife, I felt quite guilty that I was with her kids and gave them more than I gave my own kids, it's circumstantial. I'm good at being a stepdad. I have so many step kids.

■

We had one, and I love him to bits. We decided not to have any more. Then my wife got pregnant but miscarried. We'd just got our head around the idea of having another child. It put a lot of strain on our marriage. In the end I had the snip.

■

Birth was the most traumatic experience I have been through, although it was more traumatic for my wife! People say, 'It's great being at the birth of your child. Bloody hell, no! He was born by emergency c-section. He had a very big head, it was all a bit messy. It was horrendous. As a parent, I could have been more present. At weekends, I was on the football or cricket pitch while my wife was at home with two kids.

■

My son can push my buttons. He's cocky and confident. Kids are different animals at home to when they're out with other people. Friends say your kids are 'absolutely delightful', I say, 'Come and live with them.'

■

Children are wonderful things. My late son was a very popular, amusing, talented young man. I suppose every parent who's lost a child would say that. Some 850 people turned up at his memorial service. That's not bad recognition for someone aged 14. I feel him with me all the time. There's definitely a spirit there. Funnily enough I haven't told that many people about it. It's not a story that lends itself to being told very often because you're not often asked.

■

When we had our daughter it blew my mind. I couldn't believe you could love someone with that much love. I didn't want three, I thought two was enough. I was persuaded to have three and it was the best decision ever. I would have had another one after that too but my wife said 'NO!'

■

One of my favourite definitions of parenting is you find out about the best and the worst of yourself and it's true. Who gives you life lessons in being a parent? Welcome to the show that never ends! I have learnt two rules about children - don't dance around the baby; make as much noise as possible and don't ever let them sleep in your bed - you'll never get them out. Nobody tells you this stuff.

■

It's way too easy to get angry with kids. Kids need basic life skills. My kids can't even get themselves out of bed in the morning. Only two months now until A levels and he hasn't worked hard enough. He's not drinking or doing drugs but he's got this one thing - the gaming. It's become an addiction, it's his drug. He's in danger of not getting what he needs for college. We pay a lot of money for his education. I don't understand someone who doesn't make the best of the opportunities they're given. I worked hard, played hard and got it done. I took the expectations of my parents seriously. Their behaviour is out and out spoilt. That whole private school thing and their attitude. That said, if I had my time over again, I'd still have kids. It's part of the psychology of life. If you don't have kids you'll never know that kind of love.

The 60s

I was working really hard and all of a sudden my wife would say, 'I'm pregnant,' again. Life was going so fast. Before we knew it, we had five kids!

■

In my first marriage, we found out we couldn't have children. At the time they said there was no sperm. This was back in the '70s, it was all very primitive. When the doctor told me, he cried. I'll never forget it. I remember sitting there and saying to him, 'Are you all right?' Maybe I should have been the one crying. I think if it had happened, things might have been better. We'd done ten months of sperm donation which hadn't worked. My wife was desperate. She had an affair and became pregnant. I can't put it into words how I felt. I was gutted. I literally went out the door as soon as I heard the news. My gut just told me to get out and leave. She said she was in an impossible situation. She attempted to get it together with the bloke but it didn't work out. I kept in touch. We were only talking about a six month period and I was still married to her and she was still living in our home. I came back and slept in the spare room.

I was there when he was born, helping at 3am. He was handed to me, 'Here's your son.' And that was that, that's the bond, isn't it? He looked up at me, blood everywhere. My name is on his birth certificate. We carried on together as a family and were actually very happy but a few years later she wanted to have another child and I didn't. I couldn't get my head around it. I couldn't do it all again. She got pregnant again and I had an affair this time. She lost the baby quite late on. She was beside herself. She couldn't handle not being able to have the child. Why couldn't she just be content with what we had? We split up.

■

I never wanted to get married or have children. My wife was the planner. She planned everything and I didn't even realise. She was so powerful. She was amazing. I relented. It was transformative having kids. I never shirked my responsibilities. It was amazing from the beginning. When my wife became ill I had to rely on other people. Soon after I was made redundant. The decision not to go back to work wasn't hard to make. How did I know my wife was going to die and the endowment would pay off the mortgage? If I hadn't had money I could not be doing the role of 'mum at school gates.' I was there for my kids, I will say that. I ought to be proud of myself.

■

My son became ill. He'd been to Spain with his mates to celebrate finishing A-levels and school. They'd been drinking. Partying like there was no tomorrow. Nothing unusual, he was 18 years old. It just went too far. His drink was spiked. He had a psychosis, an allergic reaction. He was on a knife edge. For six months he was on a suicide watch. You blame yourselves. You can't help but think, 'What could I have done and why is this happening to us?'

■

My daughter is 25. I was 44 when we had her, so I was quite old at the time. I'm so pleased that I became a parent. I wouldn't be the same person without her. I remember her being three weeks late. This bloke said to me, 'The first time you look into your child's eyes your life will never be the same again,' and he was absolutely right.

■

What I love about children is they say what they really think. Once we've become adults, people are conditioned to say what people think they should say.

■

I didn't want kids in my '20s. The change came in my '30s. I looked at other people who were having kids around me at the time and thought, 'Perhaps this is the point of it all.' I asked my girlfriend at the time if we should have kids but she wasn't interested. A later girlfriend came with a child and he became my step-son. He's 30 now. I met him when he was four. He started calling me Dad when he was 18. He never met his birth father who did a runner before he was born.

■

I have three, and three adopted. I'm defector father with my partner and I am a step-father to my partner's biological children, so nine altogether. I never craved children but I really enjoy having them. I was a stay-at-home dad for a while.

■

The idea of me being a dad, I just never considered it. I wasn't interested. I had no need to keep the family name going.

■

The 70s

It's all right for a woman, she always knows how many children she's got but men don't! When we were young, we were bonking about all over the place! The general feeling was, if a girl was happy to do it then I was happy to do it. You kind of assumed that she'd taken care of contraception, although if she asked me to use a contraceptive then I would. I have two boys and two girls. I'm a very firm believer that the job of parents is to bring their children up to cope with the world, and kick them out of the nest. When I see grandparents wailing because they haven't seen their grandchildren for a week, I cringe. A relationship after your children have grown and left home should be triggered by them, not by you. I don't interfere in their lives.

∎

I think everybody should have children, at least two. I wish we'd have had another. In the 1960s you were doing the world a favour by only having two.

∎

I would have liked more. My daughter was seven when she died. What would she have been now? How many more grandchildren would I have had? I used to think about her every minute of every day, then suddenly, after a long time, I didn't think about her. I thought I must be betraying her. Time is the greatest healer. You don't get over it but you get used to it. After a long, long time it won't hurt.

∎

I don't think a family is complete if you don't have children. I know some people can't have children and I feel sorry for them. We get a lot of pleasure seeing our kids and grandkids growing up. The only problem is, they grow up too fast.

∎

We always wanted children. We have two although we don't have grandchildren and I don't think we will. I thought we'd be disappointed but we're not. We don't feel we are missing out. There's more pressure on people nowadays.

∎

Children are a source of vitality, joy and inspiration. They're a handful and need a lot of supervision, engagement and guidance. I have three nephews and two nieces. I feel I can have a hand in guiding them to adulthood in a way that my brother and sister-in-law couldn't or didn't. I've been a confidant for all of them when they felt troubled or had big questions. They often turned to me and still do, and that's lovely.

■

I have two sons and three grandchildren. I was happily sailing around the world when my granddaughter popped into it. I came back to the US and my son said I should stay in order to have a relationship with her so I did and she's the apple of my eye. We get along very well.

■

I never wanted children. I think in my subconscious I wasn't treated all that well as a child and probably thought, 'I'm not bringing anyone up like that.' It was a different time, very formal. I had to shake hands with my father every morning and call him 'sir'. My father was very Victorian. I don't think I ever swore until I was 20. I'd have got a thick ear if I had. He was a disciplinarian. He would say to my mother, 'I don't want those brats up when I get home.' I was in bed at 6pm every night until I was 16. My parents bickered all the time. Mother always had the last word. She was theatrical. Everyone was 'darling'. She was a show girl and a poster girl for 'Craven A' cigarettes. It was supposed to be very cultured and sophisticated to smoke in those days. Later when she was riddled with cancer, she regretted her smoking. My parents were party animals, they had no time for us. We were seen and not heard. That's how they lived. Their life was first. My parents didn't cook. School lunch was the meal of the day. When I came home it was lemon curd on a big crust of bread, that was our evening meal. When I brought friends home from school, my mother told them they should go home as they couldn't have any of our food. They were mean. When I was 16 I bought my first pair of jeans. I wasn't allowed to wear them. I had a pair of Italian winkle pickers too. I'd go to the shed to put them before I went out. I used to love

Fats Domino, Little Richard and Screamin' Jay Hawkin - they were my music tastes, but I wasn't allowed to play them. We got a television but we weren't allowed to put it on. I once went to the pictures at lunchtime, my father asked where I'd been - when I told him I was sent to bed.

The 80s-plus

I've entertained kids since I was 19, as a professional magician. You gotta love kids if you do my job. I get on very well with kids but in this day and age, you can't be too careful. I can be in the supermarket, there will be mums with their kids, you smile and show them a friendly face, but it's not acceptable nowadays. People think you're a weirdo.

■

I love kids. Our two have both caused us a fair bit of stress over the years but we love them equally. We do what we can to help them. They've done some stupid things although they both have a good work ethic, I'll give them that.

■

My son and I didn't get on when he was a teenager, he was an angry young man. I failed to understand him. We didn't know that he was gay at the time, though I sort of had an inkling. But it's one of those things you don't instantly stick a label on. When he eventually told me, we just hugged. I'm very proud of him. He has a son of his own now. He's surrounded by loving people and he earns that by being a loving person himself. I'm full of admiration for him. .

■

My mother told me there are two types of women - ones who love their husbands and ones who love their kids. She was one that loved her husband. You don't want to hear from your parents that you're second-rate.

A longer conversation…

Frank, 70,

administrator, London,
originally from County Kildare, Ireland

I was the first of nine kids. I got on well with my mother. It is her principles I live by today. I didn't see eye to eye with my father but when my mother became ill, he was very good. He looked after her. He was a hard man. He wouldn't put up with any softness or anything.

When I was 15, I worked at a hospital. That wouldn't be allowed to happen these days. I had some bad experiences. A call came in - there had been a crash. A car had run under a bus. Normally when we went out to crashes in the ambulances we'd talk about it, make it out to be as bad as we could so we didn't have any surprises when we got there. We didn't talk about this one because we were told a baby had been hurt.

When we got to the crash site, it was fucking chaos. Five people all dead. A doctor asked me to go and see if the baby was dead. I'm at the car, a policeman came up and asked me what I was doing there? (I'd got a bad reputation, I was always getting into trouble.) I turned around with the baby in my arms and told him I was trying to see if the baby was still alive. You should've seen his face. I'll never forget that. I carried that baby through a crowd of people. I saw hard people from the town crying their fucking eyes out, I've never seen anything like it in my life.

A few years on I moved to London to avoid the police. They were after me. It was only for motorcycle offences but I hadn't paid the fine and they were coming to arrest me - so I left Ireland.

I was never a career person. I went into hotel management only because somebody said I couldn't and that I wasn't qualified, so I thought fuck that - I'm going to do it. I found my way in as a trainee manager. I liked working in banqueting because you weren't tied to a nine to five. Nobody ever knew what I was doing. Half the time I'd be pissed. Years later I started a degree at the Open University. I've an active and curious mind.

I never wanted to get married. I don't care about it to be honest. Do people do it because they want to get their kids into a good school? I don't really know what I think about marriage. What purposes does it serve? It sounds terrible when you talk like that because you're disrespecting your parents, they had respect for all of those kind of things in their day.

When I got married we just had breakfast, a fry up and went home. We were pissed on champagne. I am glad to be married. I've been married for 30 years. I love what I've got.

I never wanted to have kids either. I didn't think I could cope with a child being ill. The responsibility would have been too much. I'm pessimistic and a hypochondriac. But I have coped. I've got married and had kids which has gone against everything I said.

My daughter was perfectly fine when she was born then one day at nursery she had a seizure. That seizure changed everything. We spent six months in hospital. Our son was sidelined but there was nothing we could do about it, our daughter was in a bad way. She became a drug-resistant epileptic and has a learning disability. If you have a sick or a disabled child it's very difficult to give advice because there is no advice you can give. Advice means you're trying to help. You're trying to help others heal but there is no healing process, except the same shit every day! You never get used to it. You cope because you have to. You're going through something that is quite traumatic. It's not nice. We know when we need to go to the hospital but it's not always clear cut. You go to bed not knowing if she'll wake up in the morning.

I always thought that as time went on things would get easier. It has never got better or any easier. Our daughter is 29 now and has never done anything for herself. That makes life difficult. The main thing for people like her is that they are looked after properly. You're never going to make them better, but you don't want a situation where she ends up in a nursing home having seven bells beaten out of her.

It's shit when you get old. When I was young I used to say people that were 70 were old, I am now 70! You cant do things you want to do. I've got my heart giving me shit. My knees and my blood pressure! I have atrial fibrillation, it's a result of high blood pressure. My heart is permanently irregular now. I don't like it by virtue of the fact that it stops me doing things, the same as if you were an epileptic. I have to stop what I'm doing and go to hospital and get hooked up to a lot of wires, like a cow on a milking machine!

I'm hyperactive. My OCD is really bad. I check and re check doors and locks. I check the cooker is switched off. I check the taps are turned off. All the locks in our house are broken. Every time I don't check, something has always been left open. That's why I keep checking. If I found nothing wrong, I probably would stop.

Most people think I'm a shit because I'm rude. I'm rude on purpose. It's the only way to get anything done. Maybe rude is not the word to use, direct is probably a better word. If you're dealing with a bunch of arseholes up at the town hall, trying to get social services and stuff in place, and you want to say something direct, it'll be taken as rude. I don't like swearing as such, I just think it shuts people up when you swear. I can be a right pain in the fucking arse. I'm a shit stirrer!

Out of all our situation with my daughter, my wife took on a failing organisation and has built it up into a million pound charity. Everything the charity has achieved today has been down to her. Her ideas have been realised with hard work and help from our staff, trustees and patrons. She's done everything. We're doing something because we care about people and care about what we do. Everybody should be doing the same but most people don't care. That's why things don't get done.

Underneath all the bravado and bluster, I'll admit I'm a very sensitive man. I like to help people. I don't like to see people in the shit. If anything happened to my daughter, I don't know where that would leave me. I wouldn't be interested in anything after that, that's for sure.

Where does all your energy go?

'A lot of it goes to my head and I have nose bleeds to prove it'

I've noticed a lot of men foot tap, nail bite, leg shake and fidget. It must be something to do with all that excess energy they have. One big theme to have come out of this project is that men have excess energy and they need to do something with it. It's perhaps no surprise then that commentary such as, 'I can't sit still, I can't switch off, I need to be doing something,' was in every other conversation.

One man said, 'I remember seeing my Dad pick up the dustbin full of leaves that he just swept up and then tip them back out on the path to start again.' That to me is a clear example of excess energy manifesting as OCD.

WORK ⚥ Cooking ⚥ Writing ⚥ Creating ⚥ Being productive ⚥ Politics ⚥ Football ⚥ Relationships ⚥ Family ⚥ Children ⚥ Finding purpose ⚥ **OCD** ⚥ Caring ⚥ Guilt ⚥ Negativity ⚥ Nervousness ⚥ Hyperactivity ⚥ Yoga ⚥ My inner showman ⚥ Social issues ⚥ Reading ⚥ Social media ⚥ Pottering ⚥ **OVERTHINKING** ⚥ Swimming ⚥ Poetry ⚥ Volunteering ⚥ Gardening ⚥ My allotment ⚥ Whittling ⚥ Watching stuff online ⚥ Music

♂ Insomnia ♂ Fell walking ♂ Marathon running ♂ Drinking ♂ Partying ♂ Watching shitty late night TV ♂ Sweeping ♂ Foot tapping ♂ Cleaning ♂ **EXERCISE** ♂ Fidgeting ♂ Locking doors ♂ Checking ♂ Tidying ♂ Rechecking ♂ Binge eating ♂ **ANXIETY** ♂ Counting ♂ Fixating ♂ Perfectionism ♂ Washing hands ♂ Aligning objects ♂ Nail biting ♂ Leg shaking ♂ Shouting ♂ Partying ♂ Weight training

A longer conversation...

Tom, 37

singer, musician and music teacher, from Cambridge

I am very privileged and with that comes confidence. I was always brought up knowing if I wanted to go to Cambridge, I could go to Cambridge. 'You want to do something, you can do it.' I used to be a bit embarrassed about the level of education I'd had and the stuff I've done. Now, I'm proud of it. I see myself as someone who is good at things. I'm a good singer, a good teacher. I'm confident. I'm very secure in what I do and who I am.

I can come across as being quite cocky. As a singer you're constantly being put in front of people you haven't met. Don't get me wrong, I like performing. I like showing off! But I'm really bad at introducing myself on a personal level, as in, 'Hi, I'm Tom, nice to meet you.' I tend to back away from those situations until the friendship develops organically. However, when I meet people who are like me in that respect, I tend to think they're incredibly arrogant!

I think I could have pushed myself a bit harder with my singing career. Maybe there are a few regrets there. I've always been surrounded by classical music. I played violin and sang in a choir. Then I auditioned as a chorister for King's College Choir, Cambridge. My Dad thought I might enjoy the experience of the audition, not necessarily thinking I'd get in - but I did. Then came the big debate. Now he's got in, he has to board, not only does he have to board, he has to live at school throughout the Christmas holidays. I boarded from the age of nine to 13 even though my family lived in Cambridge.

Every morning we were up early doing half an hour of piano, half an hour of violin and an hour of singing. Every evening after school we'd do two more hours of singing. All Saturday afternoon and all day Sunday. The experience and the training were extraordinary. There were the tours, the recording work and the TV work. The Albert Hall, cheesy carol concerts, radio broadcasts. We'd sing services. Christmas Eve and Christmas Day. My sister always accused me of ruining Christmas Day because they had to wait until I'd finished. It was pretty brutal.

The first few nights of a new term I was always very homesick. It was awful and upsetting but I'd always settled by day two.

I did enjoy it. I loved my time there. It was an experience that was totally unique. Everything which is good about me as a musician has come from that training. It was an incredible opportunity but the argument is - isn't it more fantastic to give your children the sort of love and attention they actually need at that age? I don't know the answer to that.

Most of my views have changed since meeting my wife. A lot of people from my background don't understand why people can feel socially displaced. I used to be like that. My wife comes from a very different background from me ('oop North'). I come from a background that says if you want to do something, the door is open. If people aren't doing it, it's because they're choosing not to and that's their decision. Not taking into consideration the fact that choice and opportunities might not be available to them. I think back to some of the opinions I used to have, and I can't believe it. My horizons have expanded.

Now, teaching, I've surprised myself with how well I get on with the kids. I like teaching teenagers. As a singer I feel I have a lot to offer. When your voice breaks it's a strange time. I've got some tricks and I see good results. I've got good relationships with my students.

Would I like my own children? We have tried. It wasn't happening. We tried a bit harder and it still wasn't happening. There's no real consensus about what the issue is. The theory is it's to do with me. The doctor said it looks like IVF because sex is very inefficient!

All a man has to do is wank in a jar. It's nothing like what my partner has to go through. Some of it is really nasty and invasive. Most of our friends have children. You can be made to feel that time is running out. I feel there is societal pressure and pressure from our parents. It is a sadness that sometimes keeps me up at night. I'm just letting the months slide by and we're still not really doing anything about it.

I am a person with too much energy. If I shut the door and am the last person to leave, I'll have to check I've locked the door about three times. It always has to be multiples of three and then I'll check the handle to make sure I can't open it. But then I'll probably unlock it again to make sure I locked it. I go through a process. Eventually I leave the house, get to the corner, come back to check again. I can't just lock the door and leave.

At night I have to check all the lights are off and all the windows are shut. Otherwise I'd be constantly on edge. There's no way I could sleep without checking the windows.

I think having the dog has given me much less mental capacity for bullshit. I'm busier so I can't waste too much mental energy on stuff like that.

A lot of my energy gets frittered away up here - in my brain. I try to put as much energy into music as possible, even if it's not in a professional context. Bashing stuff out on the piano or practising, playing with friends. I write too. My favourite guitar/singer is Devin Townsend, an extreme metal singer. I think he's bipolar. He has the most beautiful voice. He says music was this thing he tried to do. He put so much energy into music but as he's gotten older he realises he doesn't love music. He loves coffee, he loves sex. He loves other things. He has an emotional connection to everything around him. He refers to energy as the emotional exhaust fumes and his music is like the exhaust fumes from his life. If he's having a shitty day, he writes shitty music. He's just processing what's going on in his mind.

It's sort of therapeutic.

Because I've got a very academic music background I need to 'fix it'. Music is all pattern recognition. Part of training to be a good musician is discipline - you need to be very self-critical. If you're going to be any good you need to force structure on yourself. I get in my own way. I put a note in here and a chord there. I intellectualise.

I think music at its best is your way of getting rid of all the 'stuff'. If you're angry one of the best things you can do is play something angry, sing something angry, then it's out there and no longer inside. I tend to store things up so it's a useful process. I play everyday. With music there's no puzzle to be solved. There's something that comes out in the end which might be exciting, or crap!

I'll often surprise people with the sort of music I tend to listen to. When I plug my earphones in it's something either incredibly chilled out or incredibly aggressive. I respond emotionally so much better to extremes. Pavarotti, Madame Butterfly or La Boheme - Puccini knew how to put a knife in and twist it. If they're going to be angry, I want it really fucking angry. I find music like that calming. There is definitely a heavy metal and classical crossover. I think it's to do with the extremes of emotion.

What are your dreams?

'I want to be the first disabled manager
in the EFL (English Football League),
a lot of people think I'm too ambitious
because of my condition, but that's
what drives me to prove them wrong'

Where do dreams come from? Is it an itch dying to be scratched, an aspiration? A goal to aim towards, is it achievable? Is it something we just say, 'Oh, I want to be the next...' Or, 'I want to run a shop?' For dreams to be fulfilled we need effort and courage, but probably most of us use excuses not to fulfil our dreams. I have met many people who say, 'I'd like to write a book'. But if you really want to, why don't you do it? Is it a fear, fear of not being good enough, fear of rejection, fear of putting your inners out there? It's all of those things but saying something and doing it are two entirely different things. I saw a kick up the arse life quote that said, 'Comfort is a drug. Give someone regular sex, fast food, entertainment - fill in the .... and they will throw their ambitions right out the door. The comfort zone is stopping you from living the life you truly want.' So how much of us is trapped inside a comfortableness that we label, 'I'm just too tired, busy, I can't...'? If you have dreams, you got to go and live them. Haven't you?

In my experience, listening to the dreams of hundreds of people, for the most part people have simple dreams but over a quarter of these men had big dreams. To be an astronaut and space travel, or if there wasn't a rocket to hand, drive around the world in old campervan to find nirvana. Performance of sorts was key for some - the desire to be in a band, to be the front man, or on stage acting. Being someone significant in the sporting arena was a dream for quite a few, too. Altruistic motivations were prominent as was the desire to change the world via politics, but, for most, the dream of a simpler life surrounded by nature ran deep. This was in contradiction to the busy, energetic, must-do, must-achieve energy that has been consistent throughout most of my conversations with these men.

The 20s

I see myself sitting on the back deck with a couple of drinks, watching the sun going down, the music is on and I'm playing with the children

I've raised with the person I love - that's all I need!

■

To be living in America. I'm obsessed with everything American. I'd like to be performing. Getting the audience's breath in your hands - it's magical. I'd like a comfortable house and someone to share it with.

■

My dream is to have a family. Two children, a boy and a girl. I'm passionate about my disability activism but I don't get a buzz from it. I get a buzz from football, that's why I want to become a manager

■

I'd like to be an astronaut or a politician. Either discovering something, learning or changing the experience of those around me for the long-term good. If I can make a person feel better, then I have made a difference - that's my dream.

■

I never want to stop travelling and exploring. Staying in one place for a long time scares me. I want to understand and learn as much as I can. I want to become fluent in another language.

■

I want to be really well off. Money would give me freedom. I'd want to change the world, in a political sense. I want to have a big impact on where the human race is going. I've noticed people seem to have as many children as they want, they take them on holiday abroad every year, yet the other end of the spectrum people can't afford to feed their families. It's all because of capitalism.

■

I'd like not to worry about council tax bills, changing your internet provider and stuff like that. It would be nice to own a house, a car, go on a couple of good holidays every year. I'd like to get all of my ducks in a row. I'd help my parents too.

■

If I had a magic wand I'd want to open a hospital in the West Indies. A mental health drop-in centre where people can go to get support. Everyone should have food, healthcare and a roof over their head.

It boggles the mind that we can't achieve it. We are meant to be stewards of the earth but we're not treating the earth the way we are supposed to. It is down to patriarchal mindsets. The world is run by men. We shouldn't need Comic Relief, Sports Relief, Water Aid.

The 30s

I would love to live to be 100 - it's a great number. I'd love to go to space, to see how insignificant we are. My dreams change all the time. I'd like people to be more understanding of each other.

∎

Being a musician has always been my dream. My work is never finished and that's what makes me tick.

∎

Selling bananas on a beach. Living hand to mouth. Having a chilled, easy life.

∎

I'd like to be a researcher. Maybe work for the National Geographic in marine biology?

∎

All I want to do is have no responsibility. I'm happiest doing nothing. As long as I've got my guitar to fiddle around with. It's not really about, 'Oh, I'd like to do this, or I'd like to do that.' It's about, 'What in my life can I get rid of?'

∎

I would like to go into space. We take for granted all that we are - the way we are built, our shape, the thickness of our skin, the pressure inside us, the way our lungs and eyes are. But actually we live on this tiny, thin membrane which has a distance from the sun and a certain mass and gravity. We are the product of something that evolves in those conditions. It's a unique set of circumstances. The idea of going to a place where 99.99999 per cent of existence is not like ours, I'd find absolutely fascinating.

∎

I'm in my dream job so I probably wouldn't change that. I'd like to be more up-skilled. A big goal is to be financially comfortable. To provide for my family and children. Not have to worry about money is important to me.

The 40s

I want to be an actor. I would like to do something on the radio that involves lots of funny voices. It would be me creating characters. Sadly there is something enormously competitive about me. I think my dreams, like my relationships are shut away in a box. One of my dreams is to fall in love with somebody. My more realistic dream is to move from my flat into a house.

·

I'd love to be a fantastic cricket player. I would swim in the swimming pool that I don't have. I'm an early riser. I love that time in the morning. I have music on in the background as I'm unloading the dishwasher, time before anyone else is awake. It's a peaceful time that comes to an end and I like that - I don't like open ended solitude. I'd get on a plane every October and fly to Sydney and come back in May. I'd live an eternal summer. I love Australia and I love England.

·

I would love to organise evening street parties where there's fires lit in the street and they roll out on the next street.

·

I will be disappointed if I don't do one combat tour in my life. I have never actually fought and I won't sadly, that boat has sailed. It would be a in a supportive role. I'm slightly disappointed that I haven't done a PhD. It might well come in the future. I'd love to win the lottery so I don't have to worry about money and indulge my dream to do game design. I've reached a point when retirement is a good goal.

·

My dream was probably to play professional football and I did play professional football. Then I got released. I loved football. For me it was just about playing. I was playing at a level where I was asked to go to Middlesborough to play against Oldham. A week later I was signed for Brentford for £20,000. I was 21. I arrived with the reputation that I could catch pigeons, I was that quick. I was there for two years. It didn't work out. I don't think the fans liked me, I lost my confidence. I was afraid of making mistakes. That's why I said at the beginning, 'probably' become professional. I didn't have any guidance. My Mum and Dad didn't know anything about football.

I say to the kids I coach - be brave, be positive. Do not dwell on mistakes. I don't tell people I played professionally. One thing that upsets me is I had hundreds of football programmes. I chucked them all out. My own kids could have looked back at my career. They don't know much about it. If I had my time again, I'd say my dream was to be a professional footballer with a bit more focus. I was a lot more disciplined before I became pro. I should have seen it as a stepping stone, not that I'd 'made it'.

■

I think everyone wants to be adored, but for me being adored by one or two people is enough. Being happy and contented is enough at the moment.

■

I could do with 2K a month more than I have. The way I've chosen to live has left me a bit skint and I prefer not to be. I think not having debt is weirdly the new 'wealthy'. If I can get my daughter (she's three) to walk up the road at 8am to sit somewhere and enjoy a full English breakfast with me and have a nice time, then walk home by the park, then that is the fucking zenith of personal experience to me. I live my life on very low expenditure. I find it comforting. We've lost loads of people recently. If I could really know that I was going to live to 80, I think that would be the dream. Life is always in the shadow of people fucking dying all the time. If I could get to 80 without ever having to worry about that, that would be great. I think moving abroad, nowhere near anybody you know, was what I needed to be a bit more authentic. If you need to change a piece of your attitude, but you're still around everybody you've known for years who expect you to be exactly as you've always been, then it's difficult.

The 50s

I'm designed to lead a bit of a nomadic life. I'm a bit of a hippy at heart. I'm designed to be a trust-afarian, to have enough money to get by. Find out what other people are doing and what interests them. Be sociable, have campfires, decent wine and getting into the sea. Dancing, I love dancing. Shopping. I love shopping for food. I like buying for my family and clothes for myself. I love shopping for Christmas and birthdays. My curiosity really does lie in the sensuous. I am appallingly first world, aren't I? I also love cold water swimming. My dream is to be living on a beach in Cornwall surfing every day, having a spliff of an evening. A bit of wine and pottering about all day. While doing film studies at university. Watch movies and listen to what the commentators say. My favourite films - Jungle Book, Don't look Now and The Sting.

■

I would love to be living somewhere looking out at rolling fields and hills. I would quite happily have a day with nothing to do. I'd be happy pottering away in a shed making boxes out of trees all day long or polishing a chair up and sticking a £200 sticker on it. To be in the elements. To use your hands, be in nature surrounded by earthiness and grit to feel connected.

■

Honestly, I still haven't found my dream. I'm happy with myself. I'm happy doing fuck-all. Money doesn't do it for me.

■

The only real dream that's doable is to pay off the mortgage and build a house near the beach in Thailand. To open the doors and look at the ocean.

■

My dream is to have a recording contract, be produced by Seasick

Steve and go on tour. I am writing good stuff, original songs. They might not be to everyone's taste but I know they're good. There's a gap in the market for an ex-indie, alternative, middle-aged guy.

∎

I dream of a place by the sea. Walking the dog. Early in the morning watching the fishermen coming in. Not talking to anyone for a week. I like bleakness, watching waves, desolation and isolation.

∎

To move further into a remoter part of Scotland and have a little croft; a tea room, a workshop for me to sell my work. I'd have an outlet in one of the cities to sell my commissions. I'd like for us to be free spirits, to do what we want when we wanted but have somewhere to come back to, it's important to keep grounded. Who knows what true happiness is and if you get to true happiness - could you be happier?

∎

When I was a kid I was good at cricket. I got picked to trial for Lancashire. Other kids had privilege; the right gear, the right parents, the right amount of money, I didn't. Even with the best bowling average my face didn't fit. That pissed me right off.

∎

Having a second-hand book shop with a coffee bar. Sitting and reading in nice chairs, chatting and in the basement, there's a cinema, a space for gatherings or to watch films. I get lost in writing, although I still get a little niggle. 'You should be working, you should be providing.' It's a guilt thing.

∎

I would put myself in the wilderness. I want to see the Sequoias and Redwoods. I want to go to Namibia and the deserts, to see the northern lights.

∎

I'd like to find a place where there is a level of contentment just pottering. Living in London there's always shit going on, someone digging up the pavement outside your house, litter everywhere, everywhere smelling of spliff, sirens, there's always something kicking off.

∎

I would like to do meditation and go on a yoga retreat. My friend does 10 day silent retreats. I think that would be incredible. I'd like to try it. Maybe in a monastery somewhere.

.

I'd like to go back to university. I did literature and I'd like to do it again. I loved it. The discipline of reading books with people who have the philosophy and historical content. The structure of writing helps me crystallise what I think.

.

Doing something creative where I can be my own manager. I'm really good at mending things and making craft such as diorama (miniature models). My little secret is my cupboard – it's full of dioramas. My latest purchase is a 1:12 scale 1976 Porsche. It's huge. It cost £160 and was pre- ordered from Japan - a collector's item. I'll probably never build it but it takes me back to my childhood. When you used to go into a toy shop and there, on the top shelf was something big, expensive and inaccessible - I think this is one of those purchases. It's like going back in time. As a teacher, I get my students to build plastic models and work as a team. We live in a world where everything is finalised and finished. Kids are used to buying into Disney or playing games that are finished, it is death of imagination and problem-solving. Crafts fuel our imagination and problem solving capabilities.

.

I am content where I am. When there is more time I'd love to travel around America or Spain in a Winnebago. I would like to climb any of the big mountains. I've always been fascinated by them. I love being up high and seeing a view. I'd love to live in California. There's something about it that feels familiar.

.

I'd live by the sea and teach history to adults. I'd have a campervan and bomb around. My dream is to have enough resources to spend three months a year in California where my daughter lives. I'd like to spend a year up in the mountains in Italy.

.

I'd really like to be in Ibiza pottering about, sitting on the rocks fishing. I'd own a bar but not work in it. Have a dog. A campervan. I'd go anywhere as long as it's sunny and warm. I like the mountains. I well up looking at beautiful scenery.

■

I'd play in a band. I'd be able to sing. I'd be the lead singer, and playing the guitar as well. I'd be Bruce Springsteen, Robert Plant or Israel Nash. I'd also travel and see the world with no worries about having to do anything else.

■

I wanted to become a pilot and learn to fly. I did that. My ultimate dream would have probably been to move to Australia. I've always been fascinated with the Outback. I'm not a city guy. You'll find me in a pair of shorts and muddy legs in the mountains. That is my comfort zone. I'm attracted to a rough and ready terrain. Maybe in a past life I was just a wanderer.

The 60s

I would like to live in a beautiful house in Barbados, open the windows and look out to see the sunshine. To have a comfortable, easier life. Not to worry about getting up and going to work. More time to appreciate life. The lives we lead means you don't have time to completely clear your head and unwind. Sometimes when you see a picture of a couple walking along the beach - that's what I'd like. I'd like to go across America in a Winnebago, too.

■

I'm excited about falling in love - making love, a flurry of flirtation.

I love normality. There is something delicious about normality and routine. My upbringing was completely lacking in regularity. My Mum was down a lot, my Dad had left, he was always leaving - having affairs. When I got married for the second time, a big part was the routine. Getting up, going to bed at the same time. Seeing people, socialising. We had normality. I got a mortgage. We were doing it 'right'.

■

I want to meet Bruce Springsteen. It was 1985 when I first heard him. I remember because the miner's strike was '84. He gave $20,000 to support the Durham Miners. That connected with my politics. What a fantastic thing to do. Plus he's a musician. I've been a fan ever since. I'd like to meet him, have a beer and just talk it through. His lyrics are astonishing. That working class context. The humility. The common man and woman that he represents. The music is utterly uplifting.

■

I love architecture. Buildings fascinate me. I'd like to build my own house. Growing up I lived in about 15 different houses in 15 years. My Dad would buy a house, do it up and move on. I remember the first time he built a house with a laundry chute. It was so exciting. There's a space around the corner from where I live. I've had my eye on the plot for a while. I spend a lot of time imagining and planning my build. I know what kind of windows it has. I know what the entrance hall looks like. I know where every piece of art is placed. You come through the entrance and step down into the sitting room. The bedroom goes off over there. The dining room's behind a concrete pillar. I visit my house every night (in my head) and I change it slightly. Tweaks here and there. I've just seen some amazing wall lights by Tom Dixon that I'd like to incorporate. I'm living in a house in my head! My favourite place is the Barcelona Pavilion, deigned by Ludwig Mies van der Rohe and Lilly Reich in 1929. It's not practical. It's held up inside by pillars in high gloss aluminium. It is exquisite.

The 70s

I come from five generations of seafarers. After school I went to the careers office wanting to join the Merchant Navy. They said I was too young and to come back in a year's time. I got a job in a kitchen. When the year was up I was either too scared to give notice or I forgot. I wish I had joined up.

■

I did quite a lot of acting when I was younger. At school it was often a choice between rugby practice and drama. My first girlfriend was at the National Youth Theatre. We mixed with a fun crowd in the mid to late '60s. I wouldn't have minded if I'd have carried on acting. There is something about hearing the appreciation of an audience. I'm not afraid of the limelight.

∎

I'd liked to have gone skiing but never got chance. I've always had the inclination to make things, create things. To do more practical things. I love anything outdoors, nature, history, anything to do with the environment. I'm doing a dry stone walling course. I wish I'd done it sooner. When you're in a business which I was most of my life, you get tied in. All your energy is put into that. It's quite restricting.

∎

This may sound a bit boring but I don't want to do anything else. I am a content man. I've seen most of the places I want to see. I don't really want to jump on a plane for 24 hours and go to Australia or New Zealand, it doesn't grab me any more. I'd like to go to Kew Gardens.

∎

I'm happy with what I've done over the years. Maybe I could learn to play an instrument. It would have been nice to learn to ski. There's still time. I wish I had done it sooner. I wish I started running earlier, too. I'd like to see my daughter get married. I want to walk her down the aisle.

The 80s-plus

I am waiting for my next patch of luck, which might give me companionship. You have to make your own luck.

∎

I look forward to doing something challenging like putting in a new boiler in one of my launderettes. My mind is quite structured and focused. I've never been a smoker, drinker or gambler, I think that helps a lot. You can wreck your life by getting into all that. It's important to have something to do, a programme for the day. Take an interest, keep mobile and interested. Me and the wife do a crossword every day, that exercises the brain. There's always some project on. I've always been very satisfied with life.

∎

Magic makes me tick. Magic is a vehicle to entertain.

∎

I'm not driven any more. Once upon a time I had to get out of bed because I had no choice. Now when I get out of bed I mutter and grumble to myself but on the other hand, I can get up. I can swing my legs out of bed. I get breakfast for the two of us. I'm grateful for not being restricted physically.

A longer conversation...

Ernesto

41, entrepreneur, from Venezuela

My dream is to have a house in the Swiss Alps, overlooking the lakes. I want to have a beautiful study, a house full of books where I can sit, write and reflect. Maybe every two months I receive a group of people for retreats. That's how I see my life. Mountains and lakes inspire me. I always see mountains to climb. Mountains are such great metaphors for achievements and goals.

Work makes me tick. I'm a workaholic. I sometimes put work well before my relationships. My mind is constantly ticking. Most of the time, work doesn't feel like work. It makes me feel alive. Work is how I get my fulfillment. Work makes me feel happy, useful, that I'm making the best of my skills. I'm learning, I'm producing, I'm creating.

Creating a business is a form of creative expression. Creating change in people. I see myself as an enabler for others, to help them discover their own capabilities, to inspire them to do things with passion. For me, that's an art and that's why I think of myself as a creative.

I'm full of energy. I never stop. My partner's idea of a great weekend away is that I leave my mobile and laptop behind and I sit with him and do nothing. I have anxiety attacks doing that! I'm the sort of person who gets out of bed at 6am on a Sunday straight into reading a book or listening to a podcast, doing stuff in the garden. I need to accomplish things. I relax while I'm doing things! For me, there's nothing more challenging than feeling I'm not doing anything. It's not a fear of being alone because I am happy with introspection and meditation.

I once went to Thailand on an 11-day silent retreat, because I thought I needed it, to calm my mind. It was like a prison. We couldn't talk. We had to wear weird white clothes. We weren't allowed to make eye contact with anyone. After 5am, we only had one small cup of broth all day. We were not allowed to have any personal belongings and had to sit in meditation day after day. I started to question my actions - why did I have to go to the other side of the world to do this? This is crazy. I was going crazy.

I'd fall asleep during the day which meant I couldn't sleep at night so my mind was going all night long. I lost it. I started to get very short of breath. I had a panic attack. I went to the monk and said, 'I can't do it.' He looked in my eyes and said, 'See you tomorrow.' I got so angry. I went to my room and I cried my eyes out. I was so hungry. My body was exhausted. I wanted to give up, but I could hear my voice saying, 'You have to keep going. You're not a quitter.' Another voice started saying, 'Stop, rest, why are you trying so hard? Why put yourself under pressure? It's okay to let go.'

I left the following day. I realised it was crazy to try and meditate in just two weeks, when these monks spent 40 years at it. I don't need to be in a forest, meditating. I am not my voice or my body. We are greater than these bodies and we don't die when the body dies. I am not the voices in my head. I am just the stillness that lies between. I think that's when I actually learned what meditation was.

I respect people who are religious. I grew up a Catholic. When I was 16, I applied to become a priest with Opus Dei but thankfully was rejected as I was too young. It was at the time I was starting to realise I was gay and it created conflict. I felt like a sinner - dirty, non-deserving of God. These days, I don't believe in a conventional God as such, but I do consider that there may be something bigger than us out there, a bigger whole that we are part of. Faith is incredibly important, not from a religious perspective, but a conviction that there's hope. A bright future, that we're acting for the greater good.

My mother died in my arms in a car crash when I was just nine years old. She was very entrepreneurial, like me. She loved doing things. She was the leader of her pack, loved by her friends. She used to sew and to sell things she'd made. I have a Christmas stocking and a pin cushion of hers. I struggle to have memories of my childhood before my mum's passing. Losing my mother was the defining moment in my life. I refer to it as the moment I woke up to life. Everything afterwards is the result of that moment. I became quite a thoughtful, profound and serious person after that.

I was a traumatised and psychologically abused by my Dad. I had a scar from the glass he cut me with. Those circumstances taught me that it doesn't matter how shitty things get, I knew I would always be fine.

Because of the life I've had and the disruptions growing up, I know myself very well. I like change. I change jobs every two years. I change friends regularly, it's my way. My mind needs to be stimulated with new things, ideas and people, so I move on. The same with my love relationships. Marriage is terrifying. It feels like I'm locking myself into something with bigger connotations. I'm afraid of commitment and am very aware of that. I don't think I want children, although I like them very much. I reflect on the childhood I had and the difficulties I went through. The importance of the roles of father, mother, carers, parents and the education children need. I'm not sure I'm generous enough to give so much of my time to children. I'm too selfish.

Sometimes I can be judgemental. I see people who don't enjoy their work. Doing the nine-to-five. Having their 20 days holiday. They wake up, buy food, cook, shower, go to work and come home. And 20 years later they're still in the same position. Nothing changes.

For me, everything is changing. I'm in transition. I feel excited and happy. In a way I'm excited but at the same time I feel a little uncertain. I think we're here to learn. That's what jumps out at me - lessons learned. The next generation is not that far off and I wish they could listen to some of the advice, reflections and learning that I've had. I wish I could see three months into the future.

What's your most memorable experience?

'Grandma's Saturday Soup'

We are like a zillion filing cabinets, stuffed with memories and on any given day, one will surface - why? I love that about us. Humans can pull out of the ether a memory to share, a story to tell, an offering of comfort, support, meaning and experience. Ask someone to share a memory with you - it's a gift that keeps on giving.

I wish you could have been sat next to me when I asked this question, dear reader. It's like a box of surprises and you really can't assume what will come out. But always, always it's about sharing the experience, their experience, and what a privilege. That person is transported just for a few moments, and you get to go with them. It's connecting and really lovely, even the bad memories.

The 20s

I started uni with a very good group of guys, we were like kids. We would play hide and seek. I can see us now laughing together. One mate had just broken up with his long-term girlfriend. He was feeling distraught. It was 11pm, and he messaged us all saying he needed to get out and just walk. We walked and walked and walked. One guy stopped. 'I just want to take a moment to remember this night.' Somebody else said, 'Let's all make a pact, if one of us discovers time travel, this is the point we will come back to.' We noted down the time and date, then we shook hands. We took a moment to breathe it in then went our separate ways. That night I will never let go of.

.

I was attacked. I was walking to work late at night with my friend. Someone tried to mug us. At the time it didn't affect me but a few days later I realised the impact. I took some time off work. Eventually when I went back but had a panic attack at the end of my shift. I've never really felt threatened before. I feel privileged. I have my head in the clouds most of the time. I don't have many negative experiences. My friends find it shocking that I will get on the Metro (in Newcastle) in full drag and meet friends in town. I keep my wits about me. I don't have music on so I can listen to what's going on around me.

The other memory that springs to mind was the 2019 Liverpool Pride. I laugh about it now but at the time I was devastated. I'd been building up to my performance for months, it was a big deal. Tens of thousands of people were there. It was going to be the single biggest performance I'd done in my life. It needed to be perfect. When I say everything went wrong - EVERYTHING went wrong. It got off to a bad start, high heels and a wet stage. I had two costume changes and a wig reveal. There were lots of props and fifteen different stunts. The first costume didn't work. It went from bad to worse. Then I fell down the stairs coming off stage.

■

Quite late into Mum's cancer we were having an argument about something at the top of the stairs. I was being a little shit. (I was six at the time.) I shouted at her. She lost her footing and fell all the way down and broke her arm. She'd been having chemotherapy and had no hair. I remember that image clearly, her leaving in an ambulance with terminal cancer and a broken arm that was caused by me. I felt so guilty.

■

I didn't have the best relationship with my Dad growing up. I wouldn't normally play music around him because he didn't like the swearing. I'd worry that we'd have argument. But there's this song 'Florence' by Loyle Carner, I remember playing it in the car. We'd sit in silence and listen to it. He started learning the words and we'd sing along together. We still didn't chat about a lot of stuff but that started a whole string of conversations.

■

Until I was about 18 I did disability athletics. I was a shot-put and discus thrower. Without sounding arrogant I was one of the better ones from my age group in Britain. In 2016 I won the county, regional, national championship and the British school games, which is the best of the best.

■

I ended up getting a scholarship to board at school in Year 9. I was grateful for the opportunity. I knew it was going to bring big changes. I remember the first couple of weeks vividly. It was strange. I remember thinking how bizarre it was to be living in this massive house with a bunch of strangers. I remember looking at the 18 year olds, thinking wow that's really old.

∎

My last visit to my Grandpa in hospital. There were tubes everywhere. I didn't know what to do or how I should act. The full weight of what was happening sank in. I told him I loved him (crying) and that the one thing I want the most is that I make my family proud. He couldn't respond but he looked up and gave an emotional sigh. He wanted to reassure me but he couldn't. I held his hand and sat in silence for a while. I left and he passed away a few hours later. Death is such an abstract idea until you're faced with it. From that day forward I started telling my parents how much I love them.

∎

The year I had abroad from uni was the most daunting thing I've ever done. I got to Spain without speaking any Spanish. I was really in the deep end and loved it. I had to figure things out. I had to learn to ask.

∎

Finishing my Marine recruit training. After 32 weeks we marched 30 miles across Dartmoor. I got my green beret.

∎

When I went to Australia with my ex-girlfriend three years ago, we ended up working for a multi-millionaire, a head of a big financial group. My girlfriend looked after their horses. We went everywhere with them, no expense spared. I take my hat off to people like that because when you've had a life-changing amount of money yet still have your feet on the ground, that's impressive. We were there for a year. We travelled all over. Why did I come back? I missed the UK. The smell of the seasons. I missed my roast dinner, too.

∎

Saturdays at my Grandma's house, particularly when my Grandad was alive. We used to drive up from London to their house, a village on the outskirts of Leicester. My Cousins, Aunties and Uncles would all be there. It was about family and conversations. I remember them singing. There was always something to eat. Grandma's 'Saturday Soup' would be cooking. You could smell it. My Nan's soup was the elite soup. My Dad used to call it the 'premier league' soup. Boiled broth with dumplings, yams, Cho Cho, plantain, boiled banana and sweet potato and goat. She'd make a huge pot for everybody. Over time she taught us all individually how to make it.

■

Two thoughts came into my mind and they both made my parents cry. One was passing medical school and another was scoring a goal when I was eleven years old. The ball came to me on the edge of the box. I was facing away from goal, I turned around and chipped it over the keeper. That was the wining goal. It was an amazing feeling, scoring that goal and the confidence it gave me. My Dad shed a tear when I scored that goal. All the other parents came up to him, congratulating him. I don't know why but I always remember that.

The 30s

The night my Dad died. I was 21. Me and my older brother were sparring in the living room. My Mum called us into the kitchen. My Dad was slumped. I don't think anyone realised what had happened. We tried to take him up to bed but couldn't move him so called the ambulance . He'd had a massive stroke and there was no coming back from it. We had to switch off the life support. He wasn't the most healthy person but it was very unexpected. He was here one minute and gone the next.

■

I remember doing a sale when I was younger and regretted selling my favourite dinosaur. I got £1.50 for it which was a lot of money back then (laughing). The lady gave me a £5 note and said do you have change, I had four 1ps! I didn't understand what change meant.

One bad memory stands out. Me and my brother went climbing with my Dad. We got stranded overnight at the top of the mountain. It was very cold and we were hungry. The one thing you mustn't do in those conditions is fall asleep. We were high up in the Alps. My Dad was a mountaineer, 60 at the time. Thankfully he knew what to do. We got our rope and coiled it up to make cushions because sitting on rock can be dangerous. You take your boots off, empty your rucksacks and use them like a mini sleeping bag to keep your feet from freezing, then just stay up talking. We had a satsuma and a few squares of chocolate. Every two hours we ate a piece of chocolate. We developed a routine and as soon as the sun came up we set off. It was really fucking cold. We are quite slow going up as we were unsure of the route. Bad weather. Wrong turns. The longer the day goes on the more dangerous it gets because the snow starts melting. The trick is not to be climbing late in the afternoon. I managed to call Mum to tell her we were okay and would be back the next day. Eventually, a helicopter was sent to find us, by which time we were half-way back down the mountain. They saw we were safe so didn't pick us up. Needless to say my Mum was fucking furious.

■

When I was 16, I went to see my best mate off at the airport. He was leaving New Zealand to go and live in England. I was so sad. I cried and I cried.

The 40s

My daughter woke up at 4am (she sleeps on a mattress next to us.) I put my head over the side of the bed and put my hand out. She went back to sleep. That's about as memorable as it gets.

■

When my boy was born. He was born by caesarean. I was the first person to hold him. I was humbled. It's a pretty unique thing.

■

When my grandmother wanted to see me. She wasn't well. I flew back to Greece and within five minutes of me arriving, she smiled and passed away. She was waiting for me. My grandparents brought me up. She was like a mother to me. Also, when I left my hometown in Greece and went to live in the States. I saw a limousine for the first time in my life. I took a ride to downtown Chicago. I remember looking at the sky thinking, 'What the hell is that?' - the skyscrapers. I'd never seen anything like it before.

■

When I was 23 my Mum had a nervous breakdown. It was scary. My sister and Dad refused to help. My Dad burst into tears. I remember begging my sister to help but she wouldn't. There comes a point when you have to just deal with it and cry later. At the time I didn't have any faith in human nature. I didn't believe in anybody. I'd been brought up to look after me. I had to put all my trust in the paramedics, the doctor and the social worker; who were all strangers. I had no choice but to dive in with these four people and trust. That was a turning point in life. I realised there are good people who you can trust.

■

I don't mean to be flippant but tasting wine has changed the way I look at things. I was on a business trip, I got upgraded on Emirates - nice! I was given a glass of wine. OMG - I had no idea wine could taste so good. Previously I'd go into an off-licence and pick a bottle but from that moment it changed the way I looked at wine. I went on a wine course. It was a memorable experience that totally changed an aspect of my life - I now really enjoy wine. I know I should have said the birth of my children, but I am trying to avoid the cliché!

■

Doing my degree at uni was a pivotal moment in my life. It's the first time you're a grown up. I remember waking up, no alarm clock, no responsibilities. Thinking, 'What shall I do today? Finish that essay and maybe see my mates in the park. How am I going to amuse myself?' There was a huge freedom from responsibility. It's a time in life when you're young so you can drink as much as you want, eat as much as you want and still be physically attractive. A life completely devoid of responsibility apart from your own entertainment is what I remember the most. I can't quite believe we had that opportunity, although you don't appreciate it at the time. Now, there's always shit that needs doing!

∎

When I played for Farnborough against Arsenal at Highbury in the FA cup draw in 2003. We went to La Manga - the first non league team to train there. Sol Campbell, Dennis Bergkamp, were on the pitch. We lost 5-1. It was a good day out. There was a streaker that day. He got three months inside for that!

∎

Meeting John Peel. It was at HMV in Oxford Street. We spoke about bands and his wife's brain tumour. Meeting him was a moment I won't forget. Also being at the Lighthouse Rave out in Docklands in 2000. It was a one-off. Boards of Canada were playing - very trippy and lovely. Music for me is a release from everything else going on.

∎

The first time I played Rugby for Tonga.

The 50s

One time I was on a mission to find a decent wave. I swam and swam, I was out there, next stop - America! It was time to turn around. I might have gone a little far. I got on this wave and went flying. Water goes everywhere. It's like being on a spin cycle. You come out and water is streaming out your nose. When I say surfing, the surfers out there would say I was body boarding. For me a 10 footer is a beast. That's nothing, surfers ride 70, 80 foot waves. It's a great laugh.

∎

Being driven by Lewis Hamilton. A colleague invited us to Mercedes-Benz. They do these drives. He said, 'There might be a chance you'll be driven by Lewis.' And I was. I got in the front seat with Lewis Hamilton and went round the track!

∎

My Nan got killed while riding her bike. She was hit by a car. I remember my auntie coming to the tropical fish shop where I worked saying they'd been a terrible accident. Next to my Mum she was the lady that I would have loved my sons to have met. She was a great Nan. I'd go around to hers every day after school. We'd go on holiday with her to the coast.

■

My Dad was made a Druid for services to music.

■

Years ago I was at the Scala cinema on King's Cross at a rave. I was coming up on an E, the happiest I've ever been in my life. I was standing on the cinema chair listening to Adamski blaring at me. Although it was drug-induced it wasn't about the drugs, it was about being at the right place at the right time.

■

The greatest benefit from working for an American law firm for 17 years was I got to play golf at Augusta National in Georgia, where they play the US Masters. You can't pay money to do that. You have to be invited. It was surreal. I had my own caddy. I was in a place of dreams, walking down an immaculate fairway. Augusta is a childhood dream that only a fraction of people on the planet will fulfil.

■

It was on my second road trip to the States with my ex-wife and the kids. We drove to Monument Valley. We parked our RV just after sunset. The next day the kids wanted to go horse riding. It was a beautiful day. We were in the middle of nowhere, the only tourists around. We were met by some Native Americans. I was really nervous. I'd never ridden a horse before. The others had. I was terrified. I told the man I was a novice and didn't like horses. He looked at me. Listening and unflinching. He paused then tells his mate, 'Go get Flash.' I think he's winding me up and going to bring out a rampant stallion but no, he brings out this little pony. I have photos of the four of us. I'm coming up the rear, my feet just inches off the ground. This 'horse' wouldn't move. It was the way my family were all laughing at me. It was the best day of my life. An incredible experience. It's upsetting when I think about it.

■

I was nominated for 'Young Chef of the Year' - but it's not quite as good as having the kids. When my son was born the placenta was retained. They needed to deal with my wife - all of a sudden this baby was thrust at me. 'Holy shit, I helped create this person.'

■

I should say seeing my kids born, but it isn't - God bless 'em. I love them more than anything. And it's not my wedding day either, though it was a great experience. It was May 29th 1989 when we won the league up at Anfield - 2 nil. I was up in Liverpool, we weren't expected to win - it was the greatest night of my life, all the emotion came out. I cannot begin to explain how amazing that was.

■

I was sexually abused as a child. He was somebody that my family took under its wing, who'd had a horrible upbringing. He was ten years older than me and used to babysit for us. I was about 11 at the time and it happened over a period of time. I don't know how often or how many times. I do remember at times feeling my body reacting and yet knowing something was very wrong, illicit and shameful. That's a part that so many people who've been sexually abused struggle with. It's also the thing the abuser has over you. It's part of your weakness, like you were almost compliant, an illicit secret.

■

Two opposite ends of the spectrum, watching both of my children born are days I will never forget. Scared and excited at both for different reasons but at the other end was watching my Dad take his last breath peacefully, lying in a hospital bed. It gave me a good feeling knowing I was there, and a sense of closure. Unlike when my Mum died, I was away on holiday, It was a total shock and took me a while to get over it. She was only 56. Mum was a functioning alcoholic. I didn't know where I stood sometimes and the odd time she'd hit me. We never knew where her mood was. One time I asked her if she'd let me off paying rent one week as I wanted to take this lass out. She said yes. Rent day came and she asked me why I hadn't paid her - she hadn't remembered the conversations. I was so mad, I threw all my wages at her and said, 'Have the lot.' This led to a fight with my Dad, he swung for me and I punched him. I told him, 'Don't ever fuck with me again you're too old and too slow.' Later, I apologised but he didn't speak to me for about three months.

∎

When I was seven we moved North with my step-dad's new job. I was bullied. I used to get chased home from school every day by four lads and it went on for weeks. One time this lad grabbed me and started banging my head on the pavement. I was terrified about moving on to secondary school. There were fights regularly. I developed a stutter. I hated school. I was so miserable. I only saw my real Dad four times a year - it was shit. As time went on I found the best coping method was to make people laugh.

∎

I would like to know if I saved this woman's life. Years ago when I was a teenager I was a waiter at an event. Some bloke asked me to check on his wife as she'd been gone a long time. I went into the Ladies, she was locked in the cubicle. I climbed over the top of the door. She'd passed out on the toilet, knickers round her ankles and everything. I saw a piece of meat in the corner of her mouth, she'd obviously been choking. I pulled it out, pulled up her knickers, then the ambulance arrived. I never knew what happened to her.

∎

I wrote a poem called 'Gold' when I was seven - it went something along the lines of 'Gold is my jumper, gold is my hair' I was sent round to all the other classes to show the teachers, I was so proud although it was probably more about my ego than the adulation.

∎

I tend to block out a lot of my early years. I can't remember a lot of what happened before my Dad abused me. I do remember when I was about 12, my Mum went into hospital to have a hysterectomy so

I'd stayed at my mates - his parents were more parental to me than my own parents. Their house was a bolt hole, I felt safe - nothing would happen to me there.

■

One time I was playing soft ball. There was this one catch I made. I knew exactly which direction the ball was going to go almost before he hit it. The only way I could have arrived at that place, almost horizontal, my body did something I was not conscious of - I caught the ball and fell to the ground and flipped. That's what you kinda live for as an athlete. It sounds egotistical. I was watching it happen. I can't believe I caught it. People were asking me, 'How did you catch that?' I had no idea. I take no credit for it. It was a moment when all things combine in the right way that made something wonderful happened.

■

I was in Tanzania, we went up to the Ngorogoro crater on Christmas Eve. We drove into the bottom of it – in three hours, we were the only two people in that crater. It was an amazing experience. I am not about owning things, I'm about experiencing things.

■

When Chelsea won the Champions League in 2012.

■

Getting married. I passed out at the altar. It was an unseasonably hot day, I'd had a few drinks the night before and was quite emotional. All of a sudden I was flat out!

■

When my ex told me she was having an affair. That changed my life just like that. I was 28. I loved her to bits. That was really hard.

■

When my Mum and Dad died. It's those moments that are most memorable. Births, deaths, and divorce.

■

My first child being born. It's double-edged because there's a lot of fear around them surviving the experience. Once you get over the fear, life has changed for ever.

■

As a kid I spent a lot of time with my Dad. He was a scrap dealer. We used to drive around in a van to all the farms in Devon and Cornwall. Clearing stuff out. Even now when I see a skip I'll have a root around. I get on very well with my Dad. He's 86. My Dad is a very kind person. He did a lot of things for nothing. He's never been wealthy but he's always been relatively happy. We live in the same street. He and my Mum are just 12 doors down. I see them everyday.

∎

It's the moment my children were born. The first one was the most profound. From not being a Dad to the moment I realized I was a Dad was incredible. The birth itself was amazing. I cried because it was beautiful. She was very premature but I didn't know how poorly she was at that point. My wife was knackered. She went to have a shower. They put the baby in a bassinet. I walked passed her and suddenly stopped. It was at that moment, seeing her, thinking, 'Fuck me, I'm the Dad.' It was very deep. It was really amazing.

∎

The birth of my eldest boy. Chelsea winning the Champions League when we were there at Munich. Getting a scholarship to Trinity College, Cambridge. Paying off my first mortgage. Meeting my wife and knowing that I was going to marry her within a few weeks. I'm not sure if she knew she was getting married to me, but I certainly knew I was getting married to her.

∎

Going to see The Specials for the first time. I was 12.

∎

When I met my wife. It was a memorable crazy day. A Saturday. By the end of the night I was that pissed, I didn't know where I was. I fell over going to the chippy, split my head open, down to my skull. I had 16 stitches. I was sat in the back of the ambulance with a bandage on my head full of blood. She sat in A&E with me for five hours. That was our first date.

∎

I walked the 195 miles Coast to Coast trail completely barefoot. It took me 14 days. I was walking on scree for 14 hours a day and it poured down, constantly. The demons come, constantly telling you to give up. My feet were horrendous. Day 2, I slipped off the side of a mountain and had to be rescued by the film crew. Later when I was doing research for my book, I found out that somebody had fallen off that same spot and was killed. It's a notorious place.

A lot of other walkers met me at the very end. That was probably one of the most memorable and humbling things. The human spirit is absolutely fantastic. I pretty much pulled off the impossible. Afterwards, I had to go to hospital for tetanus and diphtheria shots because of the open wounds!

Previously, I did the Coast to Coast on a bike which took 12 hours. I then ran it in snow blizzard which took three days. In 2017, I travelled 10,000 miles in 336 days about 29 miles a day, every day for pretty much a year. I was walking, running and riding a bike.

∎

Watching Burnley at Wembley in 1988. We got beat 2-0.

∎

When I was six, I had an eye operation. I had a squint. I remember being in hospital having Heinz tomato soup. I remember the cream on the top. I remember the nurse being very motherly.

The 60s

The doctor said to me, 'Your Dad is a Rolls Royce car but running on a Mini engine.' I got the call at 2am. We went up the hospital. Seeing my Dad dead, that was quite hard. He looked like he was asleep. There was no pain, he wasn't struggling. It hits you hard because you're never going to see him again. He's never going to tell me anything again!

∎

I met Princess Diana in the Palace grounds. She was walking through the courtyard before she married Charles. I wished her all the very best for the wedding. I wish I'd told her not to marry him! Princess

Margaret invited us to a cocktail party. She'd walk around with a gin and tonic and a cigarette. I was working at a laundry and the royal family were one of our clients. I'd go to Buckingham Palace to deliver wicker hampers full of table linen for their banquets. We used to clean Prince Philip's and Prince Charles' uniforms. I used to go in the Palace grounds. I was allowed to walk around the rooms. I would go to Windsor, Frogmore House and the Royal Lodge too where the Queen Mum was. They would always have a glass of juice and a sandwich ready for us. The Queen Mum came down to congratulate me on the birth of my daughter. Every Christmas she would thank us for our services and give us an envelope with some cash in it. They'd give you a roast dinner too. I loved it, it was brilliant.

∎

The birth of my son. (I'm welling up now). It was extraordinary. I even managed to piss my wife off big time. She needed the gas and air. I wasn't quick enough with it, she snatched it off me and stuck it straight on her cheek, I laughed out loud. She wasn't happy! When I finally left the hospital I tried to ring my Mum to tell her the news but I couldn't speak. I couldn't get the words out. I was so emotional. I'd kept control of my emotions before then but ever since that day I cry at the drop of a hat.

∎

Finishing my first triathlon. I thought I was fucking Superman. The fact that my then wife considered jumping in the pool to rescue me during the swimming part because I was so slow and uncomfortable is by the by!

∎

I can remember exactly what I was doing on October 4th 1964 - I fished my first competition. I caught two roach and thought I'd won the day on the river Tees. Me and my mate were two young kids on our bikes, we just turned up, we had such fun.

∎

Having sex for the first time. When I found out I got a first class degree from Oxford. The birth of my first child. I wasn't there when my wife died but someone being born and someone dying is always very memorable.

∎

I was driving at night in Western Australia and I stopped for a pee. I got out of the car, turned the lights and the engine off. I looked up at the stars and almost fell over with vertigo. My mind was trying to deal with the perspective and the colour. It was sensory overload. I sort of evaporated. For a while I saw the duality of everything, The stars, rocks, me, I felt utterly and completely inconsequential and it made me feel deeply, deeply comforted that it made me cry. It was just a glimpse into a world where everything seemed to have equal significance to everything else. I realised life is short and nothing will last.

∎

Going to Petra in Jordan. You walk through this crack in the rock and come out to this beautiful temple.

∎

I had the fortune to play at Glastonbury in 1992 on the World Music Stage. As we started there were just a few people in the audience but as we played, more and more people came. The lights went down and the audience started lighting up lighters and stuff. There was this stream of light. It's like a drug. Even playing small gigs, there's something about holding the audience. You're out there. It's us against the world. When it works it just works. Sometimes you're on a stage and so in the moment that you're not bothered about the audience.

∎

The first time I had sex. At the end of it I lit cigarette and thought, 'Was that it? What's all this fuss about?' I didn't realize it takes time. If you want intimate sex, it takes time.

∎

When I was a kid, I would stand on my Dad's feet and he would dance with me.

The 70s

I was on a submarine on watch out in the Atlantic doing exercises. I was very junior in the Navy. It was a particularly rough day, and I reported sighting a yacht. The skipper thought he was in trouble and we should rescue him. This fella was sitting on his yacht, below deck, reading a book waiting for the weather to calm when we surfaced. Submarines make a terrific noise when they surface. He must have had the fright of his life, thinking he was a thousand miles away from anyone. The skipper shouted through the megaphone, 'Need any help?' He replied, 'Yes - fuck off!'

∎

We'd planned a trip to America via Toronto. I wanted to find out where my paternal grandmother was born. I had a prayer book from when she was christened saying that she was from somewhere in Pennsylvania. We flew on September the 11th 2021! Myself, my wife and daughter and our two granddaughters. We had just passed halfway across the Atlantic when the 'Fasten your seatbelt' sign came on. An aura came over the plane. The pilot said, 'There's nothing wrong with the plane but we've been told we have to land as soon as possible.' My wife was next to our oldest granddaughter who was eating toffees. My wife said, 'Stop eating all them toffees.' She said, 'Why? We're all going to die anyway!' Thankfully we arrived at our destination as all the nearer airports were already full. The captain then told us that planes had crashed into the World Trade Centre!

∎

I always wanted to work on the police dog section. After three and half years waiting I got an interview. Later that day I got a call telling me I was accepted. I'd been wanting it for so long - I'll never forget that phone call.

∎

I babysat this little boy for an American couple for a year when I lived in Amsterdam. Every day before this little boy's nap I'd read him his favourite Mother Goose book. He would sit on my lap. My arms around him as we turned the pages. He was two when I left.

When he was six and I went back to their home for dinner. He didn't remember me, but at his bedtime, he walked over to the bookshelf and picked up the same Mother Goose book without saying a word and brought it over and sat up on my lap. I was moved to tears. Those days reading to him had meant something and at such a young age. That's incredible. His parents were gobsmacked.

■

I was born during the War. We used to live right on the seafront at Selsey Bill. One night there was a huge gale. I remember getting out of bed and walking through the lounge, looking out across the garden - it wasn't there. The spray was coming over the house. The car, the garage and half the garden had gone. My father's only comment was, 'I've seen worse at sea'. He had been in the Navy. We used to have an iron table in the kitchen and when the Messerschmitts came over during the War, Mother threw us under it. My diet for the first 10 years of my life was dried egg, dried milk and porridge. We had ration books until 1952. I'd get a penny gobstopper once a week. Twice a week the ice man used to come. He'd walk up the drive with a great big block of ice. The bread was delivered by horse and cart. So was the milk. They were tough times. This is what makes me angry now. The young kids who've got so much and they can't stand being in lockdown.

Dad had a little rowing dinghy. One morning he said, 'Come on, boys, we're going out for a row'. We had our Labrador William with us. Dad took us out in his dingy, two miles from the shore and threw us over. He said, 'Now you learn to swim'. He turned his dinghy round and rowed back. My brother was four, I was eight and my older brother 10. We had to doggy paddle behind him because we couldn't swim - we could in the end! I wasn't frightened. I loved it!

■

One time I remember going to the Dolomites for work. My boss left me in the town square with a bottle of wine while he went to a meeting. He said he'd only be an hour - he was gone eight. The scenery literally brought tears to my eyes. I couldn't describe it to anybody. I was glued. I went 360 degrees around the table, following the sun looking at the mountains. I was mesmerised watching them turn from white, to blue, then pink. It was a wonderful memory, a souvenir.

The 80s-plus

I used to do Punch and Judy shows in a nudist camp, a Naturist Foundation summer event. I had my clothes on. I didn't feel uncomfortable; however, it's tricky talking to someone who's naked. It's like a magnet, your eyes are drawn downwards.

■

Discovering that the person I lived with, I was absolutely in love with. You have loves, friendship, sex and parties but this person gave me the family life that I didn't have in my childhood home. Suddenly I had a family. I was sharing a house with someone I wanted to be with.

I lost my relationship, my flat and my job in one week. Three major parts of my life all gone in one week! You just cope. You have to. You're not chirpy but you think tomorrow must be better. I tried very hard to get another job. A job is more important than a home. It doesn't mean you're not crying because things are so awful but the only person that can drive you on is you. Within two months I was back in the harness, running a newspaper. I've been lucky in life.

■

Our wedding day - that was lovely. After that I've just enjoyed the kids and the grandchildren coming along. I did achieve something at Oulton Park race circuit once. I was a racing driver for five years back in my early 20s. I broke the lap record at 96 miles per hour - that record still stands today. I am an adrenalin junkie. I'm very good on big dippers but not very good going upside down.

■

I got involved in engineering during the oil boom, and worked in Iraq, Kuwait and Saudi. I met some wonderful people. I've had such kindness from people. One time I was helped by a man whose only language was French. Myself and my work mate got stuck in the desert; our car couldn't move. This guy came along with his son and rescued us. He took us to his home and put us up overnight. I slept on the floor surrounded by all his children. As I was pulling off my boots, I remember seeing this little child, his deep, dark eyes peeping out at me. I winked, he chuckled under his blanket, it was absolutely charming. The next day the guy got us back to some sort of a civilization. I wanted to thank him. I wanted to give him some money which might have seemed crude on my part, and of course he didn't want any. Eventually in my schoolboy French I said, 'It's for the children'. He looked at me and took the money. In French he replied, 'Nous sommes tous frères,' - we are all brothers. I will never forget that.

■

I was posted to Christmas Island in the Pacific during the war as an engineer. I didn't want to go. There were no telephones in those days, we had to write letters. It took a long time to get a reply. I wrote every day. I missed my wife. I was out there for 12 months. The Army took over the island. Most of the locals were evacuated. We were testing atomic devices. I saw five atomic tests, three big ones and two small ones. The sun was very, very hot. The average temperature was 90. You could get second or third degree burns. The island had no soil apart from decomposing leaves from the coconut trees. The sand was bright white and reflected the heat. Scientists would build and test bombs. During a test you had to go to a particular area, crouch down, head down, close your eyes. The countdown began. Although your eyes were closed, a silverish light penetrated you. If anything went wrong there was a lorry on standby to take you off to the shore where a boat was waiting to whisk you away. Thankfully that never happened.

A longer conversation…

Matt, 24

consultant, from Suffolk

I've had a fascination with death for a long time. We once had a cat called Cybil. When I was seven or eight, she had to be put down. We went to the vets, I wanted to see it. I'd never seen death before. I was stroking her - then the injection went in and her breathing slowed. She died in my arms. It was weird - was I a messed up kid? Her dying was so fascinating to me - there's another realm that we don't know anything about. Death is such a taboo and no one talks about it. You'd think we'd all be talking about it - but we don't!

In Mexico there are three deaths. The first is when you actually die. The second is the funeral and you're remembered, cremated or buried. It's a very formal acknowledgment that the person has died. Then there's the third death - when the last memory of you is gone. This is the most beautiful. For example Julius Caesar - the fact that I am saying his name shows he's still around. I have thought about the death of my family and saying something at the funeral. One thing I would say about each of them in turn - yes we've had the first, we are here for the second but the third is a long way off - look at all the people around us, we will be talking about the dead for a long time to come. I think that is a great way to think about death. It reminds you of that the impact a person has. While I am alive everyone I know will never truly die because I will remember them.

I've been practising Buddhism since I was 16 so I tend to look at all aspects of myself - mind, body and spirit. I sometimes go and sit by the river and watch the water. Among the hustle and bustle, I just observe. It makes you realise that anything can be going on in your world and it has almost no effect on what's going on around you - it's calming. I can have the worst, best or neutral day and the water is going to do exactly the same every day, and I love that. Everything is going to be fine. Am I really having an affect? No!

It's been said I have an old head on young shoulders. It derives from when I was very badly bullied from the ages of nine to 16. It fundamentally changed parts of my character. At nine, I was quizzed as to whether I was gay. I was ostracised, kicked and dragged around in mud.

When I was 13, they pulled my trousers and pants down and I was hung upside down from a tree. People took pictures of me and put them on Facebook. There was a Facebook page called 'I hate Matt'. I never played the masculinity game at school, and I think that fed into how they viewed me. One of the worst cases was when someone stole a blade from woodwork class and held it to my neck. It was really weird - why didn't I tell anyone? My Mum didn't know anything about it because if you tell there will be repercussions and knowing my Mum, she'd have made sure the bullies paid. I was afraid of making the situation worse. I didn't tell her until I was 20.

I would never admit this to my bullies but in the long term it's had a positive effect - that's not to say I loved being kicked on the ground, but it led me to Buddhism. I think a lot of extremists have come from similar situations where they've been bullied and found the wrong path. Fortunately for me I went in a positive direction.

A Buddhist came into the school when I was 13 - all the other students were giggling but it really struck a chord with me. I started reading about it and thought, 'That's for me.' At 16, I plucked up the courage to go to the local Buddhist centre and loved it. I joined the men's group, we'd talk on a deep emotional level and I started helping newcomers. It was such a good support with school life which was shit! So in the long run my bullying was positive, and amazingly led me to a path which has given me such joy.

Since the age of 17 I have never been insecure and I'm fortunate in that I don't get jealous over girlfriends, or concerned by the way I look, although from the outside I can see that being misinterpreted as ego.

I don't do social media, I don't care for it. It's part of our generation and if you're not on it, you're missing out. But the scientific research shows it's really a negative thing. Social media is addictive, it's programmed to be that way. I've grown up with how important it is for a photograph to be 'just right' so it makes for a good PC (profile picture). I don't want to be doing things in life just for the recognition. I love maths, so why not change the world by using my brain and making the most of what I've got. Maths is the language of the universe.

Buddhism really underlies a lot of the way I view the world. 'Non self' is a big part of this. The way I see it is from the inside. I have acceptance and love for myself, knowing that I am the only person I am with the whole time.

One day I will turn to dust. I will be part of a higher order of chaos and my rebirth will be the energy that 'I' currently am. 'I' will be in the fly and the fly will get eaten by the bird and the bird will poop him out - these cycles continue. You can't create or destroy energy, energy just changes form and I love that. Self is an abstract idea. Everything is in flux - this is really comforting - there is no me. I take up space but I am borrowing this space. The fact that I will be a pile of dust or soil is an awesome thought.

Every year our old school meets up at a local pub, a sort of reunion. A few years after we'd left school, a guy was there who had been one of the most prominent of the bullies. He asked if he could talk to me. He told me he was really sorry for everything. I wasn't expecting it - I took my hat off to him. It was really good of him to do that. We're not the closest of friends since but I have no animosity towards him. What's the point of holding onto it? It doesn't do any good to anyone.

Who or what inspires you?

'People who tell the truth.
I don't always tell the truth'

I'm inspired by the plumber who has just painstakingly fixed a smart meter in my house. How does he navigate that puzzle? A conglomerate of wires that would send most of us into a spin and need a lie-down after one installation, let alone the other six he'll install by the end of the day.

MY MUM ⚓ My parents ⚓ My children ⚓ My daughter ⚓ My son ⚓ My Gran ⚓ My friends ⚓ My teacher ⚓ Nature ⚓ I inspire myself ⚓ Everyday people ⚓ Conversations ⚓ Mountains & lakes ⚓ Philosophy ⚓ Politics ⚓ Poetry ⚓ Science ⚓ Writers ⚓ Jordan, the smart meter man ⚓ Almost all physicists ⚓ Comic book writers ⚓ Films ⚓ **MUSICIANS** ⚓ Positivity ⚓ Being kind ⚓ My vicar ⚓ Storytelling ⚓ Young people ⚓ Women ⚓ People in the services ⚓ People who question you ⚓ Creativity ⚓ Painters ⚓ Sculptors ⚓ Henry Avery (Pirate) ⚓ Vincent van Gogh ⚓ Loyle Carner ⚓ George the Poet ⚓ Jimmy Hendrix ⚓ Bob Marley ⚓ Prince ⚓ Bob Dylan ⚓ David Bowie ⚓ John Lennon ⚓ André Previn ⚓ Oscar Peterson ⚓ **MY DAD** ⚓ Ant Middleton ⚓ Tim Ferris ⚓ Russell Brand ⚓ Terry Pratchett ⚓ Robert Rankin ⚓ Marcelo Garcia ⚓ Martin Scorsese ⚓ Guillermo del Toro ⚓ Samuel Beckett ⚓ NASA guys ⚓ The Apollo moon landings ⚓ Neil Armstrong ⚓ Malcolm X ⚓

Martin Luther King ☿ Ghandi ☿ Nelson Mandela ☿ Doreen Lawrence ☿ Steve Jobs ☿ Neil Kinnock ☿ Chögyal Namkhai Norbu ☿ Arnold Schwarzenegger ☿ Barack Obama ☿ **MY WIFE / PARTNER** ☿ Richard Rogers ☿ Norman Foster ☿ Macintosh ☿ Black Lives Matter ☿ St Thérèse of Lisieux ☿ St Bernadette of Lourdes ☿ The underdog ☿ The story of Jesus ☿ People who don't run with the crowd ☿ The Buddha ☿ Denise Bird ☿ Ernst von Born ☿ Margot Kidder aka Lois Lane ☿ Michel Roux ☿ People who make wooden boats are closer to God than anybody ☿ Bomber crews in the Second World War ☿ Courage ☿ **SPORTS PERSONALITIES** ☿ Nathan Jones ☿ Andrew Strauss ☿ Alistair Cook ☿ Brian Robson ☿ Gary Bailey ☿ Christiana Rinaldo ☿ Maradona ☿ Roger Federer ☿ Ben Stokes ☿ Mark Spitz ☿ Ivan Marks ☿ The White Rose Group ☿ Small gestures of kindness ☿ And what about the agoraphobic who manages to make it to the corner shop?

A longer conversation...

Nasir, 51

almost retired, from London

We were on holiday in the Maldives and I went snorkelling. There was a moment when I was completely on my own. Away from the other tourists. I remember swimming next to this enormous whale shark. It was like swimming next to a goddess. Whale sharks travel really slowly, the same speed at which you swim. I felt completely insignificant and blissful. This enormous head and tiny eyes drifting along in this massive ocean next to me. I didn't want to leave the water EVER. If you'd said to me you can be a fish for the rest of your life, I would have. I couldn't get out of the water - they had to haul me out. It was an incredible feeling of calm next to this force of nature. I felt unimportant, nothing mattered. It wasn't about me or anything else - it was magical. We live such artificial lives - then you realize, this is what's real, it's nature. I was just was a drop in the ocean.

When I was younger, half my family went on holiday to Pakistan. We went on a family safari, in two Land Rovers. One was new. All the parents were in that one. We four kids were in the clapped-out, knackered one driven by my cousin, who was only two years older than me. We were meant to be in convoy but the parents' car just drove off and left us in the desert. Our Land Rover broke down. My cousin was trying to get it going. Meanwhile the girls were really worried - this was in the days before mobile phones. At that moment I looked out into the desert. The silence was incredible. It felt like the whole world had stopped. All the noise was absorbed. I loved it. I just started walking. The silence was blissful. I wasn't scared, nothing about it worried me. We have lost our connection. That's where we need to be.

I want more time on my own, time for wonder. I am really bad at relaxing. I don't like sitting still. I love the London buzz. I love the crowds, the anonymity, the energy. I am a worker bee in a hive. I love going out. I waste my energy on going out drinking and partying too much, reading crappy news stuff. I think being a voyeur of someone's tragedy is awful, perverse. I am not on social media. No one I know has anything good to say about it.

I put myself down a lot but equally I am grateful for what I've got. I am very privileged. I am quite self-critical. Almost certainly it's come from my parents. My Mum has always been very critical. They set expectations, like a lot of Asian parents. They thought they were doing their best for their kids, they were driven. If I came home and said to my father, 'I've got 97 per cent today in my exam,' he'd say, 'What happened to the other 3 per cent?' It has made me strive all the time, trying to prove I am not a failure.

I feel a disappointment to them. No matter what I did, I could never reach their expectations. In our community, the focus is on family responsibility and not your individual attitude or happiness. It's about being a responsible citizen towards your family. The Asian community might say that Western culture is lonely and selfish. You'll never be lonely in the Asian community, they will be there ALL the time. It was bad enough that my character didn't fit in but when I came out when I was 21, it was awful. My parents' fake friends were all homophobic and my parents cared what they thought. They couldn't get over it. There were so many rows. Latterly in private, away from their acquaintances, they have started to accept us.

We have a daughter and a granddaughter. When I met my partner his daughter was 14, so I became a step-dad. When she was 21 she had a baby and the two of them moved in with us. It felt like the right thing to do. Being a step-father has been tricky at times. I am the boring dad with the boring dad questions but I've always loved kids.

I'm not good at the daily upbringing of kids but being a grandad and dropping in and out is great.

Life is amazing and fantastic. I don't think we appreciate it, and we should. I am very lucky. I don't have any health worries and financially everything is okay. I love life even though I have been through some shitty times.

Life is about expectations. What my parents wanted. What society wants. Do I fit in? What do I want? Self-awareness is vital. There are ups and downs but I think it's really important to be grateful and look at the positives in life. So much of life is the reaction we have to the way things are presented. Between the stimulus and the response is wisdom.

What do you think about life – what are we doing here?

'Maybe we live to become complete'

Ah the biggest question of them all - Life! Just live it. Follow your thread and see where it takes you. Try hard not to over think it because no one has any answers and that's what makes it all the more mysterious - uncertainty!

After all these interviews, I'm still none the wiser about what on earth we are doing here on this planet - no one has a clue. Everyone has their thoughts but no one actually knows. That's quite nice. It chimes with observations I made regarding men's sometimes considerable 'certainty' (see Question 14, What are your views on faith?) And the need to know. To be right and have the facts.

The 20s

Life is relatively meaningless. It's not something we choose. I don't believe in a big plan. The most pleasant view I have is that when we die we return to the earth and that's the cycle of life. Human life is this mesmerizing trance. It came about purely by chance.

■

I think we have the opportunity to leave the world a better place. If you can't find any other meaning in your life, let that be the meaning. Whatever happens to us as a species, the planet will carry on. If we become over-populated and ravaged by disease and illness, we inevitably will die out. I don't think the earth depends on us.

■

We are making it up as we go along. I get caught up in our western life - to live in a house with a white picket fence, two kids, a girl and a boy. Other countries live different lives. Maybe happier? Maybe with chickens and cows, living off the land? There's no recipe for life. It just evolves. That's the reason I like to believe in a higher being. Call it God, energy or whatever. I can't believe that this all happened randomly. It just seems too calculated, but maybe that's my way of quantifying it.

■

I'm going to be quite pessimistic and say there is no meaning of life. We are here existing because we are. I'd like to think there is some sort of higher cosmic purpose. I like the idea of what came before the Big Bang. As of yet we can't see any other purpose than reproduction - but why? What's the end goal, to keep reproducing? Two atoms came together several billion years ago and we've got to make the most of it.

■

Life is all about opinions and stories. I'm learning about states, societies and the importance of farming at uni. How we shifted from hunter-gatherers to farmers and how that created the idea of ownership of people, land and borders. That allowed people to separate themselves, create class divides and hierarchy. It came from ownership and accumulation of wealth. The invention of the plough for example, you wouldn't logically think could create sexism. The knock-on effects of all these stories have created all our social issues. All change is socially constructed. That's how we navigate life - by finding our story, telling our story and listening to other people's stories. My own family has a mix of Zoroastrianism, Christianity and Islam. I've heard so many different stories and opinions and I think they're all right.

■

It's something that I hope goes on for ever because I'm petrified of death. I think everyone has their moment.

■

You can change the way you perceive life by removing your expectations.

■

In a moment of drunken clarity while at university I had a euphoric moment. I knew it was time for me to move on to the next phase. Four years of uni was great but I realised life has different moments. School, uni, work, family. Everyone goes through the transition and there's a time for each stage.

■

I feel we are doing the wrong thing a lot of the time. Education and jobs aren't important but they get you through life. People lose sight of what's important. I never want to get past working 40 hours a week. I value my friends and family much more - I'd rather do less. A lot of people I've met say they didn't see their mum and dad while they were growing up because they were always at work. I don't want to be like that.

■

I've found a philosophy recently that says life is just meaningless and terrible. I was talking to my Grandma about it and she says I'm being daft and naive. I don't know where I stand. That's my issue at the minute. I actually don't know what to think about life. It's meaningless but we can add meaning.

■

Some people don't have mortgages and live off their pensions. They have little to worry about, yet they moan about really trivial stuff. I wonder if they've spent their whole life moaning. I think life is about enjoying stuff.

The 30s

I've never thought about that to be honest. I don't have anything to say about that.

■

Generally life is cruel, relentless and messes with you at any given time. At this point in my life, I think the joys of living far outweigh the dread.

■

Life's too short although it's long when you empty your mind. All experiences are new. As you get older the cup is getting fuller and the days are getting shorter. I have taken things out of the cup now and time is going slower. Routine makes things go faster. There's a human habit about time but time doesn't exist. No one will care in 100 years so what's the point in getting your knickers in a twist?

■

I guess we are here to form relationships and experience as much as we can in the time we've got and try not to hurt people. If you can make a difference in someone's life – then, lucky you. It might be easier if I was a monkey or a dog.

■

We like to categorise, box and frame things to make sense of life. Wonderfully, it all just is. The scale and size of it all is phenomenal. We've only been round for the last second. The fact that there is possibility of life on other planets, seeing all those planets so far away. The light coming from them means we are actually looking at something that's thousands of years old - history. It boggles the mind in a wonderful way.

■

If you look at it spiritually, then everyone gets something from it. There are people too focused on being right in a scientific sense. Ultimately science will explain everything but it's arrogant to think we've even scratched the surface of what science will tell us. Saying that, science proves there's nothing more than what we are but why do some people see ghosts? These subjects tend to get jumbled together along with religion as being nonsense but I think there is a lot of science in there waiting to be discovered.

■

Before we invented electricity, if somebody came up with electricity as a mental concept, science would prove it as complete bunkum, that it doesn't exist. But when we discovered electricity, science shows that, yes - electricity exists. It's naive to try to make sense of the world when there is so much more to uncover. We have to be accepting. A lot of people get a lot of love, strength and belonging through religion. The joy, solace and peace that it brings and that's a wonderful thing. It's mean for people to poo-poo it. We are complex. We are very keen on being right. Let people get on with what they want to get on with, as long as it's not harmful to others.

■

My conclusions are: I've absolutely no idea and no one else has either. That's the best answer I can give. People believe their own shit, 'We are here to love'. How do you know? No one knows!

∎

We are having our turn aren't we? We get on, then we get off. We need to get out of our everyday cycles, otherwise we get stuck in patterns. You have to mix it up a bit. I'm grateful for the variety I have in my life.

∎

I don't think there's any particular purpose. It's a bit bleak isn't it? I think our ability to reflect and imagine more than there is; our consciousness; choice, free will - all that stuff, is an illusion. We are incredibly complicated organic machines. We're not really in control. Everything is predetermined or chaotic and at no point does free will come into the equation and it doesn't matter. What matters is that I feel like I'm choosing. Personal experience is more important than truth. Truth is massively overrated.

The 40s

A chance to find salvation. I want to add value. I want people to be better.

∎

We are meant to be here. Make each minute count. Enjoy small activities. Enjoy people. Be grateful for whatever you have around you. Try to contribute and help others if you can. Learn on a daily basis. There is something more than us out there. Is it God? Is it some sort of a spirit? Nature? There are some things we cannot explain.

∎

Life is a series of different episodes.

∎

We tell each other stories because life is otherwise pointless. I'm reading Chekhov at the moment and he nails the human condition. What he wrote 110 years ago speaks directly to me today.

∎

On my deathbed, basking in my death rattle, I'd like to say, 'That was good.' For me it's important that I did everything I could to make the world a better place when I leave it than when I found it. That's the point of life.

■

There's so much disillusion and a culture of hate, but then here I am, at my friend's house, chatting and eating blueberries.

■

It's a bit too deep for me. I don't really do deep thinking. Maybe it's because of my short concentration span. I zone out.

■

If I look up at the stars they twinkle. I can see the Plough and that will do. Will I die with regret? Yes, but I've reconciled myself. I haven't travelled. I've got mates who really applied themselves professionally. I didn't. I think you should be happy with what you've got.

People who try to force change generally tread on other people. The capitalist society we live in means that someone, somewhere suffers. Choose your heroes carefully. I think people who have a lot have a responsibility not to add burden or make others feel worthless. But look at the people who revolt against the machine, the new age hippies and protest movements who want change - they can be as pious as anyone. It's a tightrope with intolerance on either side.

■

I marvel at the fact that if you're born into a life just how super-lucky you are – it's almost comical that we have the very top fraction of a percentage of nicest possible lives. I try every day to remember that, even though I live with my mother-in-law!

■

It's complicated. Shall we leave it there?

The 50s

There should be no fear in change. There's always an excuse not to do something. I think about what's in store and I try to make the most of the good times I've got.

Life is about flow, it's about movement. Healing and people. Lessons too: When I was 17 and first started driving, I got to the traffic lights and a bloke in a BMW came flying past me and over took me. At which point I lent out the window and started giving him loads of abuse. He stopped the car in front of me. He was a big bloke, older. He calmly walked over to my window and said, 'If it weren't for the fact that you were a kid, I'd have kicked the fucking life out of you.' He was someone with a bit of clout. It was from that experience that I learnt never to abuse anyone again. There aren't people teaching kids those lessons these days. You need to take responsibility for your actions.

■

It's a question we don't ask ourselves. Why am I living the way I am? Why am I doing the job I'm doing? Once you understand or start to quiz yourself, you probably go through a process of evaluation. Life is billions of universes. Yours, mine. You're on your own little planet, speaking with your circle of people and I am doing the same in mine. People fall into a life that pays the bills, they're in a rut. People judge but never really know what's going on underneath. I was talking to somebody the other week. She'd fallen out with a partner. She said, 'I'm moving out.' That was on the Wednesday. On the Friday I spoke to her. 'Oh, we're getting engaged! We've sorted everything out.' I was pleased for her. Then the next day she took her own life. On the surface she was the happiest person going but a series of events that I knew nothing about brought her to that decision.

■

I'm so pleased I'm gay. You couldn't pay me to be straight. I think I've had a much more interesting life as a result. Being gay forces you to question things. There are ready-made communities you can tap into. Life is complex and fascinating but I'm in such a privileged position to be able to look at it from a philosophical point of view. It's not a hard struggle for me to find the money to put food on my table. I've got the luxury of living in an 80 square meter apartment with a balcony and to be able to reflect in this way. That level of privilege is huge. I don't think it means I should beat myself with a stick for having it but it should be acknowledged at the very least. I find life amazing, curious, satisfying, destructive and cruel at the same time.

∎

There's no God or afterlife. That's it - it's very straightforward. If you'd asked me 20 years ago I'd have given you a different answer. I might have said something along the lines of, 'I don't believe in God but I believe in destiny. We all have a path and a purpose. Our spirit or souls carry on living, somewhere, after you die.' I'd have been unsure. I was keeping my options open. There's naivety in those thoughts. As I've gotten older common sense and logic kicked in. I've become more cynical. I think it's about coming to terms with your own mortality. The idea of karma is bollocks - I don't believe that now.

∎

It's a fleeting moment - I don't believe in the afterlife, unfortunately. My wife does and she's happy with that. We are just a speck. You meet brilliant people and hope you give back. It's frustrating. There's so much to do yet for some reason we do the same thing, day in day out for 60 odd years and although that's great, I've never seen China, Russia or Africa. I want to like see the Orangutans, except I go to work, come home, sit at home and watch TV. I am one of the idiots that follow the same course.

∎

Life is brilliant but when it's bad, it's bad. You get heartbroken, you lose people, then you forget and meet new people. For me it's about the people around me. That's the kind of thing I focus on. I don't think many of us live to our potential. 'Life is what happens when you're busy making plans' - I think that's what John Lennon said.

∎

Life is the flick of a finger, insignificant in the time-frame of the universe. You have 70-100 years, if you're lucky, to learn as much as you can, teach a few people some stuff and then, if you're lucky you get looked after in a nice coastal care home before you curl your toes and become a pile of dust.

∎

We are an atom in a body but if we weren't here would it really matter?

.

The odd time I've done drugs I managed to suss out the planet. One night, high on whatever it was I'd taken, I wrote it all down. I woke up remembering I'd made complete sense of the world. But when I picked up the piece of paper, I'd written five sheets of scribble in green crayon. I couldn't decipher what I'd written. The answer to life is – don't do drugs!

.

Not to be too earnest. Find balance. You can't be all things to all people.

.

It's all a big cosmic joke. It's all about sex and reproduction. People doing exactly what they want to do and being quite selfish. I was on the top deck of the bus the other day looking out, thinking this is fucking pointless. I get some kind of motivation from that.

.

We could be so much better at it.

.

I am not particularly optimistic for man going forward. As a generation I think we have had the best of it. We missed the war and rationing. We have ongoing prosperity, health care, property that we can afford. We have been blessed but the people coming after us won't have it so good - it will be a lot harder. Climate change and pollution is beyond the tipping point. I'm not quite sure this capitalist model we're all in love with is sustainable. There's such inequality between the rich and the poor. We are complicit in it.

.

I love life even though I have been through some shitty times. There are ups and downs but it's important to be grateful and look at the positives in life. I've always had a mild form of depression. I have had suicidal thoughts. I sometimes I wonder what it would be like to be on top of a building and to jump. It's almost a joyous feeling. But I would never press that suicide button because it would be awful for the people I'd left behind. The problem with depression is, it's unfathomable. It becomes like walking though treacle. It's not logical, it's like bad weather. There are things you can do to make it better and worse; drinking and bad sleep can make you spiral. Keep the physical body working, exercise, good diet. I think dwelling on the negative, or being grateful for the positive, is a choice.

■

I tend not to go deep. When you look at old photos you can become a bit morbid. Don't go there. We are only here for a short period and when we die, we go to sleep. You come, you live, you die, that's part of my ethos about animals. I don't think they're bred to be killed and eaten. Who the fuck do we think we are to do that? I eat fish, I sometimes wish I didn't. I can't empathise with a fish as much as I can with a pig, a cow or sheep. I'm not too keen on the human race. 95 per cent are nice but it's the 5 per cent that fuck it up for the rest of us.

■

Years ago I'd wake up every Saturday morning and think about dying. I don't know why to this day. But it got me thinking, 'What is life all about?' I kept asking myself that question to the point where I got bored, so I haven't thought about it since.

■

Life is about family and friendship. It's about supporting one another and helping each other to get through life's challenges.

■

I love life. I'm fascinated by it. I'm glad to be alive. I'm amazed that I've got to this age. Life is a profound and a beautiful mystery. I could be just sat on the sofa having a cup of tea, or sitting on the top of Pendle Hill. Life is fucking amazing.

■

An old headmaster of mine once said about life, 'When you have a meal, you have meat, vegetables, maybe carrots. You have a variety, a good mix of everything. You don't have your life time supply of carrots all at once. It's about sampling different things and balance.' I've always thought in metaphors, that visual interpretation has stuck with me.

■

I've told you I'm not a deep thinker. I don't think about it massively. I just embrace life and get on with it. Life is a fair gift, isn't it? I'm not going to spend my life thinking about what else is out there, things I'll never see or experience. I'm very much about the short term. I take things as they come.

■

It blows my mind when I think about how small and insignificant we are really in the scheme of things. We're only here for 80 to a hundred years, of the millions of years that have gone before. You look back at the 200,000 years that we've been on this planet as humans. I look at the smaller scale impact I have on the world, that's what's important.

■

I don't know what the higher purpose is. I don't believe there is a God as in a religious God. How can we all create these different gods and religions? Whether there's a higher sense of something I don't know. The fact that the plants grow in the way that they do and nature does what it does. Our insignificance troubles me. Why are we here? All these millions of people on the world. What is going on?

■

Are we going to die out just like the dinosaurs did? There is something going on out there that's bigger than all of us.

■

When I retire I will buy a telescope and spend some time staring at the sky. Logically there's got to be something else out there. Some form of life.

The 60s

I'm lucky to be here. We're all lucky to be here. A billion to one chance. Take each day as it comes, try not to plan too much.

■

Depending on your life stage depends on how you see your life. If I feel down I start chanting. I used to have anxiety attacks. I was bad. At one point I couldn't leave the house. It was a struggle. I took up chanting, I had nothing to lose. As it happens, it clicked. I don't spend my time convincing people it works, either do it or don't. I see life as a little ball in a massive universe. (I'm going to get very emotional.) There's so many vibrant colours of light and we fuck it up - it annoys me. There's no proof of life outside of this planet so are we really going to fuck it up? We have no respect for life. We should be nurturing ourselves and the planet, helping it survive. We are killing the planet. We could literally be the only little speck in this massive universe, it's precious and we're just pissing on it.

■

It's a mixture of the most terrible things and the most wonderful things you can imagine. It's a beautiful place of natural and human diversity. It's never going to be in a state of harmony. But somehow there is a balance between good and bad. In my experience everything comes round in a circle. I don't see many examples of things starting and stopping in a straight line - things seem to come around again and again. Seasons, war, peace, civilisations.

■

We are here purely randomly. We don't choose our parents, it's an accident of birth. I don't think we are here to propagate or have a higher purpose. My role is to continue to breathe and not to upset anyone.

■

Kids are not born racist or not to care about people and the environment. Uncaring comes from negative experiences. Maybe there should be more nurturing in the school curriculum. We should take personal responsibility. It won't solve all problems, as with everything there are some people who are just real nobheads!

■

I like Epicurus, the Greek philosopher. He postulated the atom and quantum physics. He also took time to enjoy nature. I like being in the garden, observing nature. We are quite special beings, the only entities to try and make sense of the universe and try to understand it. I think that gives more value to life.

■

In the few brief decades of life you get your own private universe and that's very important. Before you were born, that universe didn't exist. You arrive and now know it exists. You take it on trust and evidence. It won't exist when you're dead. Try to understand that life is important and not to take it for granted. Part of not taking it for granted is trying to understand one's position in life. If you just lived your life in your 'village' without thinking about anything other than the people and family within your village, you can have a fantastic life but you're a little bit blinkered to everything else.

■

When I got to 60 I realised it's different from being 40 and you have a limited amount of time left. I'm more discerning with my time. Don't live life too quickly, and do things that count. I was listening to The Smiths, 'Heaven Knows I'm Miserable Now', when he says, 'In my life, why do I give valuable time, to people who don't care if I live or die.' It's true. You spend so much time on people who don't give a fuck about you - they just want you for what you can do for them.

■

Eight hours sleep is the difference between despair and hope. Diet and exercise. Walking is the unsung hero of exercise. Love for people and passion. These are the ingredients for a long life.

■

If your mental health is good enough, life is something to be celebrated, enjoyed, and contributed to. There are so many chances where life might not have happened for us. You can worry about what you're not doing, or should be doing but you only have your slice of the pie, it's about making the most of what you've got going for you.

The 70s

It's a gift that I've been given to be on this beautiful planet. I don't know for how long but I'm really thankful for it. If there is a God - thank you for giving it to me!

■

We have no choice coming to this world but I honestly think we should have a choice when we leave it. I'm hoping there is an afterlife. I was born the day that Auschwitz was liberated. I think of all those poor people and what happened to them. So many people have a short life.

■

We are a very small part of history. Even those who are great achievers leave a very small mark on history for history's sake.

■

What's particularly difficult about modern life is the instant communication - it destroys people's lives. Everyone is turning into zombies. 'I'll send you a WhatsApp!' I don't care. I don't know what WhatsApp is and I don't want to know. I don't want to spend my life watching other people do things. I don't watch television. I don't go to the cinema or anything like that. I'd rather do something boring by myself than sit in front of the screen, watching somebody do something interesting. I play the accordion, I read a lot. I sit with a drink and dream. I let my mind drift.

■

There's no point being on the earth just as an individual. We have to relate to the communities in which we find ourselves. The family is the crux of that. Moral support, being there, turning up when difficulties happen. There's enough going on in the local world, my family, and the bigger outside world, to hold my fascination.

■

If my parents came back now they would be flabbergasted at all the things we take for granted. Life seems more difficult now, it's more complicated.

■

We are making a right mess of it. It's our responsibility. The ordinary person can improve things. We need to get rid of plastics. Everything is about convenience. We have to do our bit rather than blame other people. People don't want to listen to people who have experience. I am not a blinkered person. I can see things from other people's point of view even though I might not agree.

■

I would say life is hell on earth. We are in hell. Presumably as everyone loves to think, that when we die we go somewhere where it is all ambrosia. I don't think it is. I don't believe in a hell and I don't believe in heaven. We are here to suffer. Some more than others. Of course you can't just have suffering for 80 years, you have to have bad times to enjoy wonderful times. Likewise you have to have bad food to know what good food is and so on. It can't possibly be fabulous all the way through. Getting sacked isn't fabulous. But having a job before wasn't too bad. Life is precarious. It's a miracle that we are here, and we don't enjoy ourselves, do we?

The 80s-plus

That's a very good question. Why has God put us here?

∎

I'm not a religious person. I am not into the supernatural scene but having said that, it's weird that the coronavirus seemed to strike at a time when the world was in such turmoil. I was brought up in the Second World War. You knew who your enemy was. Now we have an invisible enemy.

∎

You need to read outside the given. I look, I change my mind. I look at stuff I did three years ago and think, 'What incomprehensible crap!' Take the artist Edvard Munch for example. What he did was so different and new. His paintings are about emotions, themes done to death by the Victorian painters who were all very theatrical and dramatic. He managed to reject those ways. What he did was just amazing. He used watercolour and managed to express anger and jealously.

∎

The greatest thing about living longer is you get to find out about yourself - whereas if you die at 65 you don't! You have a chance of getting to know your parents - somehow you come across them again.

∎

Humans have developed. We've had to. From the original ape men, we've become Homo sapiens. Are we still progressing? In a million years' time will we be totally different? Everything seems to have a logical progression. From the Stone Age all the way through to the first flight in a hot air balloon flights, to the development of cotton mills in Lancashire. It simply is. Shit happens and it does and always will. It's almost as if it's in a blueprint and we are following a path. I'm kind of taken with that idea of an inevitability.

■

The first 20 years, your parents look after you. From 20-60 you're working. I never had the opportunity to go to university. I went to a trade school, I became an apprentice carpenter. I did National Service, then went back to the building trade. In 1969 I went to work for British Telecom. I worked for them for 20 years, then took redundancy. I worked for the police for nine years until I retired. From 60 onwards - to hell with it!

■

My life is obviously pretty narrow now. It consists only of my family. I've got a cleaning woman, a gardener and a carer that comes in twice a week. I'm not lonely.

A longer conversation…

Jan, 89

from Poland, retired teacher, married, four children, four grandchildren, two great-grandchildren

Life is a miracle - astonishing, amazing. The vastness that we are part of is incredible, but so too is what's inside us. All the thinking and emotions that build up, it's so incredibly rich. Even if it is a very short life, it's amazing. Just look around - the richness of what we create, the vast universe that we are part of, yet such a tiny, tiny part. It's a paradox, a miracle.

I was the son of people who owned a very big house. They were privileged, they led a bohemian lifestyle. Everyone I knew were painters, writers, artists, actors; no one got up in the morning and went to work. I always wondered what the hell people did all day in these offices.

My parents spent the first ten years of their marriage fulfilling their dreams. They were the golden couple. They exchanged letters all their lives. He had affairs. Everyone took drugs. People were gay, no one cared. It was no big deal to leave your child with a nanny for months on end, it wasn't like dumping them in an orphanage.

As a child, I experienced abandonment. I was left in the care of my cousin for six to eight months while my mother went to be with my father in Paris. When she eventually came back, I had forgotten her smell - she was a stranger, and not only that, she didn't fight for me. That's what my parents' lives were like.

My father is near me all the time. He was a magical father. An artist. Very creative, there was always something going on. He filled my room with strange creatures and dressed me in a Napoleonic uniform or as Scottish warrior or turbaned Arab. He was enormous fun. My father said that going to an art gallery was akin to early man going into a cave in order to ponder at the marvel of the wall paintings. Being strengthened by them, he was more able to confront the dangers of life - and in the same way, we are strengthened by a visit to an art gallery. Whenever I go to a gallery, I always meet my father there.

I had no permanent friends growing up because we were always moving. I was farmed out again and again. When I went to boarding school, I had friends but they were term-time friends only, not proper friends. My teenage years were awful. It's so important when you're 11 or 12 to have friends but I was always saying goodbye to people. One Christmas I stayed with a guy who charitably invited me for the holidays as my parents didn't have a bed for me.

I was nine when the War started. I was living in Krakow, I remember someone shouting, 'The war, the war, the war is starting!' I walked out into the garden in my pyjamas. The cook came towards me, wailing. She was holding a huge, gilt framed picture of the Virgin Mary (as if that was going to save us). All I could see was this woman's arms and this great big picture covering her. I ran away and hid in the raspberry bushes (I wouldn't recommend it) and stopped eating for a week. Tensions were high.

I remember another woman staying with us. She cried a lot. She had a cardboard box with her husband's ashes - they had been sent from Auschwitz. The authorities told her he'd died from typhus but everyone knew he had been killed.

A few years later I was sent to a boarding school in Hertfordshire. It was a disaster. I learned nothing about England. I didn't know how to be in English society. At the time there was something about not having a British background, it was difficult. I couldn't get a job because of other people's preconceptions. Life has changed now, thank God, but that's how it was living in the UK in the '50s and '60s. When I became a teacher I was told my surname would have to go because no one could pronounce it. So I changed my name. It took me 20 years to go back to my original surname.

I've been married five times. Amazingly I am friends with all my ex-wives! One of them now lives in a care home. When I go and see her she greets me with open arms - the last thing I ever expected. I was keen on marriage and I am still am. It's a signal that someone loves me. It builds in stability and support. The only problem is, it can all fall apart.

I got a job as a lecturer and suddenly there were women who smiled at me. I wanted to make up for all those lonely childhood years. I had affairs. When my fourth marriage fell apart, I started to think maybe there was something wrong with me, and it wasn't them. A friend recommended that I see a Jungian psychologist. I used to have dreams of journeys going wrong. My therapy was like helping me get on the right train.

I desperately wanted to be a good father as I was always being shoved aside as a child. Not a day goes by without me feeling guilty that I abandoned my children from my first marriage but amazingly they seem to have forgiven me.

I take faith in something extraordinary. A seer once told me, 'You are going to be lucky in life,' and I have been. I have experienced loss - loss of identity and of belonging. Yet I've survived cancer twice, and all my marriages! I take faith in something extraordinary. However modest your life is, you have influence. You have no idea that what you do or say will impact on someone, but it will. Somehow, in some way, other people's lives will change by your influence. How amazing to do this interview, to function, get excited about politics, at my age. It's magical, really.

I'm amazed, that I am sat here with a family, to have children who are all doing interesting things. I haven't always appreciated it - it's taken me a long, long time to work out who I am.

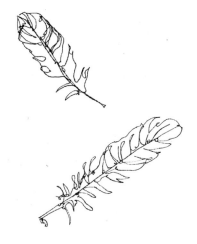

What do you think about death?

'Death is round the corner at any time'

It's coming and we know it. It's a short life. Some only make a few hours, days or weeks. Others don't make it to adulthood. Here one minute, gone the next. Death, the one and only certainty. It happens to everyone but no one's talking about it. It's not hip, it's not cool - it's feared, dreaded, unspoken. It's time to talk about death…

Conversations about death are rare, particularly in western culture. I've now spoken with 200 people about death, and I think it's a conversation that should be as easy to have as conversations about the weather. Talking about taboo subjects provokes a lot of feeling and, as we've learned, keeping all that feeling in, conscious or not, is not good for our mental health. So I challenge you to write your funeral, or at least have a chat with someone about it. Lift the veil from the taboo and take away some of that fear.

The 20s

My opinion on death is as bleak as my opinion on life. It's final and inevitable. The beauty in it of course is giving back to the earth. I think you live on for as long as your memory lives on. I'm very pragmatic and scientific. It's comforting. I don't worry about what comes after. I don't think about an afterlife. I don't worry about my eternal judgment. I don't worry about my legacy. I'm in it for the moment. Why worry about what comes after, just focus on the 80 or so years you have.

•

I had a near death experience. I was on a school trip in France. We were on canoes and I capsized. My helmet got caught on a rock. My helmet was above water and my face under the water. My life flashed before my eyes. I vividly remember picturing my home, family and friends. It was terrifying.

•

I got stabbed when I was 17. My lung was punctured. I remember being in the ambulance thinking I could die. I wasn't panicked. I wasn't crying out. I wasn't scared. I wasn't thinking about friends or family. I was thinking - it's okay if I die, everything is okay. It will be a bit like falling asleep. Ever since that moment I've worried less about my own death.

■

It's an odd, beautiful, natural process when someone dies. Nobody to the best of my knowledge knows what happens after that.

■

I am scared of dying. I'm scared of my parents and Grandad dying because I don't know how I would react. I'm a planner. I like to know what's going on. It's the fear of the unknown that scares me. You can't stop death.

■

If you go through life thinking, 'This is it, and there's nothing more to life than what we see with the naked eye,' - then it highlights that something is missing.

■

I enjoy life, I don't want to die. I want to live a long life. I am petrified of losing my parents - I don't want them to die either. I have nightmares about it. Realistically a lot of my life will be without them.

■

I've always been frightened of death. I remember asking my Dad, 'When you're dead, do you come back again?' He said, 'No, it's like going to sleep, for ever.' That really freaked me out. I used to get panicky about it. I would lie awake at night panicking and sometimes run into Mum and Dad's room. I couldn't handle the thought of not existing.

■

I feel like it's coming. When you're a kid, thinking about death is daunting and overwhelming. I remember when I was a toddler getting upset, thinking about my Mum and Dad dying. The older you get your priorities change. I think you become more accepting about the whole thing. My Gran speaks about dying. It comes up in conversations. She doesn't make a big deal out of it. If someone said I had six months to live, obviously I'd be upset but think I'd get into the zone.

■

Death is a give and take. My understanding is, when someone dies naturally a new baby is born. A life is to be taken in some way shape or form and it's usually an elderly person. When I was born my great-aunt's husband died. When my cousin was born, my Grandma passed away. Death is hard. You're never going to see that person again. Death is about acceptance. When you see how many people have gone before you, you realise you're not alone. When you die you enter into the realm of ancestorship. My parents have had to have their stories in order to understand life, as did my grandparents and so on. They understood what it meant to be young and what it meant to be old and lose people. We are here to help and guide the ones coming up after us.

The 30s

I'm not ready to die. There are so many things I'd like to live through and enjoy. It will deeply affect me when my parents and grandparents die, they are the stable people in my life.

■

My uncle passed away two years ago - he drowned. He went fishing and never came back. When I went to the funeral I was fearful and scared about seeing his body, but when I saw him my fear disappeared. The body is only a piece of meat, my uncle was already gone. There was a lot of sadness but a great deal of love, too.

■

It always used to scare the shit out of me. It's a FOMO (fear of missing out) - life will carry on and you're not there. One of my best friends died when he fell down the Tube escalator. He lost his footing and fell all the way to the bottom. I got to the hospital, he was kept alive on a respirator until his parents arrived. I've lost a lot from my life with him not being in it.

■

Death is a natural process. My Dad was buried the day after he died. It's a ritualistic process (in Muslim culture.) The body is washed, starting with the head. We purify the body. Then the body is wrapped in a shroud and put in a coffin and taken to the graveyard. We lift the body out of the coffin and carry it on our shoulders. It's a very physical act of saying goodbye. You dig the ground using a shovel and your hands. It's a physical connection. There's an idea that the person is going on to a better place.

■

I've never worried about it or thought about it until the other day. We were watching TV, something came on. This rush of blood went to my head and my thought all of a sudden was, 'What is going to happen when I die?' My heart went up to 180 beats, it was a horrid feeling. I forgot about it until you asked me that question.

■

It's sad but not scary. I don't want to live for ever, but for a while would be nice. Getting my pension would be nice. I definitely don't want to go before my time. I don't have a fear of death but I do fear cancer. I think the best way to think of death is summed up by Terry Pratchett. If you've ever read 'MORT', it has a really wonderful unique take and philosophy on death. Once I read that, I changed the way I viewed death.

■

I'm frightened of death. I think my Dad being ill (with bowel cancer) was the first time life slapped me in the face and showed me that nothing is for ever. Your parents aren't for ever, your partner isn't for ever. It's my biggest fear in life - losing people. I'm not scared about what happens after death. I'm really scared of going through pain. There's no real good way to go, is there? I'm quite a factual person - I would hate to drown, I wouldn't want a heart attack, I don't want to die in a car crash. I'm scared of it, of the pain. I'm frightened of losing my loved ones. I'm only 31 and I nearly lost my Dad a few years ago, and more recently my partner had a life-threatening illness. Those times have instilled a bit of fear in me.

■

Death is round the corner at any time. You can't avoid it. You can't stop that conveyor belt. One day you're gonna fall in. We are all simple organisms. We will break down and become carbon. You've just got to be grateful for having a beating heart.

The 40s

I don't believe in death. Death means the end. Your consciousness stops existing. I don't like that idea. I like to be conscious. I find it sad. I do live a good life, so there's reason to rejoice. Hopefully you come back again. The Christian view is you live a good life and then you get a reward. I like that idea. Try to be the best you can be. Hopefully something higher will keep your memory and preserve the consciousness.

∎

It's about those you leave behind. Have we set the kids up morally and emotionally? I want my children to be comfortable in their skin and to treat the person in front of them respectfully. I don't want to die because I love life. It's that desire to keep on breathing but when death happens, it happens. Thinking about it is meaningless. The only people who know you are dead are the people you leave behind. Death is a horrible thought. You go to a funeral and the one person you really want to be there isn't.

∎

I'm a rationalist so there's no afterlife - nothing. Our soul doesn't go off into the abyss. We are absorbed into the garden and ultimately we feed the worms. I'd have no qualms throwing myself under something if I became mentally or physically incapacitated. Euthanasia - I think it's shocking that we can't do it. I think it's criminal that I'm not in charge of how or when I die.

∎

My life is almost entirely untouched by trauma. I've still got all my family, death is uncharted territory. I have spent a lot of time thinking about my desert island discs and extracted from that is what will be played at my funeral. I would have Mahler's 5th symphony - if that doesn't break your heart nothing will. I love it. And then, Slades' 'Come on Feel the Noize', coming out because the miserable bit is over and the partying can begin.

■

It's ludicrous how over the moon I am about how my Dad died. He was fine one week and gone the next. Brilliant. The dream would be to go out like my Dad but a decade later than he did.

■

It's never frightened me. I'm fascinated by it. If there's a programme on the telly about undertakers, I'll watch it. I don't understand why we spend so much money on it. I am one of those people who says put me in a bin bag.

■

I can see where death may be a welcome option. I don't want to die from a selfish point of view, when am I ever going to have time to read all the books I want to read? For me the world is too interesting. There's too much to do and see. Ageing worries me. It starts to take away options.

■

Tongan funerals are different to English ones. In Tonga there's a protocol. Everyone is screaming, crying, laughing and joyful. We eat a lot of food, there's a night vigil and other ceremonies. English funerals are a bit stifled. Sometimes in our culture, and in the case of my Mum, when someone dies we put their body on top of their deceased spouse. We exhume the body, open the casket and take out the bones. All the grandsons take the bones to the sea. They are washed and put on a tapa mat. We then put the body on top of the bones, wrap them together and bury them again. I felt bad I didn't get to see my Mum in her last years and when she died. I struggle with that.

■

I've never thought about it. Nobody does when they're young. I'm closer to it now. I wonder how I will be as a 70 year old man? I don't want to be old. Selfishly, I want to know how many people would turn up to my funeral.

■

I'm looking forward to it. I might not be looking forward to how I die and I hope it's not painful and long but the thought of being dead doesn't concern me at all. I think it's part of the learning process. No one really knows what happens after we die. So, for me it's like we are given the chance to find out for ourselves, and that's exciting, isn't it? The way I see it is simple: if there is no life after death then it will feel exactly as before I was born and I know what that's like AND if there is an afterlife, even better!

■

I don't feel good about it. There is a part of my practice of everyday life that is about being ready to be dead so it's not a horrifying fucking shock. I don't want to be like my Mum, denying the potential of it until it's too late and then having an unbelievably distressing few months. I'd like to be ready to check out. I'd put things in the context of becoming terminally ill. I ask myself if something really matters? Whether something should be on my mind? Should I be irritated about something? I try and control my involvement and investment in things so I'm not too distracted from what's important. Mum and death are so linked. There was a four or five-year period with Mum when she started to shed her stupid concerns that she'd infected my life with for 25 years. Keeping up appearances, making sure the house was always tidy when anyone was coming round. Stupid shit about standards that needed to be upheld. She started to recognise the triviality of all that. She became a lot more chilled by the end. It was supremely liberating to me.

■

When I was 25 I don't think I could have conceived the patterns my brain has now and I would've thought that by the time I'm 65, I'll be different again. I don't really need to think about dying yet. I worry about it, then I don't worry about it. I think it's very irresponsible to bring my own neuroses about dying when there's nothing wrong with me onto other people.

The 50s

I've got my will sorted out and my music. For the reading, I'm having Matthew 5:43-48. Then for music, 'Guide me, O Thou Great Redeemer,' 'Men of Harlech,' 'Bring Me Sunshine,' and 'The Road to Home' by Amy Macdonald. That one will really get them blubbering at the end.

•

I'm not going to dwell on things or be anxious. If the bullet's got your name on it, it's got your name on it. Embrace death. Growing up in Wales, the wake is very much a celebration of life. You're there to celebrate, drink, and not look glum. When my great-aunt died, my son was 18. I hadn't forewarned him he was going to be a pallbearer. He said he really didn't want to do it but I told him he had no choice and that after me he was the most senior male and it was his duty. We lowered the coffin into the grave. He had one end of the rope and I had the other. He was looking at me as if to say, 'What sort of voodoo is this?' After he got over the initial shock he thought it was a good tradition.

•

I've been in situations where I've thought about taking my own life. I felt suicide would be the only way out. I don't actually fear death. It could be a quick thing or it could be a really drawn-out, horrible thing. But at the end it would be a finite thing.

•

It hit me when my Dad died. I carried his body down the stairs in a body bag with my brothers. I'm someone who has to see the body, for me that's part of the process. He was the first really close family member to die and it knocked me for six. I ended up on antidepressants. A few years later my Mum developed leukaemia. She went on a drugs trial, she wasn't sure if she should or not but in the end she did. Within a month or two she started to fade away. I asked her if she was scared. She wasn't. She just wanted to be with my Dad.

•

Marcus Aurelius said, 'Every grain of sand is replaced by another grain of sand. No more or less important than the other.' As if to say, 'Don't get too lost in your own importance'. I use that as a yardstick to help me try and live more fully.

I'm not ready to die but when I do I won't be going with regrets. I'll be going knowing that I've lived a very fortunate, wonderful life. My friend died in her mid-40s. She really wasn't ready to die. She was totally shocked when she found out she was dying. In her words - which I spoke for her at her funeral - she said, 'I feel like I'm in the Big Brother house and it's voting day. The public have just voted me out. I thought I was doing really well. I had no idea I was about to be thrown out. I'm shocked. I'm gutted. I'm gobsmacked that I got voted out so early. I thought I might make it near to the end.' She eventually got her head around it. She taught me how to die. Our soul lives on in the peoples lives we've touched.

What frightened me as a four year old doesn't frighten me now. What frightened me as a teen is different to what frightens me now at 52. If I get to 90 I'll maybe be frightened of things that aren't important for me now. We change along the way, but our wisdom grows with us and prepares us for what comes next.

∎

I'm not looking forward to it. I don't want to die too young or horribly. I'll accept 80. In this day and age with science and everything I think anything less than 80 would be disappointing.

∎

I want to be in good shape when I go. I want to live long but I want to be walking and talking. I want a conscious death. It doesn't frighten me. I'm even comfortable that I will probably die on my own. Death is final. I don't believe you walk up a golden staircase with angels greeting you. We should use the word die more and get used to saying the word - DIE! We should teach children how to bury their parents.

∎

I've heard you don't actually become an adult until you lose your parents. My Dad has leukaemia so I'm thinking about death a lot at the moment - his prognosis isn't great. I think he finds it hard to talk about dying. It's important to talk about things sooner rather than later. There's very little of 'later' left. He's afraid. He can see himself getting weaker. He's about to die, there might be people in the room but he's going to do it on his own.

■

I am not worried about my own death though I do dwell on other people's. I am quite morbid in that sense. Weirdly, I think I'd be quite happy about my own - finally we are getting to the end of this film.

■

It doesn't frighten me but what does is being trapped in my body with something like motor neurone disease (MND.) I imagine dying would be pretty frightening if you didn't have a support network for those you leave behind.

■

I'm not afraid of death. I welcome it in the sense that it's inevitable, it's going to happen. In my Buddhist practice there is a meditation on death. Buddhists go to the charnel grounds where all the bodies are being burned and the bones are stacked up. They meditate on death. I could die any minute. I wake up every day with that profound sense that I'm alive.

■

A couple of years ago I fell down the stairs because I chose not to put the lights on - trying not to wake my wife! I broke my forearm and kneecap. I remember being in an A&E and the doctor saying, 'You're really lucky. You could have damaged your spine. You could have been killed'. It hit me - what was I thinking? It made me appreciate life more. Death is a partner of life. It's the unruly guest that comes to the house. It's always hanging around, and then one day you end up going with it.

I was 12 when my Dad took his own life. I learnt a lot from that. I felt some empathy towards him because he must have had his reasons as it wasn't the first time he tried. He was a tortured soul. A very intelligent, charming and talented man. I came back from school one day and Mum said, 'Your Dad's passed away.' I don't think I got upset which sounds quite harsh. I didn't hate him for doing it. I just lost a little bit of respect. Time passed. Another year came and went.

■

We are like batteries, we run out eventually. When I was about six years old I used to get panic attacks. They were triggered when I thought about what happens when I die. The thought of not being here used to make me panic. When I started secondary school I decided not to think about it anymore and I haven't! The older you get, the less worry about it. It happens to everybody. You're not on your own. When you see grandparents die they seem quite comfortable with it. 'Oh, it's time for me to go.' My feeling is, you get to that stage in life and are comfortable with it. You fall asleep for a very long time. You run out of life.

■

I believe there is more to life and that our consciousness will continue. There is however a fear that my beliefs might not be true. I do fear death at times, to be honest. My Dad was clairvoyant. He didn't use it but we would talk about it. He had some strange experiences.

■

I only got really scared of death when I was about 19, it was like switching a light on. The thing about it that frightened me was not the actual nothingness or leaving the earth, but the religious aspect of it. I've been brought up Catholic, it suddenly occurred to me, 'Oh my God, what if these fucking idiots are right and we do suffer for all eternity?' I've always felt reasonably comfortable with a Catholic afterlife because many Catholics believe that when you die you get an opportunity to see the truth even if you haven't made the right choices in life. That's quite an appealing idea.

■

I feel angry at death. I feel angry that there's going to be a point where I'm no longer going to be with my wife or my kids. I find that so horrible, it upsets me. Death is a shared thing and that gives me comfort. In 110 years time everyone on the planet will entirely be replaced by new people.

■

My Mum died when I was ten from bronchitis, she never smoked in her life. My Dad remarried two years later, but died two years after that from cancer. I was 14. I lived with my step-mom till I was 18. At the time she was the wicked witch. When I look back she wasn't, she did what she could for me. I remember where I was when I was told my Dad wouldn't last the week. I remember what I was watching on the telly when my Mum died - Coronation Street. Mum had been ill for a while, I got used to the idea. I used to sit with her at night before we went to bed for two or three years before she died. Whereas my Dad, he got rushed into hospital on Sunday night and died by the Thursday. He was 56. Mum was 46.

■

I'm of a mindset that we're all here for a reason and that reason is to make a difference in the world. I'm undecided. Do we keep coming back until we get it right? Do I come back to go through it all again and refine it a bit more? Some people say we're all energy and that energy can't be destroyed therefore we will always exist. That got me thinking. Let's suppose we are watching BBC One but we changed to BBC Two, does it mean BBC One has died? No, it's just on a different frequency and if you knew that frequency, could you go back to it? I have an open mind about death. I'd love to think we will all catch up again in the next life.

■

It's not something that troubles me. I suppose, because I had a fairly early experience when my Dad died. I was 16. I realised death meant it was the end. It was final. I'm more worried about my wife dying. I don't want her to die.

■

People say to me we must have done something wrong in a past life, because this is hell. It's only hell if you make it hell.

.

I have a theory about death. When people talk about dying and going to the afterlife, I think they're talking about a different perception of time. At the point of dying, your brain is being starved of oxygen and that probably feels like an eternity. But to the people staring at you, you've gone. There's no afterlife and I'm convinced of that!

.

I lost my younger son 13 years ago. I'm very positive about it because I've proved to my satisfaction that there is life after death which is very uplifting. I know my late son is there and I know he will help me. I was sitting on an airplane from London City to Zurich in August 2008. We couldn't take off because of the crosswind. We were on the tarmac for two hours. In the course of that time, I got to know the person sitting next to me quite well. He turned out to be South African. After some hesitation, I told him that I had a bitter-sweet relationship with South Africa. Eventually he prised it out of me, and I explained that my younger son had been killed in South Africa when a campervan had overturned. This man asked me where it happened. I told him it was at a place called Thabazimbi, which is a little mining village, way off the radar, in the north-west, at which point he froze and said, 'When I was four, I was camping with my parents in Thabazimbi. I overturned a hot water urn and I got second degree burns, I ended up in Thabazimbi hospital.' It was an extraordinary coincidence. If you think about that, it's just not possible that you could sit next to somebody who would know exactly the remote spot where your son passed away. It's beyond coincidence. And not only that he knew of the place but he'd actually been treated in the same hospital. I am utterly convinced that was my son sending me a signal that day that he was okay. That was within two weeks of him passing away.

The 60s

I don't have many regrets but when I had the opportunity to visit my business partner before he died, I didn't take it. I didn't want to face it.

·

I got a text recently from a secondary school friend saying a guy we were at school with had died. His parents were Jehovah's Witnesses. I remember him never being allowed to play out. He had a car accident. When they went to operate they found a lump. He was such a nice, humble guy. It was such a shame. Death is one thing I haven't thought about. It's gonna happen and you're not going to be in control of it.

My Dad is in an urn in my bedroom.

·

After watching both my brothers, my Dad and my mother-in-law die, it's an odd thing. You just see the body stop. No response. How can it just stop? After my brother took his last breath, I watched his breathing slow down and down and down until it stopped. It's a weird feeling. I felt numb. To see the life go out of him. It's hard to see someone take their last breath.

·

My father died at 82 very suddenly. I was sitting with him just before lunch. He said, 'Can I take my jacket off?' Of course you can! He took it off, and just died. It was a wonderful way to go.

·

There's a lesson in Buddhism which is how you face your death defines who you are. The way to deal with it is to live your life so at the moment of death you are relaxed, calm and content because you know it's the natural cycle. You then manifest into a more enlightened state. It's the law of cause and effect.

·

People shouldn't be afraid of death. I think I'm all right about my own death. Last year my Dad and my brother both died. My Dad died at a ripe old age. It's connected me with life - it was natural, he'd had a full life. I feel more self-reliant now. Then my brother went shortly after. I found myself perfectly content with life and feeling peaceful. Not needing anyone. There was a feeling of calm and space. It was a solitary feeling. I don't know if it's grieving. I feel stronger for it. I can handle things better. I am becoming more conscious of time, my age and doing things I want to get on with. Death is the end. I think it's a peaceful place. An end of a chapter but definitely not the end.

•

I don't fear death because I don't feel there is anything after death. I fear pain. The pain of cancer - especially as my wife died from it. She was very afraid after having radiotherapy. She went up into the attic to sleep. She would sob night after night, working through it. Our brushes with death are going to get more and more. I don't think I'm anymore special than anyone else. I don't think I deserve anymore than anyone else. I fear dying, I don't fear death.

•

I am still here. There are many, many times in the past I thought I wouldn't be here and get to this age. I thought I might kill myself.

•

There are times when I'm looking forward to it. I am not completely resolved in my thoughts on life after death. When we become compost something grows out of it. We have become so utterly divorced from it as a society because it's unfamiliar and frightening. I came head on with it when my Mum died of cancer when I was 19.

•

It's inevitable. I am not frightened, I don't want it. I'm only just getting going. The next ten years are going to be life-changing for me if the Lord spares me, and if He doesn't then that's His choice.

•

I had a few incidents, particularly late on a night. We might be watching telly then suddenly the thought comes into my mind - you're going to die. Not right at that minute. I used to call it having the screaming ab dabs without the screaming. I'd get my shoes on and go out for a walk to calm down. I was in my early 60s. Touch wood, I haven't had one of those incidents for a while. Although a couple of times recently it's crept in. I tell myself 'shut it down, shut it down'. I've just read a book by Rachel Clarke, 'Dear Life' it's really helped. Reading about how people die. I'm not saying I won't be frightened, of course I'll be frightened!

■

It scares the shit out of me. I avoid talking about it. I don't want to live until I'm 90. I have an issue with breathing. I've seen my mother with tubes up her nose and down her throat and she couldn't cope with that. That gag reflex and the look of terror on her face. I have a phobia about that. I'm not afraid of death, I'm afraid of the process of getting there. I wonder how it's going to happen and when will it be?

■

We used to do this thing at school, it was quite fashionable at the time - we would make ourselves pass out. During one of these passing outs, I had a vivid dream involving David Bowie. It went on for ages and ages. When I came out I said to my mate, 'How long have I been out?' He said, 'Oh, about 20 seconds.' That kind of thing has happened to me a lot. I have these convoluted dreams that are happening in real time in their world, and I've got a ghastly feeling death might be a bit like that - a very long dream. I hope it's going to be painless and quick, but perhaps in that moment, it might last a pretty long time. It might be painful.

■

When you have palliative care at home they bring out their box of tricks. It basically consists of morphine. Once that's in place, they don't take it away. It's the home suicide kit.

The 70s

The one nice thing about death is that you never live to regret it.

■

I went to see my father when he died. (He was 58.) He never really recovered from the War. I remember looking in the coffin. It wasn't my father. It was just an effigy. A lifeless husk of a man.

■

The most exciting voyage I did was from Chile around Cape Horn, down to the South Atlantic, down to Antarctica and to South Georgia. Hurtling through the night. At 2am, I was at the top of the mainmast, hanging on by my fingernails. Sometimes I think it would be a wonderful way to part company with the world. It's an enormously freeing feeling. It's the nearest sailors ever get to heaven! I didn't really want to go back down to the deck where somebody was cooking dinner. It was almost trivial!

■

Death itself doesn't hold any fears for me. I know that once I'm dead, I won't know anything about it. I won't know I was alive, I won't know I'd existed.

■

I'm not looking forward to it. I'm not frightened of dying. I've still got things to do.

■

I think you should have a choice when to go. If I get Alzheimer's, I tell my grandkids to put a pillow over my face. I'd like to go like my Dad did. He'd been here for his tea, I took him home. The neighbours saw the light on the next morning. We went in and he was dead. He was 86. I don't want to end up in a nursing home.

■

Cremate me and scatter me on the grave where my wife and daughter are.

■

When you die everything shuts down. You're not going to lingering around. That's not the way it works. Once your heart stops your brain shuts off. When my mother was dying she saw everybody around her upset. She got a pen and paper and scribbled a little note, 'Don't cry for me, pray for me!'

■

I'm not frightened of death. I'd like to be pottering in my shed one day and just keel over.

■

I watched a film the other day about a dog. It was brilliant. The dog went through four or five different lives as different dogs. When its time came, the screen went hazy, then the dog came back as a completely different pup. That'd be good - to just fade away then come back as somebody completely different. I've certainly heard other people say they've had unusual experiences. I wouldn't say, 'That's rubbish, get a grip,' because things like that do happen. The supernatural must happen. It just hasn't happened to me - yet. It's not that I'm a sceptic, I just need evidence.

■

I'd like to put it off for a bit. I worked for years with people with AIDS so I've been with several people as they died. I was with my mother when she died. I used to be afraid of death. I had to come back to it about a thousand times before it comforted me. We've been dead for most of eternity. It was only the moment we were conceived that we were finally alive and it hasn't been that long, all things considered.

■

It's giving up and it's letting go of what we have. I find that very hard. I'm the kind of person who likes to stay up late. I'm a night owl. Even when I get tired, I'm fighting. Reading a book or watching a film. I'm never quite ready to let go. There's always a little more to do, to explore, to experience. I know I'll struggle with that.

■

This individuality business is highly overrated. The idea that you individually die like in some sort of terrible Shakespearian tragedy and your cousins are waiting for the good silver, is sort of silly. Part of the problem we have with death is the hallucination that you're an individual that lives in the universe. You're distinct - like a Lego brick - but none of it is true. You need a 'self' or an ego in order to get things done but it's not anything more than a convenience, like an operating system.

■

I've never given it any thought but I will think about it. I thought I wouldn't live beyond 52. I used to think that was old but of course when you arrive there, it's no age. I don't feel old. Every day is a bonus now. I said to my partner, 'You have my full permission to slit my throat if I start dribbling.'

.

I wish I knew when it was going to happen so I could make plans for the rest of my family. The fact that it's been unkind enough to hide itself date-wise from me, is very inconsiderate. My daughter has asked where I want to be buried. I really don't care. I don't have a romantic image. When it happens it happens. On my headstone write, 'He did the best he could!'

The 80s-plus

I think a lot of people welcome it. When my time comes please may it be painless. I understand suicide. I've had two friends who have asked me to drive them to Dignitas in Switzerland - but both died before I needed to help them.

.

With the greatest optimism in the world I haven't got that long. I worry more about my wife than me. If anything happened to me, what would happen to her? I am a bit of a fatalist. I think we are given a certain amount of time and then you're gone.

.

I would like to die on the same day as my wife. I don't want to leave her alone. She needs looking after. I'm not frightened of death. I've had a good life. It will come when it comes. My Dad said used to say, 'You can live too long.'

.

I'm not worried about it. I hope I go to bed one night and don't wake up.

.

I'd like to pop out - just like that. Nice and clean and quick. I don't want to struggle but I don't think I've got much control over it.

A longer conversation…

Christopher, 83

Retired film/documentary maker and writer, from Luton and Australia

I wrote this poem:

> *When times of dying come,*
> *I'd like to die outside and in the sun,*
> *where I can feel its warmth on my skin,*
> *let its heat sink in,*
> *and rekindle me as it has done through all my life,*
> *through all my years,*
> *I'd like to focus on the beauty of a butterfly,*
> *the fragrance of a rose,*
> *and think of everything and all of those I've loved,*
> *and pour myself a glass of wine.*
> *I'd savour it for one last time.*
> *Look up to see the sky, salute the sun and know,*
> *my journey onwards is begun.*

My thoughts are that if there is nothing after death, you just stop. Then there's nothing to fear. There's no feeling beyond that - no pain, no distress. It's simply a light going out. Don't worry about it. If on the other hand there is something, if we do somehow survive - and I prefer to think so, but that's romantic - then I hope it's towards enlightenment, whatever that is, so there's nothing to fear there either.

I'm hoping that there will be a continuation after death. And that it will be a rewarding thing. Not in the hope of rewards, but of being rewarded by learning more, discovering. A moving beyond the stage we're at now, into enlightenment.

I believe faith is essential to the human condition. I've often said to atheist friends of mine don't dismiss faith, it is the glue that held societies together all through the terrible medieval ages. Even though people butchered each other and burned each other at the stake. For the peasants, the story of Christ and the promise of eternity was what gave them as much hope as a king or prince. I say to some very learned friends, if you dismiss faith as mumbo jumbo or superstition, because it is vital to our society. My definition of faith is hope.

What keeps us going as a species is love. The desire to give and to take love. On the whole, I think people are good at heart. I am an optimist. My memories are all from the kindness of people. Those are the memories I live off. I can't call myself Christian, although I'm spiritual, because I'm not sure I believe in concepts such as the Immaculate Conception and the Son of God. But I do think the Christian thing of love is the most valuable word in the lexicon and in our soul.

I'm trying to write a poem at the moment - I try to write something every day. It's called 'Vital Signs'. So the doctor says, 'Shall we declare him dead?' And the nurse says something like, 'Well, no, not yet. His soul is still in there.'

I was clearing out the loft with my sons a few weeks ago, and found my old notepad from my 20s, with some early stories. They jolted my memory. I remember talking to myself, aloud. 'What is it we are trying to achieve here?' I always used the royal 'We'. It was interesting to talk to the young Christopher. I realized that the old bugger hasn't changed much.

I started writing as a kid, and had one of my short stories published in the newspaper. I have a poetry book published, 'Ambiguities'. Which pleases me a great deal. I'm looking forward to that because I'm not going to write another book, I guess.

I used to make documentary films and went to countries I would never have gone to – I travelled widely. I'm so grateful now for that and for the wonderful people that I met. I've had such generosity from people who couldn't afford things, who had nothing to be generous with.

I was in a profession that was very iffy. We were only as good as the next contract. It was also physically dangerous. I had the bank talking to me about reclaiming my business or house. Things were very bad for a while. I had a lot of anxiety and depression. But you come through this stuff, and more resilient. I stayed working until I was 75. It's been a good run. Life's been kind to me.

I was born in London but brought up in Australia. My connection to Australia grows stronger as I get older. I sometimes wonder what's wrong with me. I've been in Britain longer than I've ever been in Australia. My wife is English as are my children and grandchildren but I increasingly feel a stranger here, there is a hankering for home.

When I go back, I point a finger on the map and set off. I feel overwhelmed as you should do in such a large landscape. I head out West. There are signs, 'Welcome to the Outback, next petrol is 150 miles away.' These warnings give me a wonderful feeling. I don't know where I'm going to sleep that night, but I'll find a few beers and sit out with a book or do some writing. Local people will come over and ask what you're up to and before you know it, you're deep in conversation. I love that. They're my people. I feel totally at home there, but that's an old man with nostalgia for you.

I look in the mirror and I say, 'You really are a silly bugger'. And that makes me laugh. I'll go on doing that. I'm not going to get dragged down into some vortex of despair and doom. I'm aware of the ridiculousness of what's around us, which includes me. It's a big joke. I'm pretty cavalier about life, quite irreverent. God, you really are having a laugh at our expense and I'm going to talk to you about it some time.

(Chris died in 2021. He didn't get back to Australia.)

What brings you down?

'When I don't feel I'm in control I get desperate very quickly'

Another theme that has come up is not wanting to waste time on people who won't listen, those who moan and drain you. But I feel there are some people who need a good moan, to get things off their chest. So those of you who don't like moaning - you might want to skip this page…

Being knackered ⚥ Being embarrassed ⚥ Getting things wrong ⚥ Anxiety ⚥ **THINGS I CAN'T CONTROL** ⚥ My team losing ⚥ Being alone ⚥ When I'm not recognised for my contribution ⚥ Disappointment ⚥ Drugs ⚥ Hatred ⚥ Lack of compassion ⚥ Not sticking to a routine ⚥ Conflict ⚥ Injustice ⚥ Feeling adrift ⚥ When people do not believe what I say ⚥ Resentment ⚥ Having my schedule re-arranged by others ⚥ Hurting people ⚥ Lack of time ⚥ Not living up to my own expectations ⚥ **FAILING** ⚥ Social media ⚥ Information overload ⚥ Stress ⚥ Money ⚥ Criticism ⚥ If I don't eat enough or sleep enough ⚥ People who don't share my ethics and philosophy ⚥ Alexa ⚥ Extremist views ⚥ White supremacy politics ⚥ Being busy ⚥ The feeling of not achieving anything ⚥ Hangovers ⚥ Not having purpose and structure ⚥ White noise of negativity and anger. ⚥ Myself. ⚥ Self-doubt ⚥ Fear of rejection ⚥ Not believing in myself ⚥ Mistrust ⚥ People not cleaning up their dog shit ⚥ Inflexibility ⚥ **DEPRESSION** ⚥ Selfish people ⚥ People not having a moral compass ⚥ Wokeness ⚥ Failure to be mindful ⚥ Growing old ⚥

People who blow their own trumpet ♂ Worrying ♂ Bad drivers ♂ Late trains ♂ Lack of effort by my children ♂ Feeling like I haven't managed to communicate who I am ♂ People who cheat ♂ People who drop litter ♂ People not getting what they deserve ♂ The breakdown of manners ♂ **THINKING TOO MUCH** ♂ My father ♂ I get angry and frustrated because the world isn't perfect ♂ People flicking cigarette butts ♂ Big cars ♂ Football ♂ My mother ♂ My family has been a constant source of negativity ♂ The news ♂ Thoughtlessness ♂ My son ♂ The weather ♂ Confrontation ♂ Complete arses ♂ Aggression ♂ Hostility & Anger ♂ Alcohol ♂ Unfairness ♂ Injustice ♂ Stupid people ♂ **NEGATIVE PEOPLE** ♂ Brexit ♂ My wife ♂ My character ♂ Self-consciousness ♂ Darkness is the big one ♂ Bullies ♂ People consumed by their egos ♂ Cruelty ♂ Racism ♂ My daughter ♂ People who take advantage ♂ Lying politicians ♂ My wife's dementia ♂ Technology ♂ **MOANING** ♂ Television ♂ Scammers ♂ The danger of walking on a pavements - watch out for all the scooters and bicycles ♂ .

A longer conversation...

Keith 44

composer, from Yorkshire

I don't know what we're doing here and that doesn't bother me. It's a brilliant cosmic accident. Even if it was explained to me, it wouldn't make much difference. 'Well, God made you.' Good. Fine. That doesn't help me get to work. There's not a gaping hole of mis-understanding in my life. Life is about just getting on with it, and all we can do is experience everything and try and make sense of it. And it ends up being a story, and I'm passionate about those stories. Whether it's music, songs, plays, theatre or television, it's magic that we as human beings deal in stories, that's how we've chosen to cope.

My day job is marketing software for a computer company. I give my career the emotional commitment it deserves, which is nine-to-five Monday to Friday. I don't care. But I do care about my flat, my life, and my money - and composing. Composing is my passion. I help run musician workshops, we compose scores among many other creative projects. I'm on various committees at a local theatre, supporting small orchestras. I just love it. That's what excites me - you never know what will happen. It is organic and it's magic.

I love being creative. But I like that my living doesn't depend on it. I like the security of knowing where the money is coming from. I have friends who are actors, musicians, or writers full-time, and they're broke. I'm very cynical about people 'making it and being famous' - even the successful ones. An actor friend is in Coronation Street. And I know how much he's getting paid, and he's not going to retire on it. A work colleague, who is an engineer, writes science fiction novels. He sells his books on Amazon for beer money. Success is a myth.

Sell out! Take the money! Don't be a struggling artist! I love that. It took me a long time to get that balance right. I'm a true artist doing a mainstream job to support my art. It's taken a long time and I'm truly cool with it. I've found my world - it's taken 44 years. If you went back to my 15-year old self and said, 'What life will you be living when you're 44?' - I'm pretty much doing it. I don't have any unfulfilled, long-term dreams. I'm like, 'What's the next thing?'

I don't do self-reflection much. I'm creative, busy. Neurotic, angst-ridden and a functioning alcoholic. I really scared myself with recent drunken shenanigans. Someone sat me down and told me I'd upset someone. I had no memory of it. I was angry with myself. I was also sad because it made me think, 'Who else have I upset? How much time have I wasted being drunk?' Sometimes I think everyone else has grown up and I haven't. It's an issue and a problem - definitely. My drinking has been destructive. But it's also been fun and charming. I'm addicted not just to the alcohol but to the whole experience of going to a pub and partying and being the performer. And a lot of people are like, 'Yay, he's here - have a drink!'

But the connection between getting drunk and your mental health is huge, and I misjudged that completely. Hangovers send me into deep, deep depression. When you're 23 you feel a bit rough - whatever. In my 40s, I have two days of angst-ridden screaming into the void.

I'm terrified that something might be wrong with my health. I won't go for tests because I know the answers wouldn't be good - it's a very northern bloke thing. I'd have to be dying before I go and get help. I don't feel ill, but I feel my age. I creak and I ache and if I run for a bus, I'm exhausted. Drinking this much can't help. It's time it stopped.

I grew up in a really strong marriage. My parents have just had their 50th wedding anniversary. They sit in silence together, or bicker – it's hilarious. Famously, my brother and sister both went to private school and I at 11 just went to the school down the road. I'm not bitter about this, but I can see a difference - my brother joined the army, and my sister is a physiotherapist. We all argue about who's the most working class, which is ridiculous. My brother's running the army, my sister runs the NHS and I write music - none of us are!

School meant nothing. I vaguely turned up. I was quite a bolshie 11-year-old who just didn't engage with school. I was into theatre, dancing. That was my childhood - it was playing Guys and Dolls. I was Billy Elliot. I had the dancing lessons. I retain that. I remember watching Clare Rayner putting a condom on a banana, that's what I thought sex was. I went to a Catholic school, I didn't have a clue.

The creative process is the soul of life. I love music and art in general. Who knows where it ends up? What's going to happen next? I have no idea - that's brilliant! I don't think anyone should write until they're 35. The whole problem with the industry is that everything is about youth, about finding the next young person. It's criminal. Because at 25 what you're doing is putting your opinions on stage, not your experience. I hate being preached at, ever. Going to the theatre or cinema to see the latest thing about Brexit. No, thanks, I get my politics elsewhere.

If you ask me would I like to die tomorrow or later, I'd be like, 'Later, thank you.' Please keep me on the planet as long as possible, but not in agony and suffering – that 'please' by the way is to the doctors and nurses, not to a God. I do say, 'please God' but it doesn't mean anything. God doesn't exist. You're allowed a prayer every now and again just in case. Atheism is not a belief in the absence of God, because that's a double negative. I get obsessed with this. I'm a humanist - one of my retirement jobs would be a humanist celebrant. No prayers, just be master of ceremonies and say a few nice words about the person. I think it would be a lovely job.

What are your views on faith?

'Faith is a quiet knowing'

The word faith often brings up religious conversations which sort of surprises me because I don't automatically put faith and religion together. I think you can have faith in yourself, a football team, your family, or just about anything but a lot of people naturally assume I mean religion when I ask this question. For me, faith is a belief in something and that can be anything.

I found it interesting that some men who had 'no faith' at all were vehement about that certainty. There was no room for discussion. Science and hard facts were needed, and straightforward common sense. Faith couldn't be proven so it couldn't be believed. It was though anyone who had a faith in something religious or spiritual was a little bit unravelled. Some men had an unbending certainty. You might say some men were fundamentally fanatical in their belief that there is nothing. Their views were so strong that they stirred a bit of judgment in me - I found myself thinking, 'Wow, to be so sure, so certain, that must be quite a weight to carry - certainty! It must be like being 'right' the whole time.'

It was the first time I really felt a difference in the conversations between the women and the men. An unbudging, dogmatic certainty. It dawned on me that if the balance in society is tipped in favour of certainty, then there's little room for uncertainty, exploration and creativity. I'm beginning to think this might be how we've arrived at the world-wide mental health crisis we have! Don't we need to be unsure? Striving for certainty inevitably is going to fail - isn't it? Such rigid thinking offers little flexibility and cuts off possibility, and I question how useful it really can be. It brings back the words of Blake, 'The man who never alters his opinion is like standing water, and breeds reptiles of the mind.'

Just a thought, and a little deviation… during the writing of this book I snuck off for a little break back to the Ribble Valley to meet up with an old friend. (It's where I grew up and holds a big piece of my heart.) For the brief visit, breath was not drawn. We belly laughed, and belted out random folk songs. It was just the tonic. Energising yet thought-provoking. Being up on Pendle Hill is like being in a time warp. We visited the tiny hamlet of Newchurch. Wandering around the graveyard, our conversation turned to community, society and the role that the church played in the lives of our forbearers and what has replaced that in today's society. Shopping, football, social media? To a degree perhaps, but what about the deeper needs of people, those rituals that the church provided? The congregation created community, which is what being human is all about - I think statistics say loneliness is as bad for you as smoking 15 cigarettes a day! Confession, the place to get things off your chest. The hard seating to help you focus, so you can't fall asleep - you have to pay attention. It covers a whole gamut of human needs. Community, society, engagement. Even the timbre and rhythm of the imam, vicar or rabbi's voice is meant to soothe almost to a hypnotic 'mindful' state. The place - the church, mosque, synagogue, or temple - is there for the purpose of making time and space for focused thought, reflection, guidance and perhaps best of all, a bit of singing to release and let it all go. Have we lost our deeper connection just because we don't follow those rituals so much anymore?

The 20s

I'm an atheist. I don't believe in the supernatural, the spiritual, the divine. I've got a spiritualist mother and a Buddhist step-father. I know faith helps the people close to me. It makes them better people. I'm glad I was brought up in a spiritual household even though I don't buy into it.

·

I'd say faith is a quiet knowing. It is something you can't tangibly see or hold. You develop trust. I have faith that I'll wake up tomorrow.

·

Faith is so important. I see that with my friends who are either religious or have religious connections but don't necessarily believe in God. They use their place of worship to connect with people. That in itself is quite beautiful. I think we're all inherently tribal.

·

It's hard to have faith if you don't have a sense of belief. It's related to hope and purpose. I find it hard to have faith sometimes.

.

I quite like to chat with people who have faith. I feel sorry for people who have dedicated their whole life to something that's not there but if it gives them reassurance that's fine. It's good to question things. I don't like people shoving their faith down your throat or telling you you're doing it wrong. It's hypocritical and judgemental.

.

I have faith in a higher power. I know things always work out in the end, even when everything is shit. Nothing is forever and no one owes you anything.

.

I certainly believe in God. I've been raised a Catholic. I feel there's got to be something more. It's nice to live a life where you've got some expectation of faith. Whether there is or not is up for debate but I would hate to go through life thinking - this is it. I hope and believe, there will be something else.

.

It's necessary. I think you do need to believe in something. It allows you to breathe.

The 30s

I'm not religious but I respect people who are. It's a way for people to unburden themselves. Having faith is having faith in one another.

.

It's too easy not to explore your own feelings and hide behind a faith. Everyone needs to believe in something. The most important faith is in humanity.

.

For me, if it wasn't for my faith I probably wouldn't be here. It's an important part of my life. I pray five times a day. I'm struggling with my spiritual side at the moment.

.

I'm respectful of anyone's faith but for me faith is not a priority in my life. I'm definitely optimistic, whether you call that faith or not?

∎

I connect with nature and that's enough for me. If I've said something bad, I look up to the sky and say, 'I'm sorry about that.' I don't know why I do it but I feel better for having said it. I suppose I believe in something. I'd like to think there's some weird guardian angel keeping watch.

∎

When faith is lost, hope is lost.

∎

I define faith by believing in something irrespective of any evidence. I could have a conversation with someone who is religious and ask them to prove to me that the person you believe in is real because scientifically, I can show you evidence that contradicts your belief. When you have this sort of discussion it always ends up with those 'faithful' people saying, 'It's just faith. I believe in it and you can't question it.' I don't have faith in things without evidence. There's a difference between hope and faith. I have hope, not faith.

∎

Faith would be the ability to believe in something which you can't touch, see or prove. I believe in the possibility that there might be a God. I can accept the presence of things which I can't immediately see. Science only tests what it can observe and therefore is limited because you can't observe everything. Science by its own admission fails to answer a lot of questions. Anything to do with the human condition that can't be observed, whether or not it's real or an illusion, exists and we feel it.

The 40s

I think faith is important. I grew up a Christian. I understand faith. My issue is with religion. I think faith in religion doesn't work. You should have faith in the Creator. Try to develop a relationship with the force of the universe. I'm not sure I believe in the religious idea of Christianity. I'm not sure Jesus did either. The word Christianity was never mentioned in the bible. Jesus called it a way of life, it's the way you treat people. I believe in faith in a higher God, which is probably a religious paradox in itself.

■

Don't ask me to think supernaturally or outside the world. It's all about the here and now.

■

Faith has given society a good code of ethics which governs our behaviour. You can have the ethics without religion.

■

I like that Christianity gives society structured behaviour - it's valid but I don't give a monkey's about God or Jesus. It would be great if it were true but what other aspect of people's beliefs from 2000 years ago do we take as unchallenged? None!

■

I think you have to have faith in something or you end up floundering. At the moment, I'm floundering!

■

We had a few prayer sessions after my accident. It's been a while since I've prayed. It was very powerful. You can verbalise with your prayers. When you don't verbalise, things fester and become poisonous. I feel faith should have more status in my life but it doesn't.

■

I see faith as weakness. Embrace the raw truth of the pointlessness of it. People need to have faith that there's something else because the world is such as cesspit of misery. I get quite angry that if there was a God, He'd let this all happen. I've been to Liberia where they cut the hands off the women after they've raped them so they can never hold their child. That to me is proof there's an absence of God.

∎

People with faith use it for the wrong reasons. I've worked in church schools for years. People use the church and their faith and not always for the greater good. Religious people can be quick to condemn others. Some people who go to church think they're better than others. I don't think so. Some of the meanest people I've ever met are people who go to church. They are the first people to gossip and talk about other people behind their backs.

∎

Faith is incredibly important, it's about hope. I felt lost in my life when I lost my faith.

∎

I broke a rule yesterday. I took my daughter to a farm shop. There was an offer on - get a doughnut and a lemonade. I went over to the doughnuts and put two in the bag. Essentially, I stole a doughnut! If I were Catholic I'd be marked down. I am free of any such nonsense and superstition but I do have a different kind of faith about it. In a rational sense I just got an extra doughnut and there's really no problem, but the psychological overhead as I get better is higher every time I do anything like that. That to me is faith. I have to believe by following these religious style rules that life is ultimately better on a spiritual level. I think the consequences of stealing from WholeFoods, owned by Amazon, is literally zero. I think everybody should be stealing foods from WholeFoods. It's like a tiny corner of a major corporation that doesn't have any downside to anything that ever happens to it. But I've got it in my head that I nicked a doughnut yesterday and it's taking up space and attention that could be put to better use.

∎

People's thoughtfulness restores my faith. As I get older I think about religion more. A lot of religion is about morals. I believe in Darwinism, we all come from one mother in Africa. We are all the same with different pigmentation and a bit of inbreeding!

The 50s

I have a faith that we are not far from the campfires of kind people. We are a very lucky accident. Even luckier that we were born into a first world country, luckier still that I'm reasonably affluent.

∎

I remember when Mum wasn't well. There were three or four months of no phone calls about work. Then literally the day after she passed I got a call about work. That was freaky. I like the idea that someone's looking down, keeping me free for that time so I could be with her.

∎

Religion is clearly a comfort blanket for a lot of people. I like that it gives them support and succour.

∎

You've got to have self-belief. It comes down to confidence and being happy in your own skin. Some people follow religion because they don't have to think for themselves. We all know religion was put there to control the masses. Putting your belief system in a third party, it's too easy. It's about taking personal responsibility. Why are people afraid of taking personal responsibility?

∎

I've had three or four out-of-body experiences, they were frightening. That changed my view of life. I felt I lifted out of my body, went full circle and ended up in the far corner of the room where I could see myself. I was panicking. I've seen lots of orbs. Things don't move in that fashion unless there's a purpose. Seeing those things has changed my outlook. There is energy out there and things happen that we have no idea about.

∎

Due largely to religion, millions of people have been shot, beheaded, and otherwise murdered for being gay. I am the kind of person who will fight for the rights of anybody who is unfairly treated. But I find it difficult to fight for the rights of people who, because of their religion would spit on me or worse for being gay. Being me is against their laws. How can I get passionate about fighting for the rights of those whose religion encourages them to murder others? You've got to pick your battles in this life.

∎

When people say, 'I'm not religious but I'm spiritual' - what the heck does that actually mean? I have never had an explanation from anyone who can tell me what 'spirit' means. People with a non-religious stance are having the better time in life. Faith is a coping strategy, an escapism. Life is shit a lot of the time. It's harder to face up to how shit it is if you don't have faith in something. Life is lonely.

∎

I've done a lot of strange things out there in the wild. I've lain down and looked up through the pine trees at the stars. You are in the best possible place. It's the most beautiful thing ever. You're really experiencing it in the moment. What do religion and ritual have to do with that?

∎

My Dad went through a weird phase. He started going to classes with a group of old men and a Rabbi at the local synagogue. I suppose it's that thing of getting older and wanting to find something. He's not an intellectual - he's a cab driver. I've never seen him read a book but for some reason he wanted to find out more about his faith. He was learning Hebrew, too. Now he goes to Tesco's café with his mates!

∎

I think we're all shit scared of dying so invented something that makes you think we're going to live for ever. We don't have faith in ourselves so we rely on something that may or may not exist.

∎

My family are devout Muslim. They never forced it on us but I was definitely brought up in that environment. I don't know why but from the age of 11, I rejected it. It's all bollocks. It's just rubbish. That's one half of my brain, but there is another part where I am interested by spirituality and religion. I've studied religions. I probably know more about Islam than most Muslims.

∎

If my faith is anything at all, then it's to take joy in the people around you. I deeply dislike the word faith. Faith has an element of being unreasoned and that's the problem.

■

I don't believe in God but I believe in good. I've seen a UFO. Back in the '80s we were walking over the common near Chorley Wood. It was October time and getting dark and chilly. This cloud came over us like something out of Star Wars. All you could see were lights. We got to the pub and told all our mates. Of course they thought we'd been drinking but the next day there were reports in the press of 'sightings'!

■

I think it's a load of mumbo jumbo. It's been a way for influential people to order society. I think most people have pretty good intentions. I don't think there are that many evil people in the world. Most people would help someone struggling across the road. I've got faith in the human spirit.

■

Faith is a personal thing. I married a Catholic so I might get in the back door. Ultimately I'm a sceptic. I've never seen anything to make me feel any different. I think a lot of religion is brainwashing. I really hope there is something after death but I think your body just dies.

■

I'm a Buddhist. The Art of Happiness: A Handbook for Living by the Dalai Lama has all the answers. From the moment we're born to the day we die we are suffering and we have to try to figure our way through that suffering. I believe that everything happens for a reason. I don't know what that reason is and I never will. I pray and convey thanks. I often ask for guidance and help. That makes me feel more comfortable with the decisions I make.

■

I think it's preposterous that we should we be placed on this earth through no choice of our own and 'a God' will say, 'Well, there's one correct religion, you guys choose one and if you choose right then you go to everlasting paradise, but if you choose wrong, I'm going to fuck you up for eternity.' It's like a parent saying to their kids, 'There's eight flavours of ice cream, choose the right one. I'm not gonna give you any information and if you get it right, you can have the ice cream, otherwise I'm going to punch you in the face!' Having said that, I do believe in God. It's a possibility that there's a creative power in the universe Why do humans still have this desire to have spiritual answers? Why hasn't it dissipated when science has been able to provide answers?

■

Faith is a good thing. Whether that faith is God, the divine, the universe, or whatever. If you've got faith, you've got trust that things are going to be fine. Faith can carry you through some really tough times. I have faith that life runs a certain way. That life works itself out. I have faith that positive things will happen. I have faith that I'll be taken care of in this life. I have faith that I will be guided by whatever signs cross my paths. My path was meant to be. Piecing the jigsaw together to get me to the point I'm at now.

■

I think karma exists. I believe something will catch up with you over time if you're not appropriate. Payback seems to happen in the end.

The 60s

What is faith? Faithfully? Faithful. It's something you write at the end of a letter. I have no idea what faith is, it's just a word.

■

I am an atheist but I've become increasingly tolerant of people with a faith. I've met more people with different faiths but it's not for me. There's a street preacher at my tube station. I like stopping to chat with him. As far as he's concerned I'm going to hell, but it makes my day talking to him.

A part of the tenet of Christianity is forgiveness but because Christianity has sort of disappeared from our lives, forgiveness has too. I'm formed by Christianity. I went to a traditional school where we had assembly and hymns every morning, which I resented. I can sing hymns by heart. We had Saturday school, which I hated. We would bunk off and go to the Shed at Chelsea. Hymns in the morning and football in the afternoon!

■

I have faith in Buddhism. To make changes to the world we have to be really honest with ourselves and being honest with ourselves is hard to do. To strip away the bullshit. To dig deep and try to understand the fundamental darkness that divides us. People fight in wars. 'We won the war!' No, you didn't win a war, you still have a price to pay. There's no get out of jail free card, there's always karma. People don't really win.

■

Fundamentally I'm a dyed-in-the-wool sceptic with a nostalgia for faith and therefore I quite like people who have it even if they're a bit fanatical and limited; for instance I love going to Northern Ireland. I love talking to Protestants and I love talking to Catholics because they're lovely people. They're friendly and open. I quite like embattled people even if I have to admit that sometimes it's hardly the most liberal attitude they're expressing.

■

There is something bigger and more powerful than we are and it tends to deflate the ego quite successfully.

■

Faith came to me when my life crashed. I grew up going to church. I got confirmed later in life. The year 2000 for me was profound, my marriage was in trouble. My son had lots of issues. I couldn't deal with it on an everyday basis - I asked for help. I got down on my knees and prayed, 'God help me'.

■

I suppose I believe in God. I'm not sure I believe in the kind of bearded Jesus but I believe in an energy that is greater than us and it's probably easier to think of it in human form.

■

I left my daughter one morning to go to work. She had been jumping on the bed in her cowboy outfit. I got a call from my wife to say come to hospital. My daughter had fallen off the bed and landed on a glass of water which had gone into her spleen. The doctor was saying, 'I'll do my best.' I'd seen her bouncing around just half an hour before. I went outside to call family members to tell them what had happened. The car park attendant came and put his arm around me and said, 'He will make it all right,' and you know what - He did!

■

Several things the church has given me. One is the theory that you'll be thrown all the shit in the world but never enough to utterly destroy you, and not to the point where life is unendurable. (You'll never be given more than you can bear.) It's not a belief, it's a faith that something knows you - 'to whom all hearts are open, all desires known, and from whom no secrets are hidden.' (The Collect for Purity.) There is something that understands you intimately beyond your ability to explain. It's like a spiritual x-ray, you just allow yourself to be read.

■

I am aware of other dimensions and I believe I have a psychic antenna which sometimes twitches - helpfully. I don't think I have more of an antenna than anyone else but perhaps pay more attention than most. I remember sitting with a dying patient in a hospice. We were alone in a room, yet I knew beyond anything that we were not alone. There was some witness. We were accompanied and I felt completely supported. I had no worries.

You can't explain a faith. You can't give a rational explanation to something that isn't logical and irrational. I admire people who can embrace their uncertainly more than their certainty.

■

You've gotta stop trying to get your head around it - faith plays no part with our heads and every part with our hearts. Faith is a feeling that stands on its own. It doesn't have to shout about itself or defend itself. It simply is. It can be lost and re-found again. Sometimes it's more difficult to have hope than to it is to be hopeless. It's that old expression - despair I can live with, it's the hope that kills me.

■

If God saw all the shit that was going, surely 'He'd' wipe us all out and start afresh. From day one all men have done is try and kill each other.

■

If we don't operate at the shame and guilt kind of level and operate at a more aspirational level, then that energy becomes more visible to us. The higher the plane we can spin up to then the greater the plane we're on. Another belief I have is I am merely a conduit. None of what I am doing is me, it's a product of the energy I am creating. I don't write the book, it writes itself, I am just a messenger. I don't know what name you give to that power but there's a definitely energy greater than you or me.

■

While I was going through my transition I had a guru who helped me into mindfulness, he's a Buddhist. There's something about the way our brains are wired that are buzzy. There are ways Buddhism quietens the brain. I'm not a Buddhist, by the way.

The 70s

My upbringing instilled a belief, not a faith. The Catholic faith is about rules and regulations. I don't believe in those rules. I could never understand why I had to go to mass every Sunday and if I didn't, it was a mortal sin! 'What about all those people in Africa who are Catholics and don't have church or altars, what do they do?' I couldn't reconcile it. I make my own rules. If I want to go to church, I will. I won't go on a Sunday because the Pope says I have to.

■

Years ago I was on night shift as a hospital worker. We got a call, there had been a crash. There was a guy dead in the back of the ambulance who had to be ready for a post-mortem the next day. It was 3am. We put him in the morgue which was next to the hospital, it was really eerie. He was bleeding all over the place. I'd run out of things to clean him up so I went back up to the hospital to get supplies. An older nurse came in and told me to leave the body for an hour or so for the soul to leave the body. 'You have to have respect,' she said. Personally I don't believe in all that shit. I got all my stuff and went back down to the morgue. We had left the lights on. I saw a person's silhouette in the window. I walked up to the door, very fucking cautiously I can tell you. I saw the dead guy walking towards me, the door suddenly went BANG! I never touched the fucking door. Eventually we went in, the guy was lying on the slab. I cleaned him up quickly, we didn't hang around. The next day we told the nuns about it and in no uncertain terms we were told never to talk about it again!

∎

I read a book about a hypothesis that when you look at the solar system and then at a molecule or atom, they're very similar. With the atom you have a nucleus, which is a bit like our sun. The story was that one person's atom is another person's solar system. In that microscopic atom that we don't know anything about there might be whole little worlds just like us. One thing I do find quite fascinating is the concept of infinity. We can't grasp it. I used to frighten my children by saying that each of us is just a microscopic piece of irrelevance, clinging on for dear life to a lump of rock called Earth, which is also a microscopic scrap of irrelevance that is flying around the sun. Which in the scheme of things is also a microscopic piece of irrelevance. It's just chance. The universe is just lumps of gas and dirty old rock, we could vaporise tomorrow.

∎

I believe in God but I think God appears to people in different ways. People interpret things to suit their own outlook. I think faith and goodwill will overcome evil in the end. One thing that gets me down is when I start to lose that faith.

∎

You hear about people having reincarnations - there must be another life that we don't know about. That's hope, not faith.

∎

I'm more Darwinian than the big guy in the sky. I'm one of the most unreligious people I know but I enjoying singing hymns. I've been singing 'Blessed Be the Everlasting God, the Father of our Lord,' for the past 65 years.

■

I do go to church. I love the sense of community that it involves. Going to the Sunday service after the Duke of Edinburgh died was very moving for me because it was a collective. Just a dozen people paying their respects. It's a sense of community, those are the two primary reasons I go to church. I can't say it's faith.

■

I do have faith but I'm one of those who calls on Him when I need Him, like when I was in the throes of depression years ago. It sounds wrong and I know it's wrong, if you've got faith you shouldn't just use it for when you're desperate and in a dark place. I should give thanks for what I've got now rather than when I need help.

■

I'm more into empiricism. I have beliefs in democracy and friendship. I see that nothing is permanent. Spirituality is a passing experience. I'm aware of what's moving me forward. It's usually when I feel connected to nature or through music. I've had times at a concert hall, usually a single musician, pianist or a violinist. I feel like I'm almost levitating. It's unexpected moments. It's connection.

■

The quantum physicist Bernard d'Espagnat made the case that you have two choices; you can be a materialist, and everything's just molecules, or you can deal with the quantum, but you can't do both because in materialist term, the quantum makes no sense. I feel the same way. I've had this fight with physicists for a long time. Our ideas about consciousness relatively speaking are primitive and that's one of the things that going to have to change in physics in the 21st century.

■

I practise Dzogchen daily. The point of the practice is understanding consciousness. The removal of all the paraphernalia of religion. In the same way as storms, rain, clouds and sunsets pass across the sky, the sky itself is completely untouched by any of this. These moments pass through. Most people confuse their mind state with the weather. Emotions are moments. You just have to stop doing and watch it.

The 80s-plus

I admire people who have a faith. It's wonderful. I don't have it. I am an old-fashioned lapsed Catholic - which means agnostic. In other words, if you can't see it, you can't believe it. When you see people who really do believe it's rather admirable. The Catholic faith is all about sin and how you're going to go to hell. When I was at school the priest told me that my mother couldn't go to heaven because she wasn't Catholic. My thoughts at the time were, if God knows everything and if He has put you on this earth, and He's going to take you away at the end and He knows what you're going to do while you're here and you're going to be punished in the next world, then why did He put us here in the first place? That reeks of cruelty. Sometimes I think Catholicism is a curse.

■

Is there a God? I think so. I don't know if there's an afterlife. Religion is a code by which to live. If you do right you'll be okay, if you don't, you'll end up in hell. When I started going out with my wife, she asked me to have Catholic instruction because we wouldn't be able to get married in a Catholic church if I didn't. About 10 years ago I became Catholic. Having known what I know now, I should have converted when I got married. There's not much difference between C of E and the Catholic church - the Catholics go to church, the C of E's don't!

■

I have experienced the extraordinary. We once had a girl come to stay - she was perfectly nice. While she was staying with us, the kitchen shelf came off the wall, and everything broke - including those unbreakable Le Creuset pots. Everyone said she travelled with a poltergeist. Then one time I was staying at a moated farmhouse in Suffolk. The owner collected tall Elizabethan chimney pots. In the middle of the night they all moved across the room, making a terrible scraping noise across the paved floor. I don't know if it was paranormal activity, but it was certainly very alarming! One thing that did worry me: years ago, I was driving along a country lane when a dog ran out and got run over by the car ahead of me. It was dead in the road but I actually saw it get up and run away at the same time.

■

I think Christ was an extraordinary person, an astonishing man - very modern really. He's like Shakespeare, a good read. Because his death was so painful people can somehow relate to him when they are having horrid times. I'm not sure about the Resurrection, though. The Bible I am sure is worth reading, as is Tolstoy.

■

Faith is the glue that held societies together through the Medieval Ages, even though people butchered and burnt each other. For the peasants, the story of Christ and the promise of eternity gave them as much hope as it did for a King or a Prince. I say to some atheist friends, don't dismiss faith as mumbo jumbo or superstition. Faith is vital to our society.

■

Faith is wonderful, it inspires people. It makes them brave when they would be weak. I'm not religious but I would like to have a faith that gave me strength when necessary.

A longer conversation...

Mel, 36

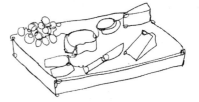

cheese seller, from Estonia

Back home in Estonia, there's a tradition of outdoor swimming. You go to the sauna, then swim in lakes two or three times a week, and if you don't, people are like, 'What's wrong with you? For me there was always a fear, I was a later bloomer. My friend was an incredible swimmer, he helped me to get over my fear. Once you learn to swim, it's like learning to fly - you're free, you're like a dolphin. I love water. Swimming is an incredible experience. I once went out in the ocean for six hours, just playing about under water. Water is incredibly calming, it's an intimate place.

I believe in nature. It's idyllic. You realise you're very small and play a very tiny part. Nature always wins. Nature takes away the stress, nature is always giving. There's an incredible freedom in nature.

Where I come from, people have a very close connection with nature. They go berry picking and foraging, walking in the forests. It gets passed down through the generations. It's like a religion, similar to the Celtic way, almost Pagan, and there are many superstitions. On Midsummer's Eve (St John's Day) there is a massive celebration (one of the biggest of the year, with family and friends celebrating round bonfires in the countryside.) My grandmother was a witch in our village - she could see into the future, she would read the cards. People don't talk about it but it's very normal in our society.

Gardening is an amazing thing - nature speaks with you. It tells you what you should do in the garden. There's a communication. My Mum has an incredible connection with nature. She talks to the flowers. She's grateful. She sees things that I don't see. I used to spend most summers at my grandmother's. There were lots of leeches and for some reason me and my mates would put them in small bottles and bury them, row upon row of them, like a cemetery. We thought leeches were bad. I think you go through phases as a child.

I came to London on a gap year and have been here ever since. London is the most diverse city, I think. People just learn to live with each other - people from all over the world. No one cares. I've only ever had two jobs since coming here. I think I am quite loyal. I try to see the good in everyone, even if there's bad. It can get me into trouble sometimes. I can be too diplomatic. Too good natured, too soft. I don't get angry often - for me to get angry it has to be on another level. I think out loud quite often. I talk to myself. Sometimes it helps me remember things if I speak them out loud, that way my brain isn't too full. Lots of people don't understand me. My mind works in a completely different way. Sometimes I can be incredibly lazy and sometimes I'm very hard-working. I speak seven languages.

I like me. I never used to. I know about myself now. There are so many 'mes' inside of me - there was a 'me' who analysed everything. I don't do that any more. I have come to terms with me. If I were a cheese, what cheese would I be? A goat's cheese? - there is always a bit of a change. Sometimes it changes three or four times in its life. Or maybe a Vaccherine - soft and smelly!

On my days off I go to the meditation centre and help my friends there. Sometimes I do nothing, watch TV, listen to music, clean the house. My God, when I clean the house, I really clean the house. It's like a switch that comes on. It's therapeutic. I like singing.

I became interested in meditation 10 years ago. I used to walk with my head down and never smile. Now, I try not to have too many expectations and I've become much happier because of it. I'm still in the middle of a journey. Men have incredible insecurities and so much pride - my God, men have so much pride! I think men used to be strong but now I think it's the women that are strong.

I learned about meditation in Korea. I stayed up in the mountains. People have such wrong ideas about meditation - they think we just sit around in a room going 'OM.' It's not like that. You look back at your life from the third person's point of view. Even though the moment has gone we are still attached to our emotions - we learn to let go of them. We see people from all the experiences we've gathered. In meditation we try to discard all those images. For example, my brother had a problem with alcohol. After getting into meditation I saw him as how he really is and that's when I could help him. If I only saw him negatively, I would never have been able to help him.

The mind is an incredible thing - you live in your own matrix, you're a slave to your own mind. Take nature - it doesn't care, it doesn't discriminate. It doesn't think, 'Oh, this flower is beautiful,' or, 'I have given you flowers today.' It doesn't have a mind - it just gives but doesn't care. That's what made me get into meditation.

Life is the great mystery of life. It's a step, a learning curve. We are not complete yet. Maybe we live to become complete. The answer to this question always changes. I don't think we just live and die. It's too short although life is long when you empty your mind. All experiences are new - everything is new. As you get older the cup is getting fuller and the days are getting shorter. I have taken things out of the cup now and I think time is going slower. Why worry? In a hundred years' time, no one will care.

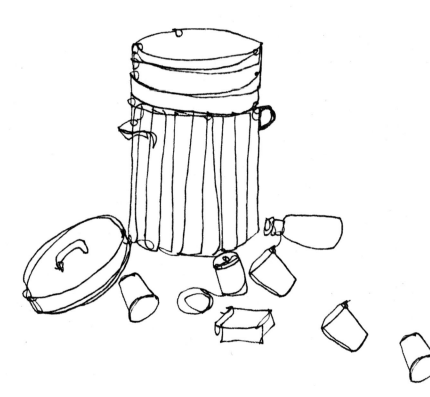

What would you like to leave for the next generation?

'When you leave, shut the door behind you and make sure that you haven't made a mess'

Reading through all the answers in this section really shows the humanity in people. I get quite emotional hearing these inspiring, kind and thoughtful comments. Imagine, all these thoughts put into actions. I feel hopeful for our future generations and thankful for the ones who have gone before.

Meanwhile, I've got a theory; how about the world has a scheme whereby as soon as you reach a certain age, say 18, you have to do six months litter picking. Everyone does it, no exceptions. That way everyone will be so sick of picking up litter they will never drop any, ever. The world will be cleaner and people will be proud of what they've worked for. I've got loads more schemes up my sleeve but it's not about what I would leave, it's about what you would leave?

The 20s

Mandatory voice lessons. I had the luxury of going to drama school and it completely changed the way I use my voice. Some people speak too much, others not enough. Imagine a world where we can really express how we feel. There are many cases where people have much to say but are worried about how they might be perceived. If you live a life of pushing your voice down things can come across quite hard and what does that do to your insides, to your mental health? Being in command of your voice is a daunting prospect. Some men feel challenged if women have their own voice, it can cause confrontation. For women to take power of their voice is an incredible thing. Letting out their natural sounds.

■

If we don't have a planet, nothing will matter. There's no point fixing other issues if the planet isn't here. If someone said you have a button to press - one will fix the environment, the other will give equality to sexuality, gender, race, ethnicity, everything will be completely equal, 100 per cent I'd push the environment button. As much as I like the idea of everyone getting on peacefully, if there is no world left, what's the point?

■

If I had a magic wand, I'd start the world all over again. It would be a cool exploration. We could make such a difference if we redistributed money, resources and focused more on equity rather than equality.

■

For West Ham to win the Premier League.

■

I think we'll look back at social media in 30 years time and say, 'How was that ever allowed to happen? How did they operate like that?' It's a breeding ground for anxiety and depression.

■

It's scary really. By the time I'm 80, what will the world look like? The ocean is already covered in plastic. I want us to look after our planet. I work in a bar - they've banned plastic straws but after 12am they use single use plastic cups for ease.

■

The next generation is going to face pandemics, global warming and inequality. The key is education to find solutions.

■

For the world to be a lot less volatile. We've had the coldest spring on record, the hottest spring on record and the wettest spring on record in three consecutive years. It's not a very happy environment, is it? Leave a good impression. Be nice.

The 30s

I think the most difficult thing about bringing up children will be dealing with social media. I'd like to remove some aspects of it. There are plenty of positives but so many negatives, too. The body image thing. I don't think people should use filters, or if they put pictures up they should say they've been edited. Anybody who makes a social media account should give their personal ID details. I've seen it in a sports context with people setting up fake accounts so they can racially abuse people. People need to be accountable. People promoting fat loss pills too, it's so unhealthy and has seriously negative effects. Social media is going to carry on getting bigger. The surge of the influencer. Millions of people can be reached by getting somebody recognisable to promote something. People aspire to be influencers, it all hinges on personal image. It's not healthy!

■

I am grateful for the people who have gone before us - gratitude is important. You always have to say thank you. When I get older I'm not going to tell the younger people how to do things. You do have to offer wisdom but not by comparing. The younger generations will live a different life - they will be influenced by other things.

■

Having respect for other cultures. For the world to be in a better place than I found it. I'd like the next generation to believe they can make things better. By the time I reach pensionable age, pensions won't exist. I feel for the younger generation, they have a hard time.

■

I'd like there to be less mobile phone use and social media influence. I have these things but I don't spend hours on them. I can't see a single benefit outside of it telling me when my friends birthdays are. I'd love to take it all away, to make kids realize there's more to life than being in tied to your phone. I wasn't allowed a phone until I was 18. I'd much rather be outside exploring the world. Sometimes you realize how much your phone has taken over your life when you lose it. I've been working on ways to engage kids in physical activity. It's a passion of mine. I've created a programme with a colleague to enhance movement skills and physical literacy.

■

The population is only going in one direction. In 50 years it's going to get a lot more crowded. Unless we find a way of living together there could be a lot of trouble.

■

Ecotourism. There are places in Mexico where all the fish stocks became depleted. The fishermen turned the habitats into nature reserves and now have more money from ecotourism and their ecosystems have recovered.

The 40s

It's a major bummer that weather is going to get really fucking horrible.

∎

I believe in an economy that's different to capitalism. Capitalism doesn't encourage love. The issue with capitalism is greed and it always will be. We should have an open economy where knowledge, food and education are free. Where the people all play our part in society.

∎

Less competitiveness and less inequality between people.

∎

A more peaceful, stable world. That's why I fought so hard against Brexit because if there's one thing I could leave my kids, it's a United States of Europe built on those pillars of freedom and a commitment to human rights. There's nowhere in my mind better than the European Union in terms of that balance of justice. I really felt Europe was a model for the world.

∎

I hope I leave my niece and nephew with a different perspective from their mum and dad. Someone who carved out a nice little life for themselves. Not better or worse but just to know they can live a different type of life. That they don't necessarily have to live with someone, get married or have a partner. I think both their parents are quite conventional. I can show them you can be unconventional and happy.

∎

Compassion is the first and foremost – it's the legacy I want to leave. I'd like to leave the ability to be able to talk to anyone whatever they do or wherever they come from. I think about the impact I am having on my kids, not just my own but all the kids I work with. I've realised the anger they have is just an inability to express what's really going on. You have to try and work out what's happening, what's trying to be said. I have greater compassion when I talk to my teenage son.

■

I'd leave them the sort of times that I had growing up because I don't think they've had the same freedoms we did. They have a lot more stuff in terms of electronics and gadgets but not as much in terms of knowledge and freedom. We went out at 10am and didn't come back until 6pm. Nowadays kids are jealous because the other kids have more stuff and they want it. They use knives. They may not want to but there's peer pressure which makes them do it. It's sad. My boys have been robbed a few times. I'd like to leave a world where teenage boys don't look at you in a strange way. Where kids can go out without getting their phones or bikes nicked. How many boys are hanging out looking menacing? You can't change them. I was in JD sports, there were these group of boys walking around. One had a spliff hanging out of his mouth. I'm like, why oh why? So you smoke weed but you do not need to walk around with it in your mouth. And the senseless vandalism. What are you doing? What are you achieving? There's no common sense, some people are thick.

■

The world is getting more complicated and demanding. You've got people who make billions, who run a few environmental projects, but are those people really saving the planet? No, some are a bunch of stuck-up wankers in love with themselves. Making a difference is more complicated than that, it doesn't need to be shouted about. If we can all leave the planet having not shit on anyone then that would be great.

The 50s

I hope I'm leaving some laughter. My golden thread is kindness, generosity and respect. I may have changed someone's five minutes, but I didn't change their world.

■

For my children to have affectionate thoughts about me as I slip away.

■

The white middle-class male doesn't get good press at the moment. Suddenly we are the bad guys. We are all pigeon-holed. Throughout my career I've been massively pushing female lawyers forward. My mate and I led a campaign to get the maternity rights improved. I'm trying to make little differences where I can.

■

For what it's worth, I'd like to leave respect, kindness and dignity. I'd like to leave a spirit of, 'Think carefully about what's important to you and never give up on it. And be compassionate to yourself, never beat yourself up.' Take an orange tree, for example. If you want it to give you oranges, then you have to really think about the soil you plant the tree in, the food you feed it. Giving it the right amount of water and so on. When it's cold you might want to bring it inside. When it's too hot, you move it in the shade. If it still doesn't give you oranges, you don't start shouting at it, calling it fucking useless or beating it. If you do, it will become infected and stressed, and then there's really no chance it will give you fruit. You stay in touch with it, looking after it and love it all the same. It may or may not bear fruit and that has to be okay.

■

Be open and honest. Don't be too quick to judge.

■

Put other people before yourself generally. Don't be rude, and pass on your knowledge - it's what we have to do, isn't it?

■

Paying attention is very important. Take a step back before casting an opinion. We can all be too quick to judge, and one comment can imprint itself on someone's psyche and leave something negative.

■

I hate big companies who have monopolies on everything. It's all about making money for their shareholders. I'd like to see big corporates open to the ideas of ordinary people and to invest in them too.

■

I don't feel I need to make some kind of impression or leave something memorable. I'd get rid of private education. Grammar schools. Religious school. Everybody's schooling should be the same. Funded in the same way. Everyone should have the same benefits.

■

I would like the next generation to have the tools and techniques to be wise and compassionate. I think everything else follows. If you're wise you can manage your relationships. If you're compassionate you care and make sure that no one's left behind.

■

Giving a shit. Listening is important - you pick up a lot when you listen. We've lost that ability.

■

Be involved and be in nature. Don't get too internalised. There's too much fear. Try to be an individual. Individualism is being strangled. Have self-expression as opposed to people thinking for you.

■

I only have a small influence on my surroundings and my little family. I've done what I can. I can't have much influence on much else.

■

I love books. I was always taught that readers are leaders. It saddens me that young people aren't interested in books. In an ideal world of retirement, I would sit and read and read and read.

■

I would like to leave a clean planet that's not in the process of dying. I would like to leave a more tolerant world than the one we have. Those are the two things that worry me the most. Conflicts between races and religions is horrible. The planet being more and more vulnerable because of climate change, what will the consequences be? Children and young people have got good grounds for feeling pissed off at our generation.

■

I hate what it's like for my daughters out there. My daughter gets cat-called every day when she's out. She was holding hands with a girlfriend. Some bloke took issue with it. She told him what she thought and he knocked her unconscious. She ended up in hospital with concussion. Women of all races get abuse every fucking day. Society is broken. There's not enough emphasis on changing the culture of men being the issue, and not women's failure to protect themselves. The only person who should be blamed is the perpetrator of the act.

■

Most people support the notion that they don't want to be racist. We need a similar change among the section of men who think it's okay to be predatory towards women. We all need to be so appalled by it. Predatory behaviour is no longer something that people can do comfortably. Too many men behaving inappropriately towards women for far too long. Us fellas need to take responsibility.

■

Without hope life is not so much fun.

■

I'd like to go back to how it was when we were growing up but there again, there were riots, wars, nuclear bomb threats. AIDS, of course. I'd just like it to be sunny and everybody to be nice. I'd like everyone to live to 140. And everyone that has died gets to come back.

■

A thought process that anything's possible.

■

The whole #metoo. I hate that sexist stuff. The way men talk about women. At university I did my dissertation on the impact of the war on women. If you go back to the 1880s when the Married Women's

Property Act came in, it was the first time unmarried women were able to own a property. There's something about inequality and the role of women in society which I find difficult. Sometimes when I go to the football with my son and hear the blokes, not much has changed from when I was younger. I'd like boys and men to treat women equally. All this sort of crap about 'woke'. Grow up and understand that people are people. Men aren't better than women and women aren't better than men. We have to have a law that requires people to treat women the same as men, that's absolute madness. And, if we hadn't been part of the European Union that would never have had happened!

The 60s

Plenty of water and for it to be free. I don't see why we should be paying for water when it comes for nothing.

∎

Old people like me have a responsibility. This younger generation is probably going to be the first generation worse off than their parents and that was before Covid so God knows what the impact's going to be now. An apology to them that we've fucked up so much.

We owe this younger generation a lot. Give them the opportunity to make the world better. We should lower the voting age to 16. The older generation should stand back and let younger people take that space. We need to listen more. There's an assumption and I'm probably as guilty as anybody that because we've lived it, we know everything but that's not the case. Men should step back and let women move into leadership positions - the world would be a better place for that.

∎

That everybody can find their place in a society not based on their ability to generate money.

∎

A sense of curiosity. Faith and optimism.

The 70s

Practically, I'm never gonna change human nature. Part of my legacy is the things I've done for the village I live in.

■

It's up to each generation to build its own life. If we try to give the next generation something and they run with it, then they're just an extension of us. It's about kicking them out of the nest. If we've done our job properly they don't need anything from us. I don't believe you benefit children by giving them money.

■

Make the world fairer for everybody, including animals.

■

I can't influence the wider aspects of life on this planet. All I can do is to hopefully leave some resources which will enhance the experiences for my family and those close to me, or support a cause which helps alleviate suffering. Things that make sense to me.

■

It's about respect.

■

Take what you need, nothing more. Leave something for someone else. People need to think rather than just do. Respect. If you're going to kill it, eat the bloody lot. The tail to the horn.

The 80s-plus

Peaceful - it's a simple as that. We have fought two world wars and now we're all big mates, I don't understand.

■

Once you've gone, you've gone so I don't think it matters. Will I leave a lasting impression? No. Look at all those blue plaques all over London, most of people you've never heard of. They were put up at the moment when that person was incredibly famous or important. They were famous in their day but those plaques mean nothing now.

■

That they keep meeting each other - as long as the generations keep meeting each other there is a chance.

■

My book of short stories and poems.

■

That the next generation have hope and confidence in their own human abilities to weather the storms. To come up with solutions. The human ability to love and care for each other is what will carry us through.

A longer conversation…

Andrew, 31

a PE teacher from Lancashire

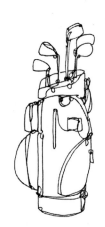

For the next generation, I'd want to address the disparity between the richest and the poorest. I feel strongly about the wealth divides in the world. It's a genuine tragedy, a disgrace that there are humans that have trillions, and humans with no water to drink. Their experience of life is literally worlds apart even though we all live on the same planet.

I teach at a deprived school and I see kids growing up in the poverty cycle. It's not as simple as people think. People from a comfortable background come out with comments like, 'Why are we giving free school meals? Isn't it their parents' job to feed them? I bet they've got money for fags and booze.'

It's not a five-year-old child's fault that parents choose to spend their money on cigarettes and alcohol. People don't understand it's very difficult to get out of that cycle. If you grow up in a postcode where you go to a rubbish school, surrounded by deprived children and all the problems that brings, the opportunities aren't the same as for those who have a better start. You become a product of the people you're surrounded by. I don't think there's anything wrong with parents wanting to do the best for their children but as a system, a country, a world, we could do better at looking after people.

The fact that some people are born in a postcode that's going to give them a shit life, unless they're lucky to escape it, I never understood. The divide wasn't on my radar until I joined the school

I now work at. I took the job out of desperation. I find it stressful and difficult at times. There are times when I'm pissed off. There are days when I'm sworn at. It's challenging. There's a time limit to it. All the same, I love my job, it's rewarding. It's tough but I get pleasure every single day giving kids opportunities that I know they wouldn't have otherwise.

At the moment, I'm tired and ready for a break. I found Covid difficult. It was a hard time. We had a baby, then four months later we went into lockdown. We were both off work with our new baby but weren't allowed to see anyone. It was seven days a week, full on with nowhere to go. It sent us a bit crazy. During the summer, places still weren't open. We'd take the baby out for an hour but still had the other 23 hours to get through. A couple of months later my partner got seriously ill, she developed a life-threatening illness. Thankfully she's okay but it was touch and go for a while. It's been rubbish if I'm honest.

I don't want the whole conversation to be about Covid but it was frustrating. I learned I can't operate without any sort of freedom and I need a certain level of control in my life. I need the freedom to do what I want to do and I need to be in control of what I'm doing. I missed not being able to go to the pub on a Friday night with my friends. And home schooling as a teacher was frustrating. I'm an outdoors person. I don't like being cooped up. Because I'm a PE teacher, I'm more in touch with the weather, in fact my life is dictated by the weather. November to March, I'm just freezing all the time! Covid wrecked my routine, which was to drive to school and listen to a podcast on the way, that was my switch-off time. I'm a bit of a dinosaur. I don't have a PlayStation, X-Box or anything like that. I'm old school. My happiness comes by being out, playing football and golf. On a positive note, we are hopefully getting married soon - fingers crossed!

I've always been ambitious for my own life. I bought my own house when I was just 22. I've always wanted to make sure I had the option to go to nice restaurants and bars. I like nice holidays and driving a nice car too. I need to relax a little and give myself the freedom and time to do things that make me happy.

The art of conversation has gone now we are living in a digital world. I don't think we make time to see people in person any more. I have a WhatsApp group with my friends and I talk to them more on that than I do in person. There's something about having a conversation that sparks ideas and makes you see things differently.

There's a reason we have traditions. Take Sunday dinner for example, something that's a bit sacred. An hour off from the telly. Conversations at the table. It's something that's regular and keeps you sane.

I've learned to allow myself time and not put too much pressure on myself. To go and play golf, and do whatever I need to do to make me happy because it can be snatched away in a moment. I work hard at my job and hard for my family. Children are one of the things I care about in life. Ever since I was young I've always loved being around them. I enjoy them as part of my job and my family life. They're hard work. I want to be fiercely ambitious for my children, pushing them to be the best they can be. One of the things I've learned is, yes be ambitious but let them be what they want to be. What makes you happy isn't the big achievements, it's the little things in life, isn't it?

How do you best express yourself?

'I wish I'd expressed myself better with my wife'

Some people are confused by this question, others think it's the best question. So how do you express yourself? Do you even know? Would you like to express yourself better than you do? There is a need in us humans to express ourselves, that's for sure.

Acting ⚲ Drag ⚲ Through language ⚲ Taking pictures ⚲ **HUMOUR** ⚲ My voice ⚲ My accent ⚲ My podcast ⚲ By my actions ⚲ Painting ⚲ Smiling ⚲ Sulking ⚲ Laughing ⚲ Yelling joyously ⚲ Crying ⚲ Through my Jujitsu ⚲ I don't think I've achieved my best form of expression yet ⚲ House interiors ⚲ **MUSIC** ⚲ I self-reflect ⚲ Playing guitar ⚲ By being drunk ⚲ Storytelling ⚲ Film & music is a graceful way to soften language ⚲ Modelling ⚲ Noisily ⚲ Through movement & fluidity ⚲ Through the process of creativity & curiosity ⚲ My partner would say I don't express my emotions ⚲ **DANCING** ⚲

Sharing ☥ Poetry ☥ **SINGING** ☥ Nature ☥ Gesticulating ☥ fidgeting ☥
If I'm expressing myself loudly, it's to keep people from looking into me
☥ Through other people's music ☥ I express my feelings at the game
☥ **VERBALLY** ☥ On my lathe ☥ My very loud laugh ☥ Cooking ☥
By what I wear ☥ I'm good at vocalising my feelings and emotions ☥
Sitting at a piano singing ☥ Through my opinions ☥ I'm very proud to be
from the North and particularly from Yorkshire, it's the heart of who I am
☥ **WRITING** ☥ Passionately ☥ Through my punctuation ☥ Sarcasm ☥

A longer conversation…

Dave, 38

a digital tech advisor, from Yorkshire

During the pandemic and lockdown I started to put on weight for the first time in my life. The wife and kids did loads of baking. I never had to think about what I ate before. I'm someone who's always got time for pudding. I was fed freshly baked flapjacks, rocky road and chocolate brownies. I had to start watching my weight and consciously having to exercise more!

I like to dance. Dancing with friends is a great thing. I've got weird philosophies on dancing. I like it when people dance. I feel like the purpose and reason for dancing is removed when there are a set of rules as to what beauty looks like. I struggle with the ballet. People love the ballet, it can bring them to tears to see such beauty but for me it's like seeing a caged bird or a lion in a circus. It is amazing, beautiful and the people performing want to, but I see the mechanics of it. Dancing is doing what you want.

Once I became a parent, I became a 'dad' dancer overnight. Thing is, I can't dance for toffee. I never learned to dance. If you learn to dance there's no freedom of expression. People either don't dance, shuffle around or, have to be on the other side of a few pints. I've always enjoyed a dance and I love music but there's only so much time in the day. Given a spare hour, do I take the time to listen to music, dance or watch a film?

I am a big fan of films. As a kid I'd watch TV back when there was only 4 channels. I'd watch all the black and whites, war films and westerns. I wasn't put off by the age of the film. I'll watch anything, good, bad, or indifferent. Once the story starts you've got to find out what happens. Who knows, it might get better? There's a level that a bad film gets to where it becomes really enjoyable.

I listen to film podcasts. I get a film magazine subscription. I know all about the new films coming out and what people's thoughts are on them. It's all the love and passion that goes into making films. You're watching something that's been created by someone with a fantastic imagination. I love the storytelling, seeing all that creativity. Technically, the cinematography, even the way a film opens. There's the visuals and the amount of people who work on them. It opens worlds for me. If a picture says a thousand words, and you're watching a film with 24 pictures per second, you're taking on a lot of information.

I don't consider myself to have a very good imagination. If I'm reading a book and it's beautifully described it, I'll only be able to frame a tiny portion of it in my mind. I can't hold it in my imagination. I can't take myself to being in that scale of place. I'm better at processing films. Books are better for your imagination but for me they limit mine.

I got told so many times that once you'd read the book, you'd never be happy with the film. I was always happy with the film. Films are like whisky, it's a mood thing. Films take me on a journey. I get lost in a film. I like to be in the right mood for certain films. A sad film will make me sad. I am a fan of the escapism. I watch things to escape, not to have reality driven home.

I've never known what I want to do with life. When I was young, I always wished that I could be a Formula One racing driver. I felt aggrieved in the school playground that it was all football, football, football. They could practise every lunch-time. There was nothing for the eager racing driver. When it comes to talking about men generally, I don't feel qualified to talk. I don't feel like a man generally. Because men talk about football, but I couldn't care less. I am a bloke and I've got lots of male friends, but I don't associate myself with the typical male tropes.

It would have been nice to have been a professional photographer or to do something with my degree, which was in electronic imaging and media communications. To work in that field, though, would have meant moving to London or another big city, and I didn't want to do that. I liked living in the country. I didn't make that sacrifice. I went for job security. My dreams are boring 'dad' dreams, to pay off my mortgage and my student overdraft!

I'm strongly led by morals. I prefer people that say it as it is. The amount of people that will appease you and say what they think you want to hear. I believe I've got a strong sense of self. I like myself. I care about people. I like that about myself. I'm happy to give people my opinions. I think the sound-bites are different from the reality, though. It's easy to be honest with yourself, but it's something different to be genuinely honest and live by it. I might not want to do something and while I'm being honest with myself, at the same time I might be being difficult for the situation or for someone else.

I'm very singular task orientated. I like routine. When my diary gets full of places I need to be and things I need to do, it overwhelms me. Anxiety used to stop me achieving things. For example, I'm terrible at taking exams. In conversation or demonstrating knowledge, I'm fine but put me in an exam situation and I'd never complete the paper. I'd confuse myself trying to work out what they actually wanted from me. Overthinking it, trying to make sure I'd got it right, being pedantic about the wording. I'd worry and end up not finishing it.

I'm terrible at calling my friends, though I'd always make time if someone calls round or phones me. Finding time to phone someone when there's so much to juggle and balance is tricky. The way we live, with social media and information overload, we are still working out how to navigate that connectivity. It's precious and dangerous at the same time. I used to read the Sunday papers every week. Page after page and Private Eye, too. I let the world get under my skin. I don't do that any more. I had to find ways of letting things go.

You could say I'm quite needy or empathic, I get my energy from others. If there's nobody around or I'm with a group of people low on energy, then I tend to feel low too. But, while I enjoy being with other people, being around an argument, even if it doesn't involve me, can crush me straightaway. People being upset will get me down very quickly. If I get emotionally hooked, that raises my anxiety and I feel terrible. To look after myself I have to remove myself from stressful situations, otherwise it makes me cross and sad.

You can have a lot of worries in life, the 'what ifs?' The parallel lives you could have had. The shoulds, woulds and coulds. Then you have kids. Kids are a major part of my philosophy. From the moment you have them you can let go of all the things you've done, all the decisions you've made in life up to that point, because it's only those chain of events, those experiences, those decisions, that's led you to the point where you've now got kids.

We have two children. I definitely wasn't keen to have more. I'd have found that overwhelming. You can only be in so many places at once. I felt I wouldn't be able to give enough attention to more. I love having my kids around. People with kids should be appreciative and thankful to those who've decided not to. If we all had kids there'd be no green spaces left. Being Green at its extreme means not having children. Overpopulation is literally the world's problem.

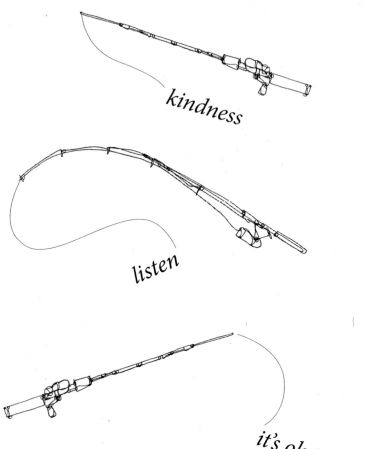

kindness

listen

it's ok to talk

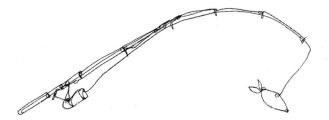

What have you taken from this experience?

'Listening is important, you pick up a lot of things when you listen'

Having spent most of my life working for myself and by myself, I've missed out on all the stuff that comes with being an employee. Pay rises, feedback, 360 degree reviews. The team effort, the joint goals, training. (oh, how I could have done with some training). The works dos. There's a lot to be said for support and collaboration. You need it. I need it. So when a friend suggested I add this question into the mix, initially I felt awkward but then realized, this is my collaboration and my feedback and it's bloody fantastic! It's reflective, validating and supportive. Pausing for a moment after you've done something to allow it to settle.

In this chapter, my own comments are in italics.

The 20s

This is a very rare thing. It isn't therapy, but I found this very therapeutic. I think anyone listening in from outside would think this is a very personal conversation. It feels very much like someone is trying to better themselves by purging old memories and finding out about themselves through this process. It's a rare thing to sit and talk for a few hours. You can really help yourself by talking out loud. So I thank you! *You're welcome!*

■

It was a really fun experience. This process massively appeals to me. I joke that my favourite thing to talk about is myself, so getting to sit and answer questions about myself is great! I just want to say you've been absolutely incredible. I want to acknowledge and appreciate that. You've done a good job and I'm excited about the outcome. *So am I. I hope I do all these conversations justice, it's been a fabulous experience!*

■

I had no idea what to expect. I don't put myself in many positions where I'm vulnerable to somebody that I've not had an existing long relationship with and who is going to potentially share some personal information about me to people I've never met. That in itself is quite odd to me. I would never usually do that type of thing. The process has been quite nice - to just chat. I love having conversations with people and hearing different viewpoints. I really enjoyed it. I really liked the questions. They were thought-provoking. *Thank you*

■

I didn't know projects like this existed. I didn't know books were being written about conversations on these kind of topics. Having now done the interview, I think these conversations need to be had more. *I agree!*

■

It's nice to stop for a minute and think about the past and the future. It's certainly nice to have reflection. It calms you down. *It sure does.*

■

It's good to ask the question, 'How are you, honestly?' It's good to talk and it's certainly made me think. The ability to show one's subconscious in a free and expressive way with no boundaries. It has made me re-think a few things. I need to find a hobby beyond work and relationships - just doing something for me. You can always find the time if you prioritise. *Yes!*

■

I've really enjoyed it. I genuinely thought I had nothing to talk about. A lot of time there's some guilt when I'm talking about stuff but if that's how I feel, then that's how I feel. *Half the battle is knowing that, right?*

■

You just need to sit down and have a chat sometimes, put technology away and talk about things. It doesn't happen often. I think you'd have a lot more energy for other things and wouldn't waste energy on lingering thoughts. *Yep!*

■

It's like Humans of New York. It's a really cool project. I'm happy to take part. *That's a huge compliment.*

Talking comes naturally to me. I didn't have to think twice about saying yes when you asked me. It's not out of my comfort zone. I imagine it's really enjoyable for you, too. I think I'd enjoy listening to all these people. *I have loved it.*

.

This has been the best few hours I have had in a long time and it was a beautiful way to end my year, so thank you, Sam. *(You're welcome!)* I think these are questions that I'm always pondering but don't necessarily having the space to verbalise. We have a thousand thoughts a minute. Think of all of the things we lock away in our minds.

The 30s

It gets you thinking. Thoughts might be in your head but you've never vocalised them. I think the end product of this project will be good. You will be able to see how other people think. I'm interested in the outcomes. *Me too!*

.

It's been an amazing experience. If you take all the excess out of the things that you're saying you can really hear yourself - there's a truth here. I've learnt so much. I feel very empty in a good way. It's like a clear-out, sorting out the rubbish. *I love a good clear out!*

.

This was a very therapeutic time. I'm mostly happy I had somebody to talk to for a change. It gets lonely at my studio. I have no access to the outside world or news unless I choose to read a newspaper. *Thank you. You're welcome.*

.

It's always great to have conversations. An interesting process. It's nice to hear things out loud. I am pretty self aware. Sometimes saying things out loud reinforces things. I have counselling so these questions aren't scary to me. When you have in-depth conversations you're always gong to learn something. People need connection. *We certainly do.*

.

It's made me think about a few things that I haven't thought about for a long time. It's made me realise that my ideal life isn't as far away as I thought. *I think most of us chase our tails, searching for something only to find it's not far away.*

∎

I've learnt a lot today. It's odd knowing that the conversation is about me. It was interesting and a new experience. I felt as time went on I could have answered the first questions better. I'm very pleased my wife thought to put my name forward. Conversations restore faith. *Yes, they do.*

∎

I think it's a super-positive project. That initial question, 'How are you?' I bet loads of people live their life every day and don't ever get asked that. *My fave question - How are you?*

∎

I really enjoyed the women's book you wrote - I was quite emotional. I was a bit intimidated because this is probably as close to therapy as I've come. *It wasn't so bad, was it?*

∎

I like what you're doing. It's got me thinking about my life. You've definitely asked me questions no one else has ever asked me before. I think everyone goes through some shit. If people can get some sort of understanding about that, it can help them on their journey. *We all need a bit of clarity, it's making time to talk, that's half the battle.*

The 40s

I have enjoyed it. It felt relaxing. Back home in Greece I have this kind of conversation with my friends. People are busy, they don't have time to listen. There's not much time to express our emotions. We should make time. Everything can become a drama and snowball. At times, life is like watching a soap opera. *And isn't it exhausting?*

∎

Everyone likes talking about themselves and you don't often get to do it - especially for three or four hours. It's a bit like the blood pressure medication I take - it opens up everything. It's 'Ramipril' for the soul. *I like your analogy.*

■

We don't talk enough. We don't chat about ourselves because it feels weird and it shouldn't but it does. I am very self-conscious about it all. *You're not alone. It's a strange thing to do - to really talk!*

■

I have been challenged without being scrutinised. What I'm struck by is what am I like compared to other people - am I really boring? Is my life so boring and my outlook so vanilla? What is she thinking? *I genuinely wasn't thinking anything, I was just listening. That's what these projects have taught me - you can assume nothing. And you're definitely not vanilla! I don't like vanilla!*

■

I find talking about myself very difficult. The question 'How do you see yourself?' was tricky for me. When I am out there doing what I do, it's about me not talking. If the focus is on other stuff, then I don't have to talk. I need to explore that. It would make the quiet times by myself have more meaning. At this time of life I should be comfortable being by myself. *I'd leave the 'should's' alone. They can be troublesome!*

■

Sometimes when I'm working I'm not in the moment. I am more worried about the outcomes and not the process. I just realised that by talking about it. People don't want to see me working all the time - I can enjoy it too. Feeling that you're worthy and for it to be okay to experience the experience too. That is a good thing. The thing I get from this is to spend more quiet time. Less Netflix, sit in silence. I think I might call it a revelation! *Me too!*

■

I always found it constructive, talking. It's good to get challenging questions. The ones that make you reflect a bit more. It's nice to feel special. I've really enjoyed it. *So have I - thank you!*

This is a really positive thing. Given that most of the problems in the world are caused by men, most of the focus should be about fixing men. There's a much higher rate of suicide in men and still too many men who see therapy as failure. Men are generally more dick-headish and problematic than women. The expectations we put on ourselves. Our need to project, and then there's all that pride! *Umm. There's a 'should' that's crept in! And a lot of judgment about what men 'should' be. After all these conversations - something needs to shift but change takes time. First comes awareness of a problem, then desire to change - then action. Men do need to talk but also to listen. There's hard evidence in this book proving that. But I think words like 'fixing' feels too rigid, another theme throughout these conversations. If men want to let go of what's troubling them, or at least try to understand what's going on inside of themselves they need to be still for long enough to allow those feelings to come through and sit with them for a while. And perhaps focus all that excess mental energy into something more holistic without giving themselves such a hard time.*

My thoughts on male suicide after listening to all these men are: men feel they need to find solutions to the feelings they can't express. Rather than just feeling them and letting them go. Solutions are linear, black and white - and suicide is the ultimate final solution. It's logical in their minds. Take away the logic, fixing, pride, and add flow, uncertainty, and vulnerability - and who knows what that might bring?

∎

It's been fun. It's been a pleasure, it's been brilliant. It's been really nice. Some things I've said I should do more of. I've enjoyed it. *Me too - thank you.*

∎

I absolutely love it. First of all, I am taking something very powerful away with me. When you shared with me, that you can never assume anything about anyone. Having spoken with all these people, your assumptions and judgments go away. Even with the most 'boring, uninteresting person' you'd ever meet, when you take a moment to sit and ask questions, you'd be amazed by what comes up and what makes them tick. I knew that in theory but how often do I do that? What an amazing and powerful thing just to sit down with somebody and ask them a few questions. A great way of deepening the relationship and depth of connection. I can see why these questions create a strong connection but it also allows insights to emerge - it's beautiful work. Thank you for inviting me. *You're so welcome. I have had such a lovely time - thank you for telling me your story.*

■

I've honestly loved it. I've really enjoyed it. Sometimes you got to expose yourself to help other people feel less exposed. *So true.*

The 50s

Ten years ago I'd have said, 'Nah, bollocks, I'm not doing it.' But therapy has been an eye-opener. I'm a bit of a therapy bore now. My therapist taught me how to deal with my mother. I used to drink a bottle of wine before a half-hour phone call with my mother and it wouldn't touch the sides. The therapist made me feel so much better about myself. I think therapy's a brilliant thing. When you're in a dark moment it gives you pointers and life lessons to help you. *It's good to talk!*

■

I've loved it. It's like self-help, asking someone to confront their shit as well as the good things. Confronting what's going on. Like the question on death. If you're not being confronted by these things, it's brushed under the carpet and you never get to grips with anything. *Exactly!*

■

I do tend to bumble through, but this has made me think a little more about doing something a bit different. This process is about being understood. You said right from the very beginning that you don't have an agenda and that really comes across in this process. You don't have any expectations. I'm not forced to perform. It's a very regulating process. I hear your questions, your lack of judgment and genuine curiosity. I can hear my own thoughts and opinions. I'm coming out of this with a sense of calm, a sense that everything in the world is okay for now. This isn't therapy but it is therapeutic. ***And it works both ways. I'm learning so much doing this. And my curiosity is insatiable so thank you.***

■

Some of the questions on the surface sound quite straightforward but they're not. I cried a lot. It's been good and I'm glad I did it. I like these sorts of conversations and getting to the nitty-gritty of life. It's hard to find men you can have these conversations with. I think women respond to men who can express themselves emotionally. ***Getting down to the nitty-gritty is for me and the point of life. Otherwise, what is the point? Thank you for crying. You'll be surprised how many men did.***

■

I've enjoyed it. I love sharing my grumpiness - spreading the word! The question 'How do you see yourself?' I found very interesting. ***Love a bit of grumpy, it's expressive, just don't overdo it!***

■

It's been an absolute amazing experience and I feel a lot lighter inside. I have been able to talk to you freely, someone who isn't a medical professional. I've talked to medical people in the past and psychologists who've listened in a practitioner sort of way but you've sat there as a total outsider who doesn't know me from Adam - it's a breath of fresh air. I'm breathing easier. I don't feel so heavy, something has lifted. It's been a cleansing experience. I didn't know what to expect. Each question can form another 10 questions. I've never actually sat and spoken to some one for four hours. I don't feel like I've been talking for all this time - where did the time go? It seems to have been almost an exorcising process for me. I feel better. I need to exorcise that devil somehow and this has helped. I feel like I've known you for years, which is weird as I don't normally let people in. I have felt a comfort and ease with you. *Aren't strangers just friends you haven't met yet? It's been brilliant - thank you.*

■

I said things I didn't think I'd say. I feel really good. I'm glad I did it. It felt really cathartic. It's refreshing - I like it. *Me too!*

■

I've enjoyed it. I don't know what I expected. I have achieved one thing - I didn't want to cry and I didn't, although I do cry. I come from a tiny market town with the same amount of idiots as everywhere else - boys aren't taught not to cry. *I don't cry either, I laugh! I laughed when my Dad died - hysterically. It was very inappropriate but a purge is a purge and it needs to be let out.*

■

Today has been like a journey from one place to another - a whole network of answers. I found out more about myself today. That energy question - wow, all the stuff I like doing is in pursuit of something to make me feel and find out who I am. I am answering the questions with the same stories. I didn't see that happening. I like communicating like this - I like being open and honest. I don't think anyone is ever going to ask me to be this open again. You probably didn't anticipate it but you've probably become a really important person in some people's lives. Conversations like this are rare enough and you are good at facilitating them. *It's really weird when we hear ourselves out loud - you can hear patterns. Somehow it validates your thoughts and sometimes we realise how much bullshit swirls round in there too.*

■

I think this is a great idea. I have enjoyed our conversation. The bad thing about therapy is you only go when you need something fixed. I think, like a car we should get a service. Get someone to ask you a couple of meaningful questions every now and then. *I agree!*

■

I think this is a great thing to do but then I'm a narcissist and I like talking about myself. I love this process. Self-awareness. What makes you tick? Getting other people's views. I would love to be a fly on the wall to hear what other people have said. *You can read the book - then you'll hear it all, then it's not just about you. See what I did there? Unleashing you from your narcissistic traits!*

.

It's not intrusive. I like your thinking around what you're doing. It's a snippet out of everybody's life that appeals to me. I like to read about people but couldn't read a full book on one person. Different people from different lives. I like the concept. I'm interested in hearing about men of all ages. Do men in their '20s still think about clubbing and sex like I did, or is it all about university and feelings these days? *Weirdly we didn't talk about sex much. But there again - I didn't ask. And, you know what? Men in their '20s aren't going to tell me about their sex lives - it would be like talking to their mother!*

.

What a great chat! It's been brilliant. When I said I was anxious about it, I wasn't lying. I was extremely nervous and extremely anxious but once I got talking, it was natural. *Fear and anxiety are just thoughts and imaginings. There was nothing to worry about, was there?*

.

You've been a fabulous interviewer. *(Thank you!)* I think your questions are great. They're challenging. I felt relaxed though. I think what you're doing is very important. You're operating on the level of magic. You're asking me to tell you about me which is nice, but also uncomfortable. I like that you've created a process that could loosely be described as a therapy but actually it's a springboard to help reflect further on how I can be a better version of me. That's what I've got from this. I've got to say this has been a fantastic experience. I'm really grateful. *You're very welcome. I like that it's not therapy. Therapy would mean I had to write notes, possibly give you an 'ism' or label and see you every week. That's not me, I'm a one time only, sort of gal! I have things to do!*

.

I think people should have more conversations. Conversations are good. I think some people see it as extravagance, to afford the time to have conversations. Stories are everything. *We have to find time to talk - how bad is that?*

■

Now you've asked me these questions, you've prompted me to think more. It's nice to talk to you. I might go and do a cartwheel after this or even an Arab Spring! *Send me a photo! (He did.)*

■

I would talk to you gladly again and again. I've absolutely love it. Congratulations on hitting upon the idea. *Thank you - it was lovely talking to you too.*

■

You're probably one of the first people in a long time that has asked me such questions. It's making me think. I'm good at keeping people at arm's length. I'm good at talking about my adventures but not about my personal life. I'm good at finding out about other people's stories but I suppose as long as I'm asking the questions, they're not asking about me! *You're not on your own, I think there's quite a few of us that deflect. But that's okay. Just as long as you're not deflecting so much that you lose sight of what going on inside of yourself.*

The 60s

I found it very interesting. It was nice to reflect on everything in life, from where I started to where I've come to now. What's ahead of me? It's brought back a lot of memories. I think we should talk about the past more. *I love a venture into the past. Especially to our ancestry. What they went through? I 'call' upon my lot when I need a bit of encouragement. In fact when I did my TedX talk - I called all my ancestors up on stage with me, there's no way I could have given that talk without their help!*

■

It's been quite fun, cathartic. I didn't want to be self-conscious about any of it. I've told you things that I probably haven't told anyone else. *Better out than in.*

•

It's very helpful to talk like this. *This I know for sure!*

•

I like how you're not passive. It's not a one-way conversation. *I'm never passive, maybe I should try it sometime!*

•

I've loved it - lots of things I mentioned that I didn't think I would. It's always a great relief to know you've been listened to in a non-judgemental way, it doesn't happen very often. *It's interesting don't you think that we sometimes don't even know what we think until we think it out loud? And get an 'Ahh' moment!*

•

You're very good because you worked through your questions as a conversation. You seamlessly segue from one question to another without it being a questionnaire. It's been a very nice and interesting conversation. *Thank you*

The 70s

It's better than therapy. You can talk about things instead of paying £55! I've enjoyed it. It's been nice talking to you. You're doing a good job! *I should have charged you!*

•

To collate all this must be a task and a half. *You're not kidding! - THREE MILLION WORDS! (In case you'd forgotten!)*

•

It was a good to have a natter. You're treating me as a 71-year old sounding board. Inquiring is healthy. You are a super inquirer. *Thanks.*

•

I was apprehensive. May I congratulate you on the way you kept the conversation so interesting and there's never been any awkward pauses. You ought to be a radio interviewer. *I don't really do dull conversations - always better to seek out the interesting stuff.*

∎

Conversations are important. If we are not careful, our grandchildren's generation will lose the art of conversation very quickly. They all seem to be on their gadgets. It's really sad and a definite problem. If we go out for a meal, for example, they're all sat at the table on their iPads and phones. *I blame the parents!*

∎

I haven't talked so much in ages. I've found it really good. I've enjoyed it. It's thought provoking. You've asked me things that people don't. Talking does you good. People should talk to each other. It's what makes the world go round. *I've said it before and I'll say it again - it's good to talk!*

∎

I am very impressed by your ability to listen well and to probe. So many people can't do that. You do it well and it's refreshing. Because I'm a therapist, I'm usually the listener. This was an uninterrupted conversation. I didn't know how I was going to find it but I've enjoyed it very much. *Well that is a compliment indeed. Thank you.*

The 80s-plus

I think it's brilliant. I am very honoured to have been asked. *It's been a joy - thank you.*

∎

There's something very powerful hidden in stories. It invites internal dialogue. You've seized on something that is a very good idea. *Thank you.*

∎

I think this session between you and me has been very beneficial to me. I think this form of questioning draws the interviewee out gently, which is what you've done. It's turned me in on myself, often to face things that one would normally try to avoid. It makes you question yourself and, we should always be questioning ourselves. *I think so.*

Sitting back with my feet up, I have taken some time to reflect on this whole process and what I have taken from it…

…listen, question, don't assume, shut-up, be polite, be kind, don't judge. There's not enough time to hold a grudge.

Talk it out or let it go.

A longer conversation…

George, 57

from Manchester

Fundamentally I'm a sad person. I'm happy in moments, but I struggle with melancholy and sadness a lot. I feel irritated with myself and unhappy with where I am in relation to what I've achieved. That's really tricky. I don't like myself at all. I am really angry with myself and it's really hard not liking yourself. It's been bad for a long time.

I was 19 when I started suffering from anxiety but I handled it well until I was about 27, then it got really bad - to the point where it was so debilitating it absolutely paralysed me. I couldn't leave the house at all.

I developed monophobia in that I became frightened to be by myself. That lasted for a good five or six years. When my wife went to work I would either have to find a friend to hang out with or go to somebody's house. I wasn't alone for almost a decade. I took medication. It was continuously humiliating searching for people to protect me or give me company. Eventually I started alienating my friends. People can only do so much for you, they have their own lives.

When I first started developing panic attacks I would tell everybody because I thought it felt so profound and so important. People would say, 'That's awful!' But then, eight months down the line when you told them about your panic attacks, they'd just say, 'Oh well, that's a shame.' They don't want your problems because what I was asking for was endless. Support me here, support me there. It was horribly humiliating. I really, really hated myself during that time.

When you're in pain or even depressed you can go to a reservoir of inner strength to deal with it but when it's anxiety it's your inner strength itself that has been attacked - it's gone and that's why you're panicking.

It got to a point when it was really bad where I didn't feel anything. I didn't feel love. I didn't feel happiness. I only felt scared. I only felt sad and that went on for a long, long time. I couldn't even be with my kids and feel anything for them. It was horrible.

After our third child was born, things got better. I didn't need to beg people for help. This last 20 years have been better. I still suffer from anxiety a lot but my panic attacks are few and far between. The trigger can be anything. It could have been from my childhood but I don't think it matters. Knowing the source of the anxiety doesn't necessarily help. What would be more helpful is dealing with the reality of what you're feeling in that moment.

Anxiety has fundamentally changed my life. I think my life would have been very different. I probably would have been a university lecturer by now. That's where I was heading. I feel sad. I've underachieved.

I am really fucking frustrated, sad and angry with myself. Then I think, what can I achieve with anxiety disorder? There's nothing stopping me being a great musician, recording, writing and trying to get published. No matter how much of a long shot those things are, the fact that I haven't tried to do it really grates. I'm so preoccupied in failing that I don't even try.

I haven't got false modesty. I know I'm above average intelligence. I understand that I've got academic skills. I'm quite a good musician but I don't do anything with the skills I have. I won two academic awards as an undergraduate. I did my master's degree, got a distinction, applied for the funding - got it! Did a PhD! I'm an academic. It's just so cool! I fucking love history. History is the story of human experience. There's no other subject whose only focus is that. I would go further and say you can't understand anything properly without understanding its history. That's why I like it. It ties us all in together. Human experiences I find really moving. History helps us understand the world we live in.

I could have done a lot more but the fact is I am very limited. I can't get out there. I can just about be at home by myself now and that has taken 30 years to manage, which feels really fucking pathetic to be honest with you! Everything I've done, I've done half cocked. I've got a mother fucking PhD but haven't done anything with it!

I'm not a terrible person or anything. I think I'm probably quite nice. I get a lot of safety from my family. If I'm with somebody I trust I can pretty much do anything. If I'm with my wife, I can get on a plane to California.

I started on antidepressants and they're working. They've made a big difference to my general mood.

I think I'm a compassionate person. I think I'm generous. I'm kind of funny sometimes - I like that about myself. I'm a good cook. I'm very good at DIY. I learn by using common sense. I think I'm loyal. I think I'm loving, particularly to my family. I think people like me more than I like myself. I think they think I've got more value then I think I have. My immediate family like me. They tell me I'm funny and nice, and they like my company. My daughter is always telling me how much she loves me.

If my kids were in the same boat, I'd say, 'Do what you can, don't be ashamed of what you're going through. It's not your fault. Dealing with anxiety makes you brave because it's easy to do stuff that you're not frightened of but really hard to do stuff that you're frightened of.' What I wouldn't say is, 'Pull yourself together, you snivelling wimp,' which is essentially what my mother used to say to me.

Nobody enjoys being frightened. Being frightened to the point where you're desperate and there's no resolution is horrible.

I am endlessly forgiving in relationships but my Mum's been really horrible. She was abusive. Me and my brother took beatings like you wouldn't believe. She was horribly unpredictable. We were frightened of her. When we used to go to my Gran's, it was the only time we would go to bed and feel safe. To feel that somebody wasn't going to come up and pull the bed sheets off and hit us because we forgot to do something.

A psychologist said it's much more damaging to have a mercurial parent. If you have a parent who is only abusive there is no dilemma in loving them. It's when it switches from abuse to tender and fun-loving it becomes mentally problematic.

I didn't have much of a relationship with my Dad. We got on okay in terms of affability and chit-chat. He was friendly enough but we didn't have a nice relationship. We didn't really know each other. Both me and my brother definitely feel that we are the second class children of both our parents as they both prioritised a new set of children.

I don't feel hard done by, but I do feel sad. I look at my wife who had a genuine friendship with her mother. I look at my own kids and how they feel about us. I think it must be really fucking nice to see a parent as somebody you have a real, genuine relationship with.

When I became a parent, all I cared about was being a good dad. That was the start and end of what I wanted to achieve. I didn't understand why somebody would have kids and not feel that way. Having children was the only thing I was certain about. I remember when I was seven years old, people would say, 'What do you want to be when you grow up?' And I'd say, 'I want to be a dad.' Kids are brilliant. I love children. I love being around any children, they're just really, really fun. Anybody who can get delight from an old Weetabix box has got to be somebody that's worth spending time with. Kids are fascinating, learning constantly. If a child falls over it cries. It's in deep sorrow, then literally three minutes later is perfectly happy again.

Conclusion

WOW - that was a huge emotional rollercoaster of a project. It's been educational. Ultimately that's why I do these projects - I learn so much and I like sharing what I've heard. Why did I interview a hundred men? After transcribing how many words? I did ask myself the same question! But in all seriousness it was a natural transition - first a hundred women, then a hundred men. So here we are at the end of another fantastic adventure.

I'm an instinctive person and definitely not a focused thinker. This means I often don't know where a project is going or how long it will take - I follow as it unfolds. It's like when you're gardening - you start in one corner, and branch out. And as our conversations unfolded, more questions surfaced. I'm always amazed what simple questions reveal, and again it highlights the need for people to share and tell their stories.

Without a shadow of a doubt the most overriding theme that stood out beyond everything else was the sheer amount of energy men have - both mental and physical. 'I can't relax,' was a common remark. The need to be active, to be doing, to exercise, was predominant in many of the men I spoke to. They expressed a need to be purposeful, to do rather than to be. I would say having too much energy was a weight most men carry.

Men are massive over thinkers, too. They don't seem to able to stop their brains from whirling around and around.

Forty men out of the hundred expressed obsessive compulsive behaviours. Locking and checking doors was very common, along with sweeping up leaves or just the desire to sweep! Picking up apples from the grass because they'd stain the lawn. I had no idea ODC was such a big deal in the lives of men. But I do remember a time when I was about 10, a neighbour across the street would be out in his anorak come rain or shine, literally straightening blades of grass on bended knee! Clearly he had way too much energy. Or was something more foreboding going on in his mind, and this was the only way he could express it?

The next finding was a bit of a shocker. The abuse men suffer. Twenty eight out of a hundred had been abused in some way; verbally, physically or sexually. And, even more disconcerting, 9 per cent of those were by their mothers and 12 per cent by their fathers! It's hardly surprising then that over a quarter of these men suffer with mental health problems, although I sensed the number was higher in light of what I was told, but they hadn't given their symptoms any labels yet.

Society depicts that men historically have their 'shit' together so it was eye-opening to hear that 20 of the men I spoke to experienced imposter syndrome and self-doubt. They experience inner turmoil and low self-esteem - this is not an assumption, I found it to be a fact.

Male suicide rates are an a concern, accounting for the majority of UK deaths from suicide - 75 per cent, according to the Office for National Statistics, 2020. Suicide is the most common cause of death for men under 50. And I'm sad to say that 16 of the men I spoke with had experienced suicidal thoughts.

The stigma around mental health issues appears to be greater for men than for women. The stereotype of the strong silent man is a dangerous notion. The concept of 'manliness', along with our laddish culture and the emphasis on drink as a coping mechanism, means it is seen as a weakness to ask for help. Men are more likely to resort to harmful coping methods such as alcohol abuse and drugs. One man I interviewed said, 'Men cocoon themselves. We use vices to dull our emotions - for me it was beer, I drank a lot of beer. But there's always a price to pay. We don't seek help soon enough. I cannot recommend getting support as soon as you know something is wrong'. On a positive note, seventeen out of a hundred had undergone or were in therapy. I'm glad to hear men are at least starting to get a few things off their chest.

Football was massive, as you would expect. Passionate, dedicated and fanatical for the game, or sheer disregard and couldn't care less. But for me, listening to these fellas was addictive. 'The greatest night of my life was 1989 - I think it was May 29th when we won the league up an Anfield - 2 nil. I was up in Liverpool, we weren't expected to win - I cannot begin to explain how amazing that was.'

Despite the fact that men can sometimes be uncommunicative - a little monosyllabic perhaps? - get them talking on 'their' subject, it is music to my ears. It might be how wood is turned on a lathe or how meditative it is to cast a line into the river and wait to see what bites. Or how working with paper all your life gets so under your skin that you can smell and feel the differences between hundreds of types of paper types. Their descriptions are poetic. These men have poetry in their blood. And nineteen out of a hundred read or write poetry, with two or three published poets featuring here.

Politics was another major interest with twenty two out of a hundred expressing opinions that ran deep. I'd ask why hadn't they gone in to politics with all that passion, opinion and energy? The will was there, just not the way!

Surprisingly perhaps, Buddhism was a theme, too. Many men were actively engaging in the Buddhist way or at least practising its philosophies. Chanting proving to be a great comforter as well.

Music was another lead interest. Listening, playing, idolising. Artists that have had lasting impact. Whether it's Bowie or Brahms, Prince or Previn, Cohen or Carner, Mahler or Mitchell, Glyndebourne or Glastonbury, music has influenced the lives of most of these men in some way, shape or form, with some being professional musicians.

There were many more themes. I asked about the weather. There wasn't enough space to put their answers in the book but it was surprising how descriptive men are about this topic. Almost a fifth of them - 19 out of a hundred - described the rain in a sensual, even romantic way. 'I wrote a poem, it's about crying in the rain and no one can see your tears. It's romantic. I like kissing in the rain.' 'I'm attracted to desolate wild weather, blasted heaths and crashing waves.' 'I love going to bed with the sound of rain. It's so cleansing. It's melancholic.' 'Being under an umbrella all wrapped up, it's a bit like being in the womb.'

The subject of technology and social media came up, too, with another fifth – nineteen out of a hundred - hating it, while seventeen out of a hundred felt pressurized by life. But dreams of travelling the world in 'my campervan that I haven't bought yet,' exploring space and quantum physics or a brewing a crafty beer, all stood out. One theme I particularly enjoyed was the need or desire to dance. Not in a showy-off, performative way but just a quick jig around the kitchen while unloading the dishwasher or a good old fashioned 'dad dance' in your living room. Throwing some shapes just because you can!

I have heard so much wisdom doing these projects that you would think we would live in a world without fear, violence and stigma, but one consistent theme throughout is the contradictory nature of being human. We say one thing and do something else.

Listening to all these men has been a joy and enlightening. I've loved it. I'm only sorry that you weren't in the room listening in on our conversations because sadly, as the reader, you only get an essence of what's been said - you've missed out on the side of the conversations which can't translate to words. The pauses, the eye contact, the space between language. The unsaid. But I hope you take away something to share from this project. My hope is that the conversations continue… because the thing I've taken from all of my time collecting conversations is -

It's crystal clear, we need to talk but we also need to listen!

My Top Twenty Takeaways

ꝏ Imagine a world where we can really express how we feel.

ꝏ I watched a documentary about people who take their own life by jumping from the Golden Bridge in San Fransisco, the two only survivors both said, as soon as their hands left the rails they realised - everything is reversible.

ꝏ I'm trying to slow down. I'm finding it very difficult.

ꝏ I don't have my airpods in so I can listen to what's going on around me.

ꝏ I'm generally a pretty poor communicator. I don't share my emotions. There's an app I have that can helps you express your emotions!

ꝏ Sometimes the best help is when you doing nothing.

ꝏ You can die a little everyday just by thinking.

ꝏ Be good, be bad, but don't be indifferent!

ꝏ You can't spend your life analyzing the fuck about what might happen. You've just got to get on with it.

ꝏ I am brave except when it comes to holding large spiders in my the palm of my hand.

♪ I am not too proud to say I cant do it all by myself.

♪ I don't always tell the truth.

♪ The difference between despair and hope is 8 hours sleep.

♪ How can you love anyone unless you love yourself.

♪ It doesn't need to be beautiful, it needs to be from the heart.

♪ When you hurt - go quiet.

♪ To make changes we have to really be honest with ourselves. Being honest is a hard thing to do.

♪ You miss things if you don't stay around.

♪ Look beyond yourself. It's not just your life it's everyone else's life.

♪ I am sorry that I gave up on my creative side because being creative means you don't get caught up in intellectualism and being grumpy.

So, are men and women that different?

Eleven years on from starting my projects, millions of words heard, two books and a whole heap of new friendships and connections I thought it might be an idea to share my observations; the comparisons between the sexes. I'm not saying one is better than the other, or making any judgments - just sharing the stand out differences - and by doing so, we 'might' be able to understand each other a little more.

My observations…

The over riding theme with men was their excess physical and mental energy and how they deal with it. For women theirs was the amount of worrying they do. From my observations men direct a lot of their energy into OCD, anxiety and depression. These definitely weren't themes with my conversations with women.

Women have more open ended conversations and tend to deviate off topic mid conversation whilst men are more linear and finite in their conversations - perhaps looking for solutions and conclusions. When I asked the question, what do you like about yourself? Most of the women said 'I can tell you what I don't like' and go off on self sabotaging negatives. I found this eye opening. I had to ask them to answer the question again but this time with a positive response. On the contrary, men just answered the question. They're literal. That's not to say they weren't uncomfortable and awkward at times.

Men hate moaning and 'nagging'. Women talk, some may say too much! Maybe it's because they don't feel listened to? I definitely felt there were mis-communications between the sexes. Lack of understanding or inability to express what was going on inside.

Men talked about the abuse they suffer. Physical, mental and sexual. Those who'd experienced it, mostly received the abuse from their parents. The women I spoke to suffered less abuse but those on the receiving end, it had come directly from their partners.

I asked about dreams, most women had everyday achievable, dreams. Whilst men also having ordinary achievable dreams they also have extraordinary ones too, such as becoming an astronaut, the lead singer of a band, a footballer, cricketer or a sports personality.

Men are less open to 'other realms' women are much more so. Men are steadfast in their certainty - ie unless science proves it, it's mumbo jumbo. Women are more open to uncertainty.

Women have instinct and intuition - men have logic and solutions. Women have inner knowing, that's their tragedy, some men don't, and that's theirs!

The five word cloud questions were interesting comparisons too:

How do you think other people see you? Womens top four were - caring, confident, kind & strong, whilst mens were: friendly, arrogant, intelligent and socially awkward.

Where does all your energy go? Women's top four were: my husband, my children, my family and work. Whilst men's energy goes on their OCD, over thinking, work and exercise.

Who or what inspires you? Women's top four inspirations were - my Mum, the weather, nature and ordinary people. Whilst men's inspirations were their Mums *and* Dads, their wife or partner. Musicians and male sports personalities.

A side note - Men tell me they have a lot of pride. Research shows men don't engage as much with female creativity in terms of art, literature, music etc. as much as they do with 'art' created by men. Yet the number one inspiration for both sexes was MUM! I wonder what would happen if men spent a significant period engaging only in 'feminine' creations. Would that have an impact on their pride?

What brings you down? Women's top four were: my husband, my children, worry and responsibility. Whilst men's four downers were thinking too much/negative thoughts, people moaning. Feeling out of control and failing.

How do you best express yourself? For women their number one best form of expression was singing. Singing anywhere but mostly in private, belting out a tune in the car or shower. For men it was writing; be it poetry, stories or their thoughts.

Humans aren't that confident - it's shown in women via their body image and in men as being competitive. If we were happy in our own skins, literally and metaphorically - self confidence would be rife - it's not.

Men and women are contradictory by nature. We over worry (women) and over think (men). We love singing and being poetic. We are kind. We need to talk but we also need to be heard. We don't address issues - they fester and get out of control, yet we are control freaks - trying to control the uncontrollable. I'm genuinely curious, what it is that we are trying to control? I'm not a psychologist - and no one knows why we are here, but here we are. We can't control that. So what's the point in trying?

'Leaves of Grass'
(Extract from original Preface)
Walt Whitman

*Love the earth and sun and the animals, despise riches,
give alms to every one that asks, stand up for the stupid
and crazy, devote your income and labor to others, hate
tyrants, argue not concerning God, have patience and
indulgence toward the people, take off your hat to
nothing known or unknown or to any man or number of
men, go freely with powerful uneducated persons and
with the young and with the mothers of families, read
these leaves in the open air every season of every year of
your life, re-examine all you have been told at school or
church or in any book, dismiss whatever insults your own
soul, and your very flesh shall be a great poem and have
the richest fluency not only in its words but in the silent
lines of its lips and face and between the lashes of your
eyes and in every motion and joint of your body.*

Acknowledgements

My step-brother said, 'Remember Eddie Stobart, the haulage company? Eddie used to say, "I built this business by myself. I built this from the ground up." Actually, no, he didn't, because he didn't build the roads or the towns. He didn't build the infrastructure or the businesses that he supplied. Those things were there before he was. Without those he wouldn't have his company because nothing works in isolation. My life, your life, whatever it is, it's all interlinked'. He's so right. You can't do anything with out the impact of others. This book has come to life with so much help:

A huge thank you to all the one hundred men who took part in the project - it was lovely getting to know you. I've learnt a lot. To everyone I've met along the way who has given me kind words, support and encouragement. Amy for helping me get my head around the mammoth task I set myself. Tash for her IT skills. Katy my web designer. Ali for the so needed social media training! To Anne S who has encouraging words. Deborah, my yoga buddy and sounding board. Sarah Drew Jones for that long conversation. Sue B for a whole lot of discussion, singing and laughter. Saffron & Mike, Julia, Jonathan, Lorna and all the ears at the writer's workshop, you've been invaluable. And where would we be without Zoom? To Alex at the 'Black Lab' cafe in Clapham where I went to drink an awful lot of coffee whilst typing! To Al for managing to read the manuscript all whilst sailing across the Atlantic. To David T who has been with me every step of the way. To Sophie, Mel and Rachel for proof reading - a hard task for anyone - THANK YOU. Alison who made the book so beautiful. Ruth for the front cover and all the gorgeous drawings. To Dig for getting the book printed. To my editor, enough said. To Phil for friendship, and writing the foreword. And to June for always encouraging me when I'm complaining especially about those three million words! And to my family Martin, Connie, Anna and James.

■

And finally to YOU for buying a copy. Thank you!

About the author

Sam has enjoyed listening to people most of her adult life. With a fascination for conversation, she has spent the last 7 years putting together her findings into three beautiful books. She has an insatiable curiosity, and eager to keep learning.

Sam was born and raised in Lancashire. She lives in London with her family. When not asking questions, she'll be pottering in her garden, practising yoga or drinking coffee!

Other books by the same author

available from **collectingconversations.com**

collectingconversations
@SamBunch1967
Collecting Conversations

*"When an old man dies
a library burns to the ground"*

African proverb